GREGG DICTATION

Diamond Jubilee Series

GREGG
DICTATION

Louis A. Leslie

Charles E. Zoubek

Madeline S. Strony

Shorthand written by Charles Rader

GREGG 75 *Diamond Jubilee Series*

Gregg Division

McGraw-Hill Book Company

New York   St. Louis   Dallas   San Francisco

Toronto   London   Sydney

GREGG DICTATION, DIAMOND JUBILEE SERIES

Preface

Gregg Dictation is the second volume in the Diamond Jubilee Series of Gregg Shorthand. It is designed to be used after *Gregg Shorthand* or *Gregg Shorthand, Functional Method,* and serves as a bridge between the student's study of the principles and advanced dictation and transcription. For some, *Gregg Dictation* may also serve as a terminal course in shorthand.

OBJECTIVES

Gregg Dictation has five major objectives:

1. To review and strengthen the student's knowledge of Gregg Shorthand.

2. To develop his ability to construct outlines for unfamiliar words under the stress of dictation.

3. To increase his dictation speed to the highest point possible.

4. To extend his knowledge of the basic nonshorthand elements of transcription.

5. To lay a solid foundation for rapid and accurate transcription —the student's ultimate goal.

ORGANIZATION

Gregg Dictation, Diamond Jubilee Series, is divided into 16 chapters, each containing five lessons. Each lesson consists of three parts:

1. Developing Phrasing or Word-Building Power
2. Building Transcription Skills
3. Reading and Writing Practice

Developing Phrasing or Word-Building Power

The five lessons in each chapter contain a carefully planned cycle of phrase and word-building drills that provide a quick, intensive recall in list form of the important elements of Gregg Shorthand. Many of the words and phrases in these drills are used in the Reading and Writing Practice exercises.

Lesson 1 in each chapter concentrates on developing phrasing power. It opens with a group of frequently used phrases. This phrase group is followed by a phrase letter, which serves as a source for warm-up practice throughout the chapter.

Lesson 2 in each chapter reviews, in chart form, the brief forms of Gregg Shorthand. Many derivatives of the brief forms are used in these charts as well as in the Reading and Writing Practice.

5

In addition, a drill on cities, states, and other geographical expressions is provided in Lesson 2 of each chapter.

Lesson 3 of each chapter is devoted to the study of shorthand word families. These shorthand word families enable the student to take advantage of a very effective aid in word building—analogy. The study of shorthand word families develops the student's ability to construct outlines for unfamiliar words.

In *Gregg Dictation* the student studies 69 shorthand word families.

Lesson 4 in each chapter provides recall and practice on the word beginnings and endings of Gregg Shorthand. Through the medium of word drills, the student reviews intensively all the word beginnings and endings at least once; some of the more important ones, several times.

Lesson 5 of each chapter contains a shorthand vocabulary builder that concentrates on the major principles of Gregg Shorthand—blends, omission of vowels, quantities and amounts, etc.

Building Transcription Skills

One of the distinguishing features of *Gregg Dictation, Diamond Jubilee Series,* is the constant emphasis placed on the nonshorthand elements of transcription. It is a well-known fact that the weakest link in the transcription chain is the student's inability to handle the mechanics of the English language. The cry of the businessman has long been that his stenographer cannot spell, cannot punctuate, and has no feeling for correct grammar.

In the first book of the Diamond Jubilee Series, *Gregg Shorthand,* a number of features designed to develop the student's mastery of the mechanics of the English language were introduced. In *Gregg Dictation* the emphasis on this phase of transcription is intensified and extended. From the very first lesson, mastery of the mechanics of the English language and the development of shorthand speed proceed side by side.

Spelling

1. Marginal Reminders. As in *Gregg Shorthand,* words selected from the Reading and Writing Practice have been singled out for special attention. These words appear in type, syllabicated, in the left margin of the shorthand.

2. Spelling Families. These spelling families group words that have a common spelling problem—words that are spelled *ance-ence; ible-able;* etc.

Punctuation

In *Gregg Shorthand, Diamond Jubilee Series,* the student studied nine of the most frequent uses of the comma as they appeared in the Reading and Writing Practice exercises. In *Gregg Dictation* he will continue to drill on these uses of the comma.

In addition, he will study more advanced problems of punctuation, such as the use of the semicolon, the hyphen, and the apostrophe. The reason for the use of each punctuation mark is indicated above the encircled punctuation in the shorthand.

To test the student's grasp of the punctuation rules studied, each lesson, except the fifth in each chapter, contains a Transcription Quiz letter in which the student must supply all internal punctuation. In the later lessons each Transcription Quiz contains an additional transcription problem — the student must supply from context words that have been omitted in the shorthand.

Vocabulary Development

1. Business Vocabulary Builder. In each lesson the student studies words and expressions, selected from the Reading and Writing Practice, with which he may not be familiar. The definition provided for each word or expression is the one that applies to its use in the Reading and Writing Practice.

2. Similar-Words Drill. One of the main reasons for transcription errors is the student's inability to choose the correct word from a pair of similar-sounding words—*there-their,* for example. In *Gregg Shorthand* the student studied several of the commoner pairs of similar words; in *Gregg Dictation* he studies 14 additional, more challenging pairs.

3. Common Word Roots. As the student learned in *Gregg Shorthand,* common word roots are an effective device for increasing the student's command of words. In *Gregg Dictation* he studies seven new, more advanced word roots.

Grammar Checkup

There are nine lessons that contain drills dealing with common rules of grammar that are often misapplied or misunderstood by stenographers. Correct applications of these rules are woven into the Reading and Writing Practice exercises.

Typing Style Studies

In the Typing Style Studies, the student learns the correct way to transcribe dates, street addresses, amounts of money, and times of day.

Office-Style Dictation

In Chapters 13 through 16, four of the simplest problems of office-style dictation are introduced. Each problem is explained and then illustrated in a letter that is written in shorthand. This feature will be especially valuable to those students whose shorthand training will end with *Gregg Dictation.*

Reading and Writing Practice

An essential part of every student's practice program is the reading and copying of quantities of well-written shorthand. This reading and copying provides a constant, automatic review of the principles of the system. In addition, it stocks the student's mind with the correct joinings of shorthand characters and with the shapes of the individual characters, so that he can quickly form an outline for any word that is dictated. *Gregg Dictation* provides the student with 52,551 running words of shorthand practice material in the form of business letters and interesting, informative articles. More than 60 per cent of the material is new, fresh, modern. The material retained from the previous edition has been revised and brought up to date.

In order to give the student the dictation "flavor" of many kinds of businesses, the connected material in each of the 16 chapters in *Gregg Dictation* relates to a specific business or department of business. Each chapter opens with a brief description of the business or business function that is the subject of the chapter.

An extremely helpful and interesting feature of the Reading and Writing Practice of the fifth lesson of each chapter is an actual secretarial case study entitled "The Secretary on the Job." Each case emphasizes the importance of some desirable traits or characteristics of a good secretary, effective secretarial procedures, and so on.

The authors wish to express their gratitude to the many successful teachers who have shared with them their experience with previous editions of *Gregg Dictation* and have contributed many helpful suggestions and ideas. These ideas and suggestions were of immense value in the preparation of this edition. The authors hope that these teachers — and teachers everywhere — will find real pleasure in teaching from *Gregg Dictation.*

The Publishers

Contents

Part 1

Your Speed-Building Program

Before you begin your work on the second phase of your shorthand training — shorthand speed building — let us take an inventory of what you have already accomplished. You may not realize it, but you have taken a long step toward your goal to become a stenographer and secretary.

> You have learned the alphabet of Gregg Shorthand and thus have the means with which to form an outline for any word in the language — whether the word is familiar or unfamiliar.
>
> You have learned many useful abbreviating devices, such as brief forms, word beginnings and endings, and phrases that will help you to write more easily.
>
> You have improved your ability to spell and to punctuate, you have increased your vocabulary of business terms, and you have brushed up on a number of rules of grammar.

If you have faithfully practiced the lessons in *Gregg Shorthand* (and of course you have!), you now have a firm foundation for the task ahead — developing your ability to take dictation on new material easily and rapidly and to transcribe on the typewriter. With this firm foundation you will experience the thrill of watching your shorthand speed grow and your ability to handle the mechanics of the English language improve almost from day to day!

Your Practice Program—At Home

Here is what you should do at home as you practice the lessons in *Gregg Dictation:*

Read the word and phrase drills. For some of them, a time goal is provided. Try to reach or, better still, exceed that goal.

Study the Transcription Skill Builder.

Read and copy the Reading and Writing Practice in this way:

1. Always *read* all shorthand before you copy it. Read aloud, if possible. This is important!

2. If as you read you come across an outline you cannot decipher, spell the shorthand characters in it. If this spelling does not give the meaning of the outline to you, refer to the Transcript if one is available to you. If one isn't, write the outline on a slip of paper and find out its meaning the next day. Do not spend more than a few seconds trying to decipher an outline. Fortunately, at this stage there will not be many outlines that will "stump" you.

3. After you have read the material, make a shorthand copy of it. Read a convenient group of words — aloud, if possible — and then write that group in your notebook. Write as rapidly as you can, but be sure what you write is legible.

4. If time permits, read what you have written. You will be glad you did if you are called upon to read back from your homework in class the next day!

Your Practice Program—In Class

In class most of your time will be devoted to taking dictation at constantly increasing speeds. Your teacher will see to it that you get the right kind of dictation at the proper speeds so that your dictation skill will increase steadily and rapidly.

Sales

A business organization manufactures goods or offers services for one reason only — to sell them. Sales are the lifeblood of a business. A business may manufacture the finest products and render the best services in the world, but it cannot survive unless it can sell them at a profit.

How does an organization sell its goods or services? There are many ways. The following are perhaps the most important:

Advertising. Through the medium of newspapers, magazines, radio, television, and so forth, an organization tells the public about its wares. A very substantial part of the sales budget of most organizations is made up of advertising and promotion expenses.

In-Person Selling. Any organization of appreciable size will have a sales department, headed by a sales manager who selects, trains, and supervises a staff of salespeople. These salespeople are called by such names as salesmen, representatives, service specialists, or agents. In many companies, each salesman has a definite territory in which he works — seeking new customers and giving service to old ones. A person in a position of this type must like people and make friends easily, must enjoy traveling, and must be able to adjust to the inconvenience of living away from home a good deal of the time.

Selling by Mail. Business organizations in this country send out millions of sales and sales-promotion letters each year. Most of these letters try to attract the reader's attention to a product or service and to stimulate him to take some action — send in an order, request a booklet or other descriptive literature, or ask for a representative to call. Letters of this type are usually prepared by trained letter writers.

Other letters written by the sales office answer inquiries, thank customers for orders received, follow up on customers who have not sent in recent orders, and offer assistance to current customers in getting the most from their purchases.

In the final analysis, of course, every letter that goes out under a company's letterhead is a sales letter. If it is friendly in tone, neatly typed, and accurately transcribed, it creates a good impression of the company — and a good impression is an important factor in building sales or good public relations that lead to sales.

The letters and memoranda in this chapter will give you a good sampling of the type of dictation you will take if you are employed in the sales department of an organization.

✳ Comma Brushup

As you learned in *Gregg Shorthand*, a stenographer or secretary must be able to do more than take dictation rapidly; among other things, she must be able to punctuate correctly if she is to turn out letters that her employer will have no hesitation in signing. In *Gregg Shorthand* you studied a number of the simpler uses of the comma as they occurred in the Reading and Writing Practice.

In *Gregg Dictation* you will take up new and more advanced points of punctuation. Before you are introduced to these new points, however, you will "brush up" on the uses of the comma that you studied in *Gregg Shorthand*. In Chapter 1 of *Gregg Dictation* you will review five of those uses; in Chapter 2, the remaining four.

Practice Procedures

To be sure that you derive the greatest benefit from your study of punctuation and spelling in each Reading and Writing Practice, follow these practice suggestions:

1. Read carefully each punctuation rule and the illustrative examples.

2. Continue to read each Reading and Writing Practice as you have always done. However, add these three important steps:

a. Each time you see an encircled comma, note the reason for its use, which is indicated directly above the encircled comma.

b. As you copy the Reading and Writing Practice, insert the commas in your shorthand notes, encircling them as in the textbook.

c. When spelling words appear at the left of the shorthand pages in the textbook, spell them, aloud, if possible, pausing slightly after each syllable. Spelling aloud helps to impress the correct spelling more firmly on your mind.

In Chapter 1 you will review:

, parenthetical

In order to make his meaning clearer, a writer sometimes inserts a comment or an explanation that could be omitted without changing the meaning of the sentence. These added comments and explanations

14

are called *parenthetical* and are separated from the rest of the sentence by commas.

If the parenthetical word or expression occurs at the beginning or end of a sentence, only one comma is needed.

> His main job, of course, is to sell our products.
> I am sure, Mr. Jones, that you will like our representative.
> We shall send you a copy, of course.

Each time a parenthetical expression occurs in the Reading and Writing Practice, it will be indicated thus in the shorthand:

par

⊙

, apposition

Sometimes a writer mentions a person or thing and then, in order to make his meaning perfectly clear to the reader, says the same thing again in different words. This added explanation is known as an expression in *apposition*.

An expression in apposition is set off by two commas, except at the end of a sentence, when only one comma is necessary.

> Our representative, Mr. Harry Smith, will call soon.
> The meeting will be held on Friday, April 16, at the Hotel
>   Brown.
> Meet my assistant, Mary Brown.

Each time an expression in apposition occurs in the Reading and Writing Practice, it will be indicated thus in the shorthand:

ap

⊙

, series

When the last member of a series of three or more items is preceded by *and, or,* or *nor,* place a comma before the conjunction as well as between the other items.

> He likes our goods, our services, and our prices.
> I saw him on July 1, on July 3, and on July 18.
> Her duties consisted of receiving callers, answering the
>   telephone, and opening the mail.

Each time a series occurs in the Reading and Writing Practice, it will be indicated thus in the shorthand:

ser

⊙

, conjunction

A comma is used to separate two independent clauses that are joined by a conjunction:

> A customer stopped sending in his orders, and we are wondering why we have lost his business.
> Perhaps you cannot send us an order, but won't you be good enough to answer my question.

Each time this use of the comma occurs in the Reading and Writing Practice, it will be indicated thus in the shorthand:

conj

⊙

, and omitted

When two or more adjectives modify the same noun, they are separated by commas.

> He was a quiet, efficient worker.

However, the comma is not used if the first adjective modifies the combined idea of the second adjective plus the noun.

> She wore a beautiful green dress.

Each time this use of the comma occurs in the Reading and Writing Practice, it will be indicated thus in the shorthand:

and o

⊙

LESSON 1

Building Phrasing Skill

1. PHRASE BUILDER

The following list contains 58 phrases that are used frequently in business letters. Can you read the entire list in one minute?

1. Of the, in the, Yours truly, to the, Dear Mr., we are, Dear Sir, for the.
2. Yours very truly, on the, it is, we have, will be, of our, that the, with the, Very truly yours.
3. I am, and the, at the, to be, of this, you can, I have, you have, you are.
4. By the, to make, from the, there is, in our, in them, is the, is that.
5. That is, we can, in this, to have, to get, so that, of course, they are.
6. There are, have been, to see, we shall, to us, you may, about the, we will.
7. To you, may be, with you, should be, if you, as the, you will, in which.

17

2. WARMUP PHRASE LETTER

The following 129-word letter, which is your warmup letter for this chapter, contains 28 frequently used phrases. Can you read the letter in one minute? Can you copy it from the shorthand in two minutes?

(129)

Building Transcription Skills

3. BUSINESS VOCABULARY BUILDER

In *Gregg Dictation* you will continue to improve your command of business terminology through the Business Vocabulary Builders, in which business words and expressions selected from the Reading and Writing Practice of the lesson are briefly defined. As in the Business Vocabulary Builders in *Gregg Shorthand*, only the meaning or explanation of each word or expression that applies to its use in the Reading and Writing Practice is given.

Study the definitions carefully.

high-pressure (*verb*)   To force.

appropriate (*adjective*)   Specially suitable; fit.

treading on someone's toes   Giving offense unintentionally.

Reading and Writing Practice

4.

an'a·lyze
prac'ti·cal
rec'om·men·da'tions

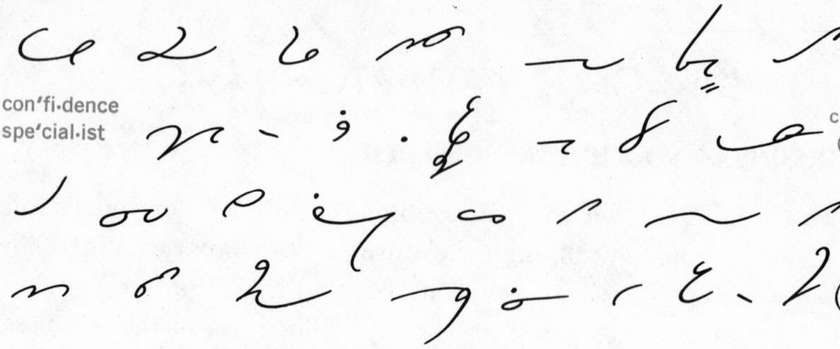

con′fi·dence
spe′cial·ist

conj

(116)

5.

los′ing
ap·pro′pri·ate

par

won′t
e·nough′
an′swer

conj

and o
(121)

6.

oc·ca'sion
ours

conj

conj

par

lose
dis'ap·proved'

ser

par

par

a·fraid'
tread'ing

(152)

7.   TRANSCRIPTION QUIZ

You are already familiar with the Transcription Quiz from your work with *Gregg Shorthand*. This quiz gives you an opportunity to see how well you can apply the comma rules you have studied thus far. In Chapters 1 and 2 of *Gregg Dictation*, the Transcription Quiz will contain the same type of problems as those in *Gregg Shorthand*. In later chapters, as new points of punctuation are introduced, these quizzes will become more advanced.

As you read the Transcription Quiz letter, decide what punctuation should be used. Then, as you make a shorthand copy of it, insert the correct punctuation marks in the proper places in your notes.

For you to supply: 5 commas — 1 comma conjunction, 2 commas series, 2 commas parenthetical.

(100)

LESSON 2

● **Warmup.** A profitable way to use the few minutes between the time you enter the shorthand classroom and the time your teacher starts the day's lesson is to "warm up." Unless your teacher instructs you otherwise, turn to the phrase letter on page 18 and see how fast you can copy it.

Developing Word-Building Power

8. BRIEF-FORM CHART

The following chart contains 30 frequently used brief forms and derivatives. Because you have practiced them many, many times while you were studying from *Gregg Shorthand*, you should be able to read them rapidly. First, read the brief forms from left to right. Your reading goal: 35 seconds. Then, read the brief forms down each column. Your reading goal on this second reading: 30 seconds.

1					
2					
3					
4					
5					

1. A-an, about, after, am, and, are-our-hour.
2. It-at, be-by, between, but, can, could.
3. During, out-how, from, gone, good, have.
4. For, important-importance, in-not, is-his, merchant, merchandise.
5. Character, Mr., Mrs., must, never, next.

23

9. GEOGRAPHICAL EXPRESSIONS

1. San Francisco, New York, Newark, Hartford, Seattle, Chicago, Los Angeles.
2. California, Oregon, New Jersey, Connecticut, Washington, Illinois, Tennessee.

Building Transcription Skills

10. BUSINESS VOCABULARY BUILDER

designated   Named; specified.

suite (pronounced *swēt*)   A group of rooms occupied as a unit.

reaction   Feeling; response.

tentative   Not final; subject to change.

Incentive Compensation Plan   Method of granting additional pay to employees in order to encourage them to do their best work.

11. SIMILAR-WORDS DRILL

In *Gregg Dictation* you will continue your study of similar words — words that sound alike and words that sound or look *almost* alike.

Similar words are responsible for many of the errors that stenographers make when they transcribe.

Study each definition carefully. As you read and copy the Reading and Writing Practice of the lesson, watch for these similar words; you will find them used a number of times.

Accept, except

accept   To take.

O   ᒪ   ᵍ   ℯ   ⌐   ℒ ﹏

I believe we should accept their offer.

except (*preposition*)   Omitted; left out.

◦   ᒪ   Ɛ   ᷠ   ⌐   ⌐   ᷠ

All salesmen, except one, have met their quotas.

Reading and Writing Practice

12. *—ᷤ   ᒿ   :   —   ᷡᵇ   ⊙   ᷢ   ᒪ*

des′ig·nat′ed
an′nu·al

ex·cept′
mi′nor

ad·di′tion·al
of′fered

ser

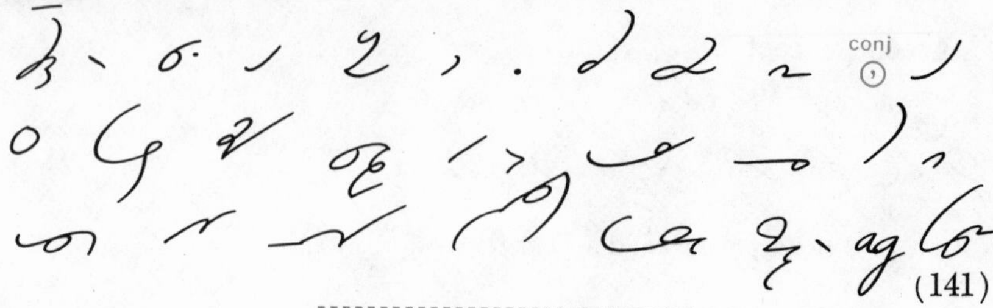

(141)

13.

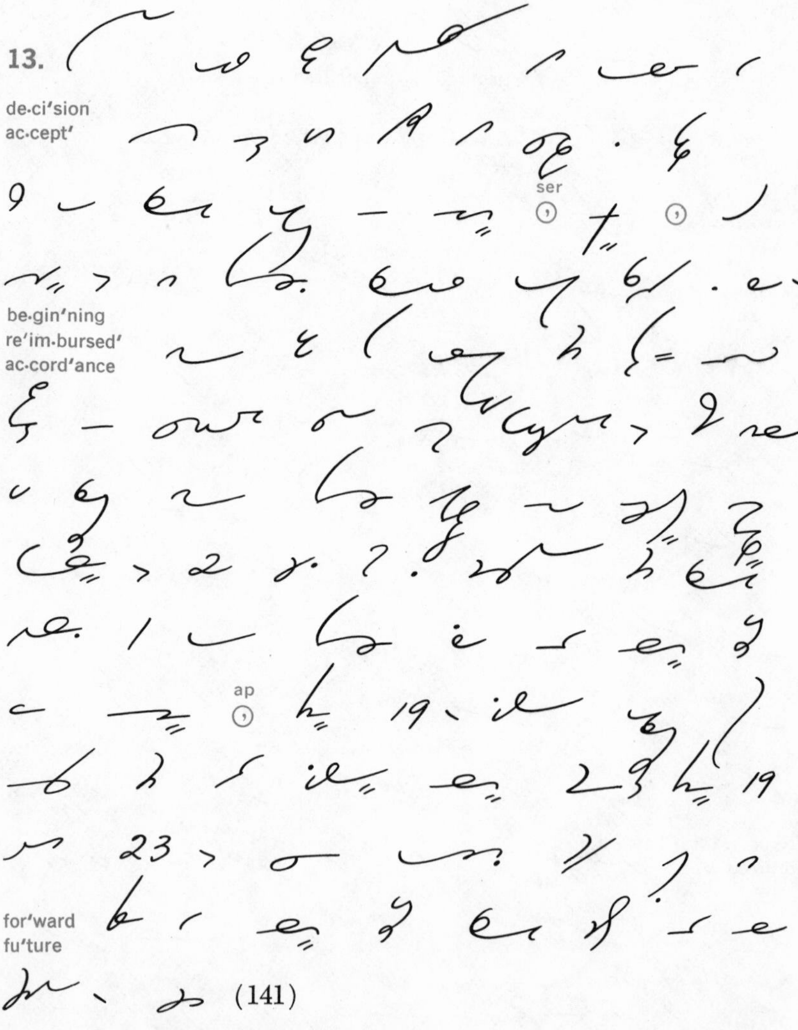

de·ci'sion
ac·cept'

be·gin'ning
re'im·bursed'
ac·cord'ance

for'ward
fu'ture

(141)

14.

com·pet′i·tors
wor′ried

par

anx·i′e·ty
ex·cept′

par

par

(117)

15.

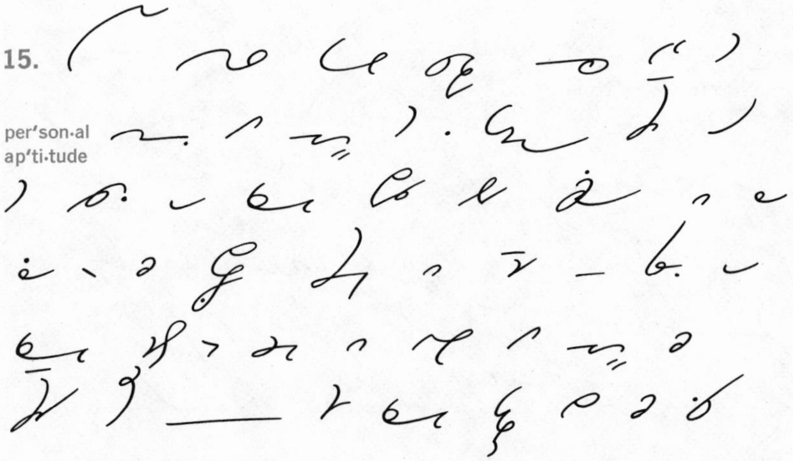

per′son·al
ap′ti·tude

[Gregg shorthand outlines] (103)

ap'pli·ca'tion
fur'ther

16. Transcription Quiz.

For you to supply: 6 commas—2 commas apposition, 1 comma *and* omitted, 1 comma conjunction, 2 commas parenthetical.

[Gregg shorthand outlines] (131)

LESSON 3

● **Warmup.**   A minute or two of warmup will help you get off to a good start on your day's dictation. Turn once again to the phrase letter on page 18; copy it as rapidly as you can and still write readable shorthand.

Developing Word-Building Power

17. WORD FAMILIES

-let

1

-form

2

-sure

3

-thing

4

---

1. Let, booklet, pamphlet, leaflet, outlet.
2. Form, inform, informative, information, reform, perform.
3. Sure, pleasure, measure, treasure, assure, insure, pressure.
4. Thing, anything, everything, something, nothing, plaything, things.

29

Building Transcription Skills

18. BUSINESS VOCABULARY BUILDER

exhibit   Show.

offset   To compensate for; to balance.

informative   Instructive.

19. SPELLING FAMILIES

One of the most troublesome spelling families in the English language is the *ie, ei* group. Grammarians tell us that:

1. i comes before e:

a·chieve′	brief	yield
piece	chief	friend
be·lief′	niece	re·lief′

2. except (a) after c:

de·ceit′	re·ceipt′	re·ceive′

and (b) when the combination has the sound of a:

their	heir	eight

But, of course, this rule, like any other rule, has its exceptions. Here are a few words that are used with some frequency in business that are exceptions to the rule.

ei′ther	nei′ther	lei′sure
for′eign	ef·fi′cient	suf·fi′cient

In your Reading and Writing Practice you will find a number of these words; watch for them.

Reading and Writing Practice

20.

[Gregg shorthand outlines]

fur'ni·ture
in'suf·fi'cient

par

course
em·bar'rass·ing

conj

a·pol'o·gy
off'set'

ah (114)

....

21.

col'league
neigh'bor

ap

ap

ter'ri·to'ry
be·lieve'

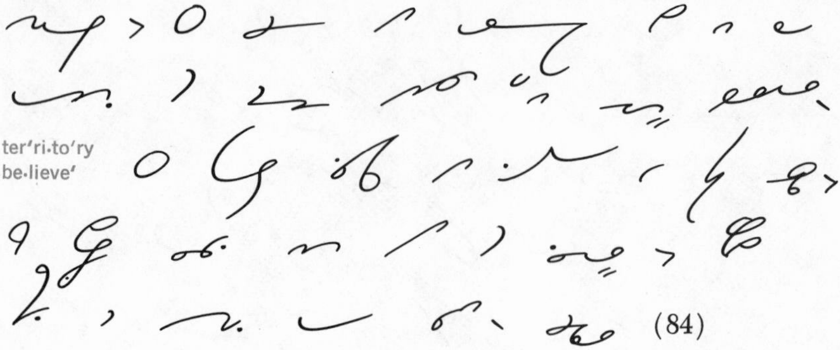

(84)

22.

ap
par
par
par
par

qual'i·ty
piece

ad·vice'
write

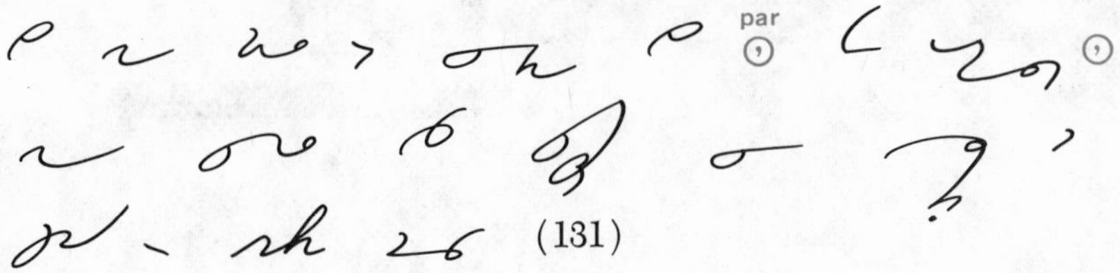

(131)

23. Transcription Quiz. For you to supply: 8 commas – 4 commas apposition, 2 commas series, 2 commas parenthetical.

(117)

LESSON 4

● **Warmup** Don't you find that a minute of warmup before the shorthand period starts really gets you ready for the day's dictation? For your warmup, turn to the phrase letter on page 18 and write it as rapidly as you can.

Developing Word-Building Power

24. WORD BEGINNINGS AND ENDINGS

-ly

-tion

Im-

Re-

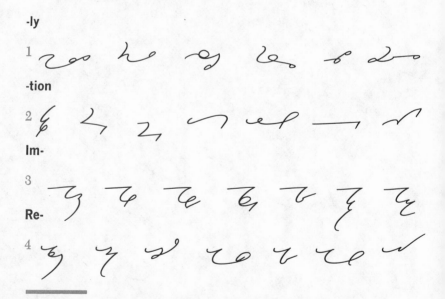

---

1. Completely, fully, carefully, frankly, neatly, firmly.
2. Position, function, information, organization, relation, mention, contention.
3. Improve, impression, impressed, impartial, import, impossible, improper.
4. Reserve, reasonable, recently, reply, report, replace, reorder.

Building Transcription Skills

25. BUSINESS VOCABULARY BUILDER

> **functions** (*noun*)   Operations; activities.
>
> **made a quotation**   Named a price for goods.
>
> **prompted**   Moved to action.
>
> **mutual friend**   One whose friendship is enjoyed by two persons.

26. GRAMMAR CHECKUP

Pronouns

A pronoun must agree with its antecedent in person, number, and gender.

> These *tests* can save you many times *their* cost.
> After studying your *plan*, I think *it* is a good one.
> *Each* of the students wrote down *his* (not *their*) answers
>   to the questions.

Reading and Writing Practice

27.

sat′is·fied
de·vel′op·ing

spe′cial
lat′ter

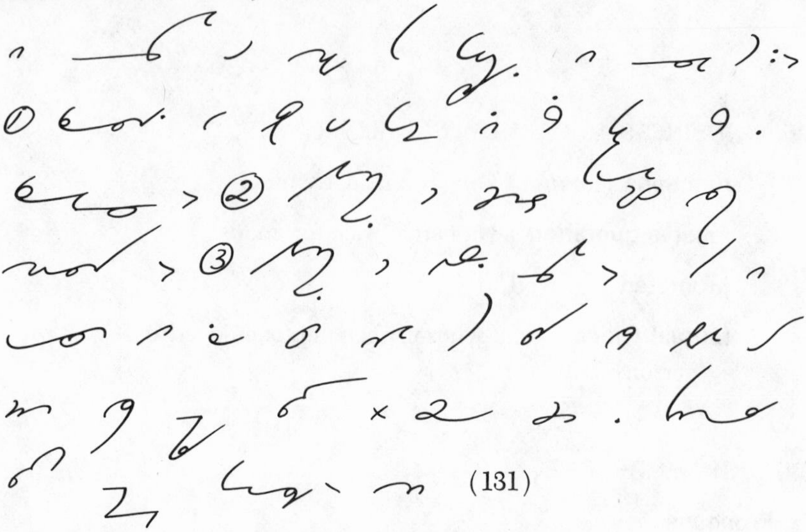
(131)

28.

in·quir'y
buy'er
steel

ap
ser
conj
and o
par

ours
im·pres'sion

mod'ern
man'age·ment

(132)

29.

re'cent·ly
mu'tu·al

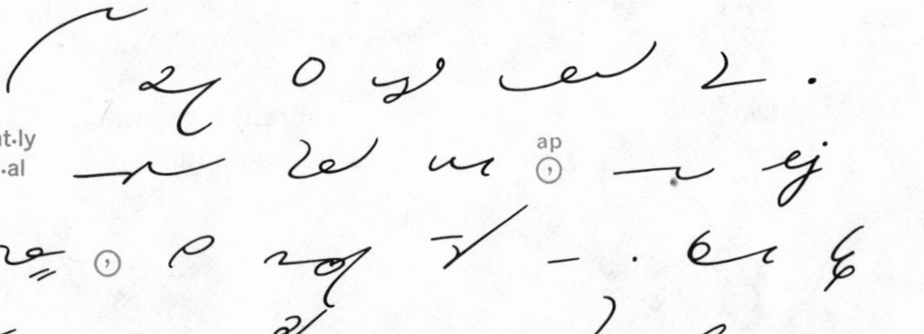

op'por·tu'ni·ty
for'ward

(101)

30.

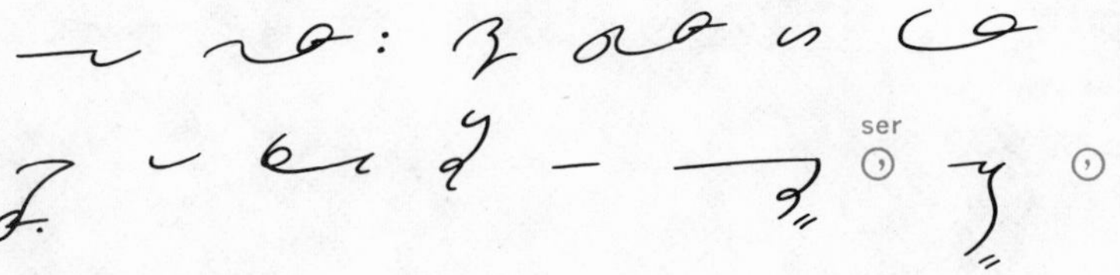

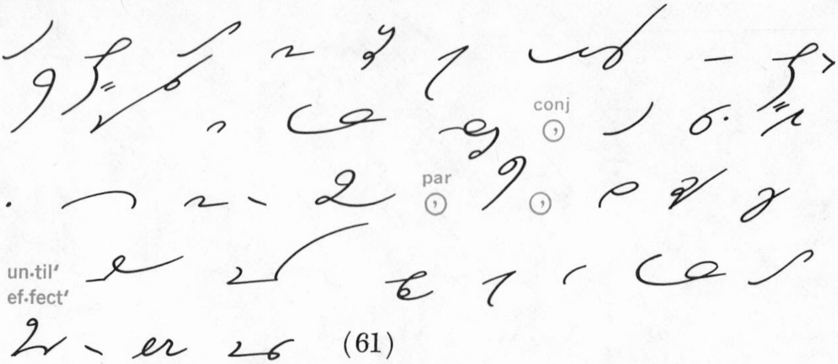

31. Transcription Quiz. For you to supply: 7 commas – 2 commas series, 4 commas parenthetical, 1 comma conjunction.

LESSON 5

● **Warmup.** Turn once again—for the last time—to the phrase letter on page 18. The phrases in that letter should now be familiar to you—so familiar, in fact, that you should be able to write the whole letter in about a minute. Can you do it?

Developing Word-Building Power

32. SHORTHAND VOCABULARY BUILDER

Ted

1

Dif, Def, Div, Dev

2

Men, Min

3

Ent-, Ind-

4

---

1. Adopted, adapted, tested, delighted, treated, wasted, resisted.
2. Different, difference, definite, divided, individual, devoted.
3. Salesmen, comments, recommend, determine, examination.
4. Entire, entirely, entitle, entrust, indicate, industry, independent.

39

Building Transcription Skills

33.   **BUSINESS VOCABULARY BUILDER**

warrant   To justify.

applicant   One who applies for something, as employment.

a good "mixer"   A person marked by easy sociability.

Reading and Writing Practice

34.

write
passed

de·vot'ed
daugh'ter

in·quir'ies
un·til'

[Gregg shorthand outlines]

(121)

....

35. par ⟨.⟩

wheth'er
ap'pli·cant

qual'i·ties
ef·fec'tive   and o ⟨.⟩

par ⟨.⟩

conj ⟨.⟩   "ʃɪ"

de·vel'oped
in'dus·tries

a·dopt'ed
com'pa·nies
a·dapt'ed

(130)

36.

rec'om·mend'
some'one'

trav'el·ing
ad·just'
weeks

conj

(140)

37.

ap

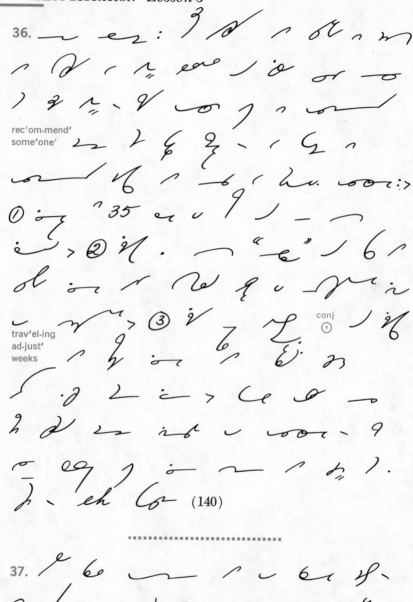

[Gregg shorthand outlines]

dis'trict
ac·com'pa·ny

ap

conj

'ea'ger
suc·ceed'

(135)

....

38.

ah (37)

39. The Thirteenth Doughnut

[shorthand content]

What does this *[shorthand content]*

Giving the little

(278)

No field of special interest is closed to the young woman who chooses secretaryship as a career. —Clare H. Jennings, former president of National Secretaries Association

Adjustments

Pamela Jackson immediately fell in love with a dress that she saw in the window of a department store in a nearby city; so she bought the dress. That very evening she wore it to a party. The next day, however, she decided that it was not quite the color she wanted; so she decided to write the store that she wished to return the dress and wanted a refund.

A letter from the store granting Pamela's request would have been an easy and pleasant one to write. However, the store's policy states that "clothing that has been worn cannot be returned." Someone must write to Pamela and break the news to her. What is more, that someone must do it in such a way that Pamela will understand the store's position and will continue to be a happy customer. Such a letter is not an easy one to write — in fact, it is one of the most difficult of all letters to write.

Writing letters answering complaints and requests for adjustments —whether justified or unfair — is an important responsibility in every business. The organization that loses as a customer every person who makes a complaint or asks for an adjustment will not be in business long. Sometimes an adjustment is in order; sometimes it is not. The trick is to keep the customer satisfied whether he gets a "Yes" or a "No" answer! Many organizations find this phase of their business so important that they maintain a special adjustment department in which trained "trouble shooters" are employed to investigate complaints and to make adjustments that are justified and refuse those that are not. One of the most important qualifications of such a trouble shooter is the ability to write courteous and convincing letters that will make the customer accept "No" for an answer and like it!

Taking care of complaints represents a considerable expense for any business, of course. But complaints from customers also serve a very useful purpose to the business executive. They bring to his attention the things that are wrong in the operation of his business, in the quality of his merchandise, and in the performance and attitudes of the people who work for him. They show him where he can make improvements that will result in greater customer satisfaction — and greater customer satisfaction means more business!

Many of the letters in this chapter are actual letters written by those who work in adjustment departments — letters that you may have to take in dictation (or write yourself) if you should become a secretary to an adjustment department manager or supervisor.

✳ *Comma Brushup* *(Concluded)*

In Chapter 1 you reviewed five of the uses of the comma that you studied in *Gregg Shorthand*. In Chapter 2 you will review the remaining uses of the comma that were presented in that book — commas with introductory expressions. As in *Gregg Shorthand*, introductory commas will be treated under the four headings listed below. Next to each of these headings is the indication that will appear in the shorthand for that use of the comma.

, when clause	when ⟨⟩
, as clause	as ⟨⟩
, if clause	if ⟨⟩
, introductory	intro ⟨⟩

All dependent clauses beginning with words other than *when, as,* and *if* will be classified as ", introductory."

> When the original shipment is located, we will make the necessary adjustments.
> As you know, we guarantee our cameras for a year.
> If you are in urgent need of the notebooks, wire us.
> Unless we receive our supplies soon, we shall be in difficulty.

When the main clause comes first, however, no comma is used between the main clause and the dependent clause.

> We shall be in difficulty unless we receive our supplies soon.
> Wire us if you are in urgent need of the notebooks.

A comma is also required after introductory words and explanatory expressions such as *frankly, consequently, on the contrary, for instance.*

> Frankly, I cannot wait any longer.
> On the contrary, you are the one who made the error.

LESSON 6

Building Phrasing Skill

40. PHRASE BUILDER

The following four groups contain 38 phrases. Can you read the entire list in 55 seconds or less?

We

1

You

2

He

3

I

4

---

1. We are, we will, we can, we have, we have not, we may, we should, we did.
2. You are, you will, you can, you have, you have been, you might, you may be, you know.
3. He is, he may, he will, he might, he should, he did, he made.
4. I was, I wrote you, I am sure, I would, I did, I could, I made, I should, I do, I do not, I can, I cannot, I am glad, I may, I know.

49

41.   WARMUP PHRASE LETTER

The following 113-word letter contains 21 frequently used phrases. Can you read the entire letter in one minute or less? Can you make a shorthand copy of it in two minutes?

This will be your warmup letter while you are working on Chapter 2.

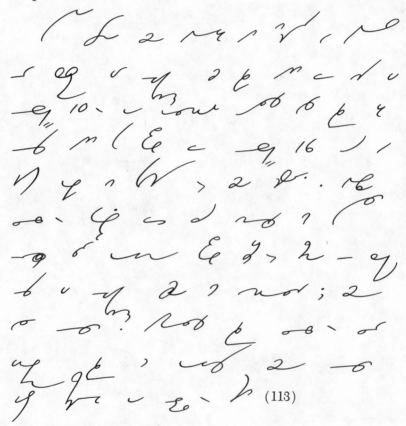

(113)

Building Transcription Skills

42.   BUSINESS VOCABULARY BUILDER

exhausted   Gone; used up.

wire collect The receiver rather than the sender will pay for the telegram.

prevails Is current.

Reading and Writing Practice

43.

slight
ac·knowl'edg·ing

ap

when

par

intro

fac'to·ry
weeks

if

intro

(110)

44.

as

short'age
re·ceived'

15

20

(Gregg shorthand outlines)

weth'er
trace

(104)

····································

45.

re'al·ize
an·noy'ing

when

be·lieve'
neigh'bor

par

intro

in'con·ven'ienced
vi'a

when

conj

(135)

46.

dis·turbed'
tech'ni·cal
re·ferred'

con·tin'ue
pub'lish

conj

as

ser

pro·duc'tion
ris'en

intro

30,

intro

10,

in·fe'ri·or

par

and o

[Gregg shorthand outline] (151)

47. Transcription Quiz. For you to supply: 4 commas—1 comma *as* clause, 1 comma apposition, 2 commas parenthetical.

[Gregg shorthand outline] (97)

LESSON 7

● **Warmup.**   For your warmup during the first few minutes of the period, copy the phrase letter on page 50. Write as rapidly as you can, but be sure that your shorthand notes are readable.

Developing Word-Building Power

48.   BRIEF-FORM CHART

This chart contains 30 brief forms and derivatives. You have seen these brief forms many, many times; therefore, you should be able to read the entire chart in less than 25 seconds. Can you do it?

1. Of, about, shall, should, such, than.
2. That, the, them, they, this, those.
3. Throughout, upon, very, was, will-well, thank.
4. Why, with, would, yesterday, yet, you-your.
5. There-their, street, several, purpose, probable, I.

49. GEOGRAPHICAL EXPRESSIONS

[shorthand outlines]

1. Minneapolis, St. Paul, Des Moines, Miami, Boston, Indianapolis.
2. Minnesota, Iowa, Florida, Massachusetts, Indiana, Pennsylvania, Ohio.

Building Transcription Skills

50. BUSINESS VOCABULARY BUILDER

temporarily   For a short time only.

featured   Advertised as a special bargain.

distressed   Worried; concerned.

51. SIMILAR-WORDS DRILL

Billed, build

billed (past tense of *bill*)   Charged.

[shorthand outlines]

I have been billed for a call I did not make.

build   To create or produce; to construct.

[shorthand outlines]

I will try to build as much good will as possible.

Reading and Writing Practice

52. *[shorthand outlines]*

[Gregg shorthand outlines]

fac'tors
be·yond'
mod'el

intro

par

if

(94)

53.

pur'chased
In'di·an·ap'o·lis

98 50 as

1 50 ap

par

an'nu·al

15 ser 16 ⊙ 17 (95)

54.

par 15 ⊙

762

15,

1,205/ 1,385 ⁷⁵

billed
for'mal

conj

conj

ap·pre'ci·ate
sit'u·a'tion

and o

intro

(190)

55.

ours
wheth'er
as
when
(88)

56.

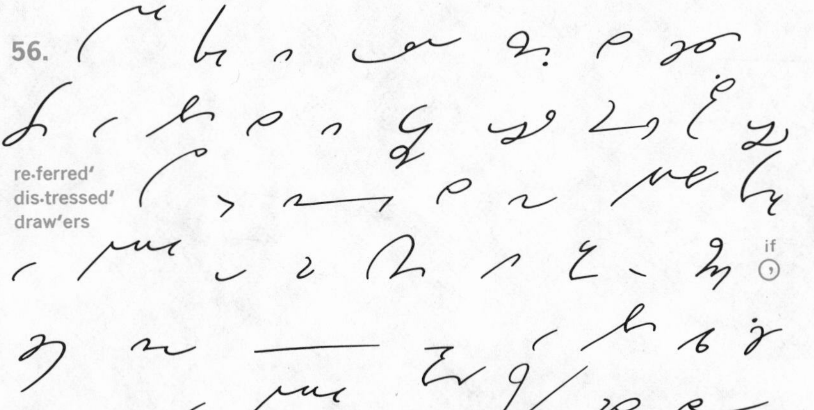
re·ferred'
dis·tressed'
draw'ers
if

eas'i·ly

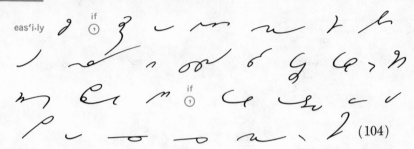

(104)

57.   Transcription Quiz.   For you to supply: 9 commas—1 comma *as* clause, 4 commas parenthetical, 1 comma introductory, 2 commas series, 1 comma conjunction.

(129)

LESSON 8

● **Warmup.** Your warmup letter is on page 50. Can you copy it faster than you did in the last lesson?

Developing Word-Building Power

58. WORD FAMILIES

-count

1 *[shorthand outlines]*

-age

2 *[shorthand outlines]*

-er

3 *[shorthand outlines]*

-cate

4 *[shorthand outlines]*

---

1. Count, account, discount, amount, accountant, recount.
2. Package, manage, manager, damage, mileage, luggage.
3. Later, matter, customer, daughter, writer, wider.
4. Locate, indicate, duplicate, communicate, educate.

Building Transcription Skills

59. BUSINESS VOCABULARY BUILDER

in transit   On the way.

dye A coloring agent.

flaw Imperfection; defect.

communicate To get in touch with.

60. SPELLING FAMILIES

-ize, -ise, -yze

Always be careful when you must transcribe a word ending with the sound of *ize*—sometimes the ending will be spelled *ize*, sometimes *ise*, and occasionally *yze*.

-ize

au'thor·ize	re'al·ize	sym'pa·thize
e·con'o·mize	rec'og·nize	a·pol'o·gize
sum'ma·rize	crit'i·cize	or'gan·ize

-ise

ad·vise'	com·prise'	mer'chan·dise
ad'ver·tise	en'ter·prise	su'per·vise'

-yze

an'a·lyze	par'a·lyze

Reading and Writing Practice

61.
ath·let'ic
ad·vis'es
sup·plies'

im·me′di·ate·ly
un·less′

[Gregg shorthand outlines]

intro

(88)

62.

shipped
du′pli·cate
mer′chan·dise

conj

[Gregg shorthand outlines]

intro

oc·ca′sions
un·u′su·al·ly
rough

[Gregg shorthand outlines]

when

[Gregg shorthand outlines]

par

ac·cord′ance
de·scribed′

[Gregg shorthand outlines]

(shorthand outline)

(137)

································

63. *(shorthand outline)*

par ⓘ

dye
an·a·lyzed
dye'ing

conj ⓘ

par ⓘ

at·ten'tion
ex·pe'ri·enced
ex'er·cise

brought
re·dou'ble

intro ⓘ

(142)

64.   Transcription Quiz.   For you to supply: 10 commas—1 comma *as* clause, 1 comma apposition, 4 commas parenthetical, 1 comma introductory, 1 comma *if* clause, 2 commas series.

[shorthand outlines]

(149)

LESSON ⑨

● **Warmup.** Your warmup once again is the phrase letter on page 50. By this time you should be familiar with this letter and thus be able to write it quite rapidly.

Developing Word-Building Power

65. WORD BEGINNINGS AND ENDINGS

-ment

1

Per-, Pur-

2

-ble

3

In-

4

---

1. Shipment, treatment, moment, replacement, compliment, experiment.
2. Permit, performed, personal, persist, personality, purchase.
3. Considerable, possible, advisable, questionable, obtainable, suitable, flexible, comfortable.
4. Increase, incomplete, information, inconvenient, intend, insist, insult.

66

Building Transcription Skills

66. BUSINESS VOCABULARY BUILDER

gracious   Kindly; courteous.

disclaiming   Denying.

fragile   Easily broken; delicate.

67. GRAMMAR CHECKUP

Between, among

Between is used ordinarily when referring to two things or persons; *among*, to more than two.

Between you and me, I do not think he will get the order.

Caution: Remember that when *between* is used as a preposition, any pronoun that follows it must be in the objective case. Careless writers and speakers often incorrectly say, "between you and *I*" instead of "between you and *me*."

He divided the territory equally among the three men —
Mr. Smith, Mr. Green, and Mr. Baker.

Reading and Writing Practice

68.

sat'is·fac'to·ri·ly
dif'fi·cul·ty

guar'an·teed'
nec'es·sar'y

[shorthand outlines]   as

(118)

ac'cu·rate·ly
oc·ca'sion·al·ly   conj

when

be·lieve'
sea'son
ap·proach'ing   as

par

ap

in'crease
prof'it

(150)

if

70.

when

bought
wore

ser

mer'chan·dise
gra'cious
cour'te·ous

and o

[shorthand outlines] conj ⊙ (128)

∙∙∙∙∙∙∙∙∙∙∙∙∙∙∙∙∙∙∙∙∙∙∙∙∙∙∙∙

71. *[shorthand outlines]* intro ⊙

re·quired'
cus'tom·er
fur'ni·ture *[shorthand outlines]*

[shorthand outlines] ap ⊙

23 *[shorthand outline]* (102)

∙∙∙∙∙∙∙∙∙∙∙∙∙∙∙∙∙∙∙∙∙∙∙∙∙∙∙∙

72. *[shorthand outlines]*

dam'age
dis·claim'ing

frag'ile
re·place'ments

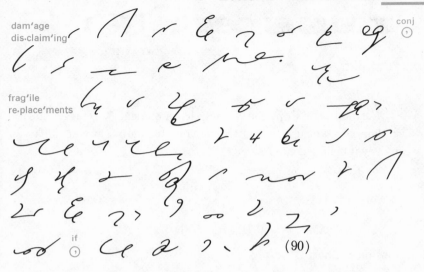

(90)

73.   Transcription Quiz.   For you to supply: 5 commas—1 comma introductory, 4 commas parenthetical.

(79)

LESSON 10

● **Warmup.** Copy the warmup letter on page 50. This will be the last time you will use that letter for your warmup. Do you think you can copy it in 90 seconds?

Developing Word-Building Power

74. SHORTHAND VOCABULARY BUILDER

Omission of Short U

1

-ld

2

-rd

3

-nd

4

-md

5

---

1. Some, something, become, son, rush, brush, judge, much.
2. Old, sold, failed, entitled, mailed, installed.
3. Repaired, delivered, marred, stored, guard, cared, dared.
4. Opened, second, friend, returned, find, wondering, bind.
5. Seemed, named, framed, tamed, claimed, famed.

72

Building Transcription Skills

75. BUSINESS VOCABULARY BUILDER

marred Damaged.

liberal Generous.

markdowns Decreases of prices for goods on sale.

Reading and Writing Practice

76.

(shorthand outlines)

pur'chased
beau'ti·ful

when

marred
ap·pre'ci·ate
dis'ap·point'ment

intro

sat'is·fac'to·ri·ly
cer'tain

intro

conj

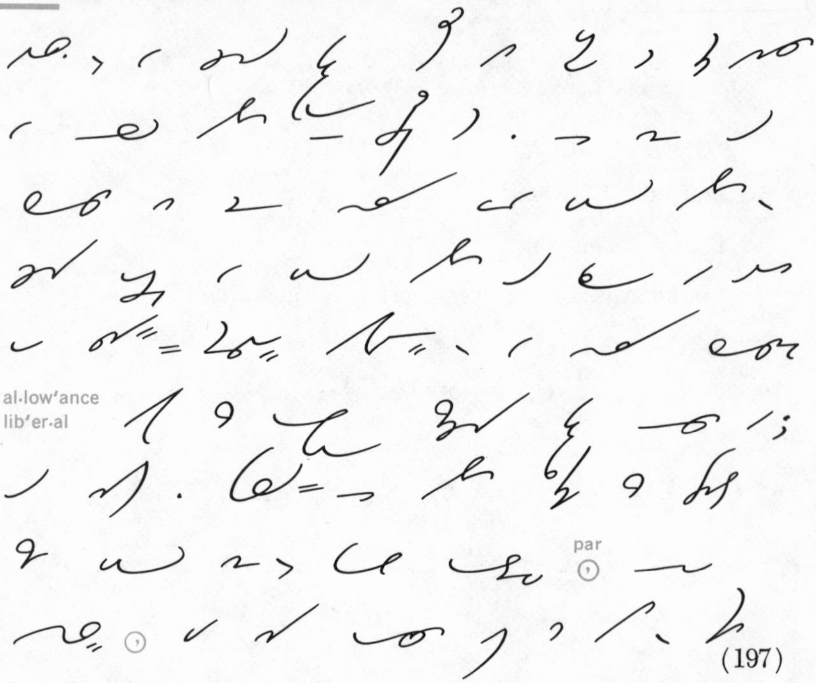

al·low'ance
lib'er·al

par

(197)

77.

par

will'ing·ness
ac·cept'

par

cit'ies
u'su·al·ly

cloth
re·duced'

(123)

78.

ser

intro

nat'u·ral·ly
rea'son

conj

en·ti'tled
dis·pleased'

intro

(103)

79. Check and Double-Check

[shorthand]

He was afraid *[shorthand]*

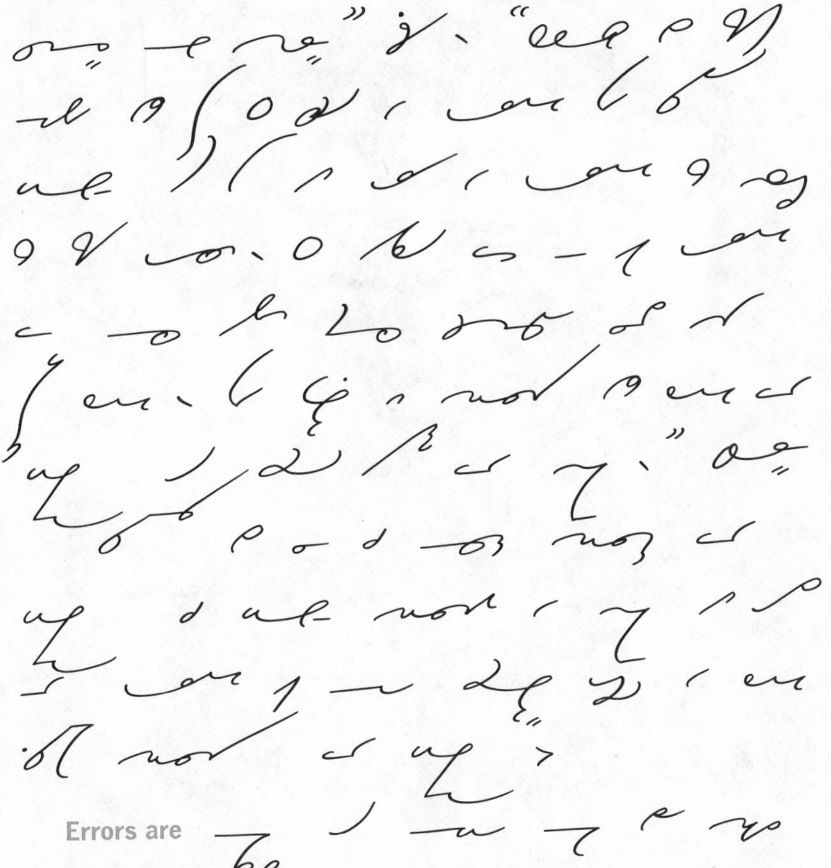

[Gregg shorthand outlines — not transcribable to text]

Errors are *[shorthand outline]*

(348)

Credits and
Collections

"Charge it" is probably the most frequently used expression in business today. You may purchase a coat in a department store and say to the salesclerk, "Charge it." Or you may buy a tankful of gas and tell the attendant to "Charge it" after you ask him to "Fill her up." A business house may order goods, equipment, or services and say — if not in the same words, in effect — "Charge it." These two words are the basis of credit; that is, accepting goods or services now with a promise to pay for them later. Much of today's business is done on credit.

Most organizations have a credit department under the supervision of a credit manager. The credit manager has two primary responsibilities: (1) to decide who shall be granted credit, and (2) to see to it that those who have been granted credit pay their bills. The credit manager's job is an important one indeed. Not only must he collect the money from charge customers, but he must also guard against creating ill will as he does it. If he succeeds in collecting an overdue account but loses the customer in the process, he may hurt rather than help his company. Credit managers must have the knack of being firm but tactful!

Fortunately, most people make their payments when they are due —as they should. Occasionally, however, some do not. Some just forget, and a brief reminder is all they need. Others discover that they are short of funds, for one reason or another, when their bills become due; and, consequently, they cannot pay. Special payment terms often have to be arranged for these people. Still others — only a small minority — make no effort to pay, even though they have the money. These often have to be threatened with legal action before they will pay. As most collections must be handled by mail, you can see the important part that collection letters play in the success of a business.

The letters on which you will practice in this chapter are, for the most part, actual letters that are used by successful companies all over the country. Among them you will find some simple reminders to people who have simply overlooked the fact that their accounts are overdue; some follow-up letters to those who are chronically slow; and a few get-tough letters that threaten legal action when payment is doubtful.

The letters in this chapter are typical of those that you will take from dictation should you become secretary to the credit manager of a store or other type of business organization.

LESSON 11

Building Phrasing Skill

80. PHRASE BUILDER

The following groups contain 25 phrases. Can you read the entire list in 40 seconds or less?

In

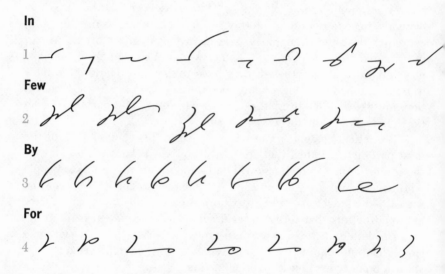

Few

By

For

---

1. In the, in which, in our, in time, in his, in this, in addition, in fact, in order.
2. Few days, few days ago, for a few days, few minutes, few moments.
3. By the, by this, by those, by that, by its, by them, by that time, by mail.
4. For the, for that, for many, for my, for me, for these, for your, for his.

81. WARMUP PHRASE LETTER

The following 113-word letter contains 25 frequently used phrases. Can you read it in 30 seconds and copy it in one minute?

80

[Gregg shorthand outlines]

(113)

Building Transcription Skills

82. PUNCTUATION PRACTICE

You have now reviewed all the uses of the comma that you studied in *Gregg Shorthand;* from this point on, you will take up new punctuation pointers. In this lesson you will take up another common use of the comma.

, nonrestrictive

Nonrestrictive clauses and phrases are set off by commas. A nonrestrictive clause or phrase is one that may be omitted without changing the meaning of the sentence. The nonrestrictive clause or phrase might be classified as parenthetical. It is important that you follow the meaning of the dictation in order to be able to identify the restrictive and the nonrestrictive clauses and phrases and to punctuate them correctly.

> Restrictive—no commas: All persons who are old enough
> to vote should register.
> Nonrestrictive—commas: John Smith, who is old enough
> to vote, should register.

In the first sentence above, *who are old enough to vote* is a restrictive clause and must not be set off by commas. The expression *who are old enough to vote* identifies the persons who should register. In the second sentence, *who is old enough to vote* is a nonrestrictive or descriptive or parenthetical clause that must be set off with commas. It is not needed to identify the particular person who should register; it could be omitted without changing the meaning of the sentence.

Each time the nonrestrictive use of the comma occurs in the Reading and Writing Practice, it will be indicated in the shorthand thus:

nonr

⊙

83. BUSINESS VOCABULARY BUILDER

sober reflection Serious thought.

auditors Those who examine accounts.

lax Lenient; not firm.

Reading and Writing Practice

84.

debt
in'de·pend'ence —

when
⊙

re·flec'tion
right

[Gregg shorthand outlines with annotations: par, par, and o, nonr]

e'co·nom'ic
po·lit'i·cal
de·lin'quent

[Gregg shorthand outlines with annotations: intro, par, nonr]

(117)

....

85.

au'di·tors
re·ceiv'a·ble

[Gregg shorthand outlines with annotations: intro, nonr, par, if, if, as]

[Shorthand outlines] (87)

....

86. *[Shorthand outlines]*

5/ *[shorthand]* nonr *[shorthand]*

[shorthand] intro *[shorthand]*

[shorthand] 5/ *[shorthand]*

[shorthand]

[shorthand] par

fail'ing
past *[shorthand]*

[shorthand]

[shorthand]

[shorthand]

[shorthand] conj *[shorthand]*

[shorthand]

en've·lope
post'age *[shorthand]* nonr

[shorthand] (144)

87. Transcription Quiz.   In this and succeeding Transcription Quizzes, a new factor will be added that will be a challenge to you. In addition to supplying the commas necessary to punctuate the letter correctly, you will have to supply a number of words that have been omitted from the printed shorthand.

Occasionally a stenographer will omit a word when he is taking dictation, either through lack of attention or because he did not hear it. Then, with the help of the meaning of the sentence, he will supply the missing word when transcribing.

You should have no difficulty supplying the missing word in these Transcription Quizzes, as in each case only one possible word makes sense.

For you to supply: 5 commas—2 commas conjunction, 2 commas parenthetical, 1 comma nonrestrictive; two missing words.

(107)

LESSON 12

● **Warmup.** For your warmup during the first few minutes of the period, copy the phrase letter on page 81. Write as rapidly as you can, but be sure that your shorthand notes are readable.

Developing Word-Building Power

88. BRIEF-FORM CHART

The following chart contains 30 brief forms and derivatives. Can you read the entire chart in 35 seconds or less?

---

1. Time, timed, times, timer, timely, timeless.
2. Present, presently, presented, represent, represents, representative.
3. Publish, published, publisher, publishing, publications, unpublished.
4. Over, overdue, overcome, overpay, oversee, overcoat.
5. Order, orders, ordered, orderly, disorder, reorder.

89. GEOGRAPHICAL EXPRESSIONS

2 

1. St. Louis, Portland, Denver, New Orleans, Fort Worth, Salt Lake City.
2. Missouri, Oregon, Colorado, Utah, Idaho, Montana, New Mexico, Texas.

Building Transcription Skills

90. PUNCTUATION PRACTICE

Commas in numbers

1. When a number contains four or more digits, a comma is used to separate thousands, millions, billions.

$1,000 (not $1000) 167,841 1,321,000 4,500,000,000

2. A comma, however, is not used in large serial numbers, house or street numbers, telephone numbers, page numbers, and dates.

No. 14568 6314 Third Avenue Longacre 4-1414
page 1212 1963

These uses of the comma in numbers will be called to your attention in the margin of the Reading and Writing Practice thus:

Transcribe:
No. 14568
$1,000

91. BUSINESS VOCABULARY BUILDER

revenue Income.

delicate Requiring careful handling.

hesitant Uncertain as to what to do or say.

Reading and Writing Practice

92. 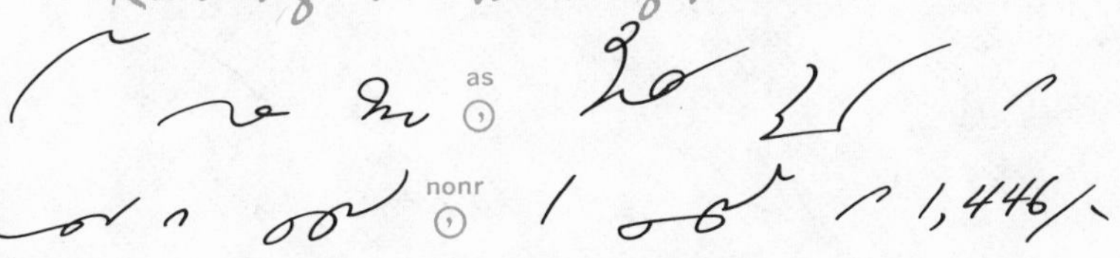

[shorthand outlines]

par

[shorthand outlines]

intro

law'yers
dis·like'

nonr

[shorthand outlines]

1,446

if

4-1616 (136)

························

93. *[shorthand outlines]*

Transcribe:
No. 14568
2820 Baker Street

ap

14568

2820

conj

Transcribe:
$100,000
1961

1961

conj

ap

Le'gal
rev'e·nue

par

guid'ing
prin'ci·ples
grate'ful

and o

if   (169)

94.

Transcribe: 15816
No. 15816

ap

ar

[Gregg shorthand outlines] (78)

95. Transcription Quiz. For you to supply: 6 commas—1 comma *as* clause, 1 comma *when* clause, 1 comma introductory, 1 comma conjunction, 2 commas parenthetical; two missing words.

[Gregg shorthand outlines] (120)

LESSON 13

● **Warmup.** Can you copy the phrase letter on page 81 faster than you did the last time? Each day, try to cut a few seconds off your copying time.

Developing Word-Building Power

96. WORD FAMILIES

-st

1

-rate

2

Or

3

Ol

4

---

1. Past, last, first, rest, test, best, list, cost.
2. Rate, operate, co-operate, concentrate, separate, accurate.
3. Or, nor, more, store, ignore, floor.
4. All, call, recall, collect, stole.

Building Transcription Skills

97. PUNCTUATION PRACTICE

; because of comma

As you already know, a comma is used to separate two independent clauses that are joined by one of the conjunctions *and, but, or,* and *nor.*

Example:

> Mr. Lee will make an automobile trip through the Southwest, and he should arrive in your city by the end of the month.

Sometimes, however, a comma occurs within one or both of the independent clauses. When that occurs, a semicolon is used between the independent clauses.

Examples:

> Our representative, Mr. Lee, will make an automobile trip through the Southwest; and he should arrive in your city by the end of the month.
> Mr. Lee will make an automobile trip through the Southwest; and, weather permitting, he should arrive in your city by the end of the month.

The reason for this is simple enough. If there are other commas in the sentence, something stronger than a comma is required to separate the two parts of the sentence.

Each time this use of the semicolon occurs in the Reading and Writing Practice, it will be indicated in the shorthand thus:

bc

⊙

98. BUSINESS VOCABULARY BUILDER

routine (*adjective*) Done regularly, as a matter of course.

remittance Payment.

reciprocate Return good for good.

Reading and Writing Practice

99.

re·ceived'
ex'pla·na'tion

re'al·ize
con·nec'tion

(101)

- -

100.

col·lect'
due

[Gregg shorthand outlines]

ig·nore'
plain'ly
of·fense'

when

conj

stick'ers
dif'fer·ent   10

and o

bc

re·mit'tance
in'voice

nonr

30   (121)

• •

101.

ap

10

set'tle
re·ceive'   5

bc

10   *conj*

Transcribe:
$1,000

par

cer'tain·ly
ap·pre'ci·ate

(84)

102. Transcription Quiz.   For you to supply: 5 commas—2 commas series, 1 comma introductory, 1 comma conjunction, 1 comma *if* clause; two missing words.

(117)

....

There is no substitute for shorthand speed. — H. H. Green

LESSON 14

● **Warmup.** Can you copy the phrase letter on page 81 a little faster than you did the last time? If there is time to do so, copy the letter a second time in your best shorthand, for control.

Developing Word-Building Power

103. WORD BEGINNINGS AND ENDINGS

Un-

Circum-

De-

-ful

1. Unfair, unless, unpaid, unwise, until, unbiased, unplanned.
2. Circumstance, circumstances, circumstantial, circumnavigate, circumvent, circumference.
3. Delay, delinquent, deliver, deliberate, depress, depart.
4. Successful, careful, usefulness, faithful, wonderful, thoughtful, helpful, roomful.

96

Building Transcription Skills

104. PUNCTUATION PRACTICE

; no conjunction

A semicolon is used to separate two independent, but closely related, clauses when no conjunction is used to connect the clauses.

> Mary received an appointment in the Personnel Department; her sister was not appointed.

The above sentence could be written as two sentences.

> Mary received an appointment in the Personnel Department. Her sister was not appointed.

Because the two thoughts are closely related, however, the use of the semicolon seems more appropriate.

Each time this use of the semicolon occurs in the Reading and Writing Practice, it will be indicated in the shorthand thus:

nc
⊙

105. BUSINESS VOCABULARY BUILDER

distasteful   Unpleasant.

hallmark   A mark that guarantees quality.

jeopardy   Danger.

Reading and Writing Practice

106.

suc·cess'ful
busi'ness·man'

[Gregg shorthand outlines]

en·dan'ger·ing
bal'ance

3) *[nonr shorthand symbol]*

o'ver·due'
de·lin'quent *[intro]*

lo'cal
bu'reau

[nc]

(132)

··

107.

busi'ness·men'
re'al·ize

[nc]

444/

[if]

(92)

108.

re·quest'ed
re'cent

par

Transcribe:
No. 15161   15161   if

nc

(90)

109.

par   nc   par

jeop'ard·y
owed
a·ware'

as

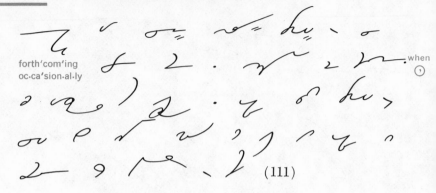

forth'com'ing
oc·ca'sion·al·ly

(111)

110.   Transcription Quiz.   For you to supply: 7 commas—6 commas parenthetical, 1 comma conjunction; two missing words.

(128)

LESSON 15

● **Warmup.** This will be the last time that you will copy the phrase letter on page 81 as a warmup. If you have time, copy the letter a second time in your best shorthand, for control.

Developing Word-Building Power

111. SHORTHAND VOCABULARY BUILDER

Ng

1 *(shorthand outlines)*

Nk (ngk)

2 *(shorthand outlines)*

Omission of Ē from Ū

3 *(shorthand outlines)*

Tern, Term

4 *(shorthand outlines)*

---

1. Wrong, strong, spring, longer, single, among.
2. Frank, banker, ink, blank, function, banquet.
3. Due, overdue, suit, lawsuit, new, renew, renewal.
4. Turn, turner, determine, determination, stern, term, termed.

Building Transcription Skills

112. BUSINESS VOCABULARY BUILDER

purchasing agent   The person in an organization who does all the buying.

enviable   Desirable.

Reading and Writing Practice

113.

wheth'er
pur'chas·ing

(shorthand outlines)

conj ⊙

intro ⊙

an'swers
won't

(110)

114.

prompt'ness
in·val'u·a·ble
en'vi·a·ble

and o

yours
un'ap·pre'ci·at·ed

nc

intro

ef·fi'cient

and o

par

bc

(114)

....

115.

12⁵⁰

nonr

and o

(52)

116. Eleanor Baker, Timesaver

[shorthand]

Eleanor put *[shorthand]*

104

1. <u>Urgent.</u> *[Gregg shorthand outline]*

2. <u>Correspondence to Be Answered.</u> *[Gregg shorthand outline]*

3. <u>Correspondence to Be Read.</u> *[Gregg shorthand outline]*

4. <u>Miscellaneous Reading.</u> *[Gregg shorthand outline]*

(348)

Advertising

No doubt you have heard the saying that if a person builds a better mousetrap than his neighbor, the world will beat a path to his door. This saying has been attributed to Ralph Waldo Emerson. Emerson was indeed a great poet and essayist; but we suspect that he would not have been very successful as an advertising man, for what would it avail a man to build the world's best mousetrap if he did not let the world know about it?

After a man builds his mousetrap, he must announce the fact to the mousetrap-buying public; he must set forth the reasons why his mousetrap will catch more mice than the mousetraps already on the market; he must let the public know where they can buy the mousetrap and how much it costs. In short, even the world's best mousetrap must be advertised — and that is the function of the advertising industry.

Advertising in America goes hand in hand with our system of business. In order to produce goods in large quantities, we must have means of letting the people know that the merchandise is available. Advertising uses various media — newspapers, magazines, radio, television, billboards — even skywriting! Sometimes we may think we are exposed to too much advertising, but we must remember that advertising enables us to have good television programs at no cost to us and that it keeps down the cost of newspapers and magazines. More important, however, is the fact that advertising enables us to enjoy more goods and services at less cost than would otherwise be possible.

Working in an advertising department of a business firm or in an advertising agency can be an interesting and exciting experience. Perhaps you have already given some thought to a career in some phase of advertising — as a commercial artist, copy writer, market analyst, or research assistant, for example. Of course, you cannot hope to be hired in any of these capacities immediately upon your graduation; only experienced people get these coveted jobs in advertising. You can, however, get your foot in the door of the advertising business through a stenographic position — advertising concerns *need* thousands of stenographers. As a stenographer you will have the best possible opportunity to demonstrate any special talents you may have to the executives who make appointments.

The letters in this chapter are representative of those you would take from dictation if you worked in the field of advertising.

LESSON 16

Building Phrasing Skill

117. PHRASE BUILDER

The following four groups of phrases contain 32 phrases. Can you read the entire list in 30 seconds?

As

1 

If

2 

That

3 

Of

4 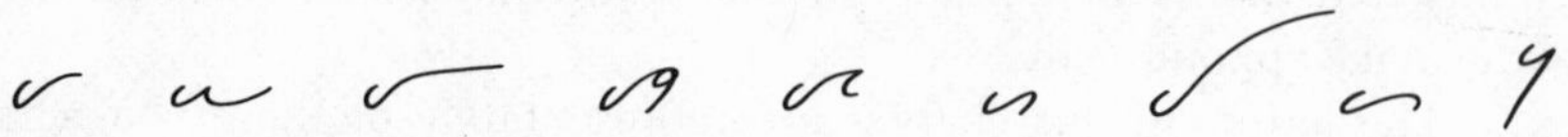

---

1. As the, as you, as you know, as you may, as you will, as you can, as you are, as if.
2. If you, if you will, if you can, if you would, if you know, if you have, if it is, if it will.
3. That is, that is not, that are, that will, that would, that it will, that it will be.
4. Of the, of our, of them, of these, of those, of you, of time, of course, of which.

118. WARMUP PHRASE LETTER

The following 120-word phrase letter contains 23 phrases. Your reading goal: 1 minute; your copying goal: 2 minutes or less.

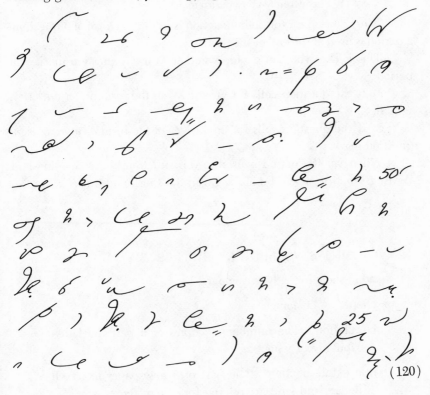

(120)

Building Transcription Skills

119. PUNCTUATION PRACTICE

courteous request

Very often one businessman may wish to persuade another to take some definite action. He could make his request for action with a direct statement such as:

I want to hear from you by return mail.

A direct statement of this type, however, might antagonize the reader. Many businessmen, therefore, prefer to make such a request in the form of a question.

> May I hear from you by return mail.

Where a request for definite action is put in the form of a question, a period is used at the end of the sentence.

This is how you can decide whether to use a question mark or a period:

1. If the question calls for an answer in the form of *action,* use a period.

2. If the question calls for an answer in the form of *words,* use a question mark.

Whenever the period is used in this situation in the Reading and Writing Practice, it will be indicated in the shorthand thus:

cr

⊙

120. BUSINESS VOCABULARY BUILDER

ad Short for "advertisement."

client A customer.

circulation The number of copies of a periodical distributed per issue.

real estate section The part of a newspaper in which houses and land are offered for sale or rent.

Reading and Writing Practice

121.

pleas'ant·ly
col'umns

ap

at·tract′ed
de·sir′a·ble

Transcribe:
$40,000
worth

(93)

....

122.

as·so′ci·ates
judg′ment
ad′ver·tis′ers

con·tin′ues

Transcribe:
59,000
3,000

pro·gres'sive

when

cr (172)

123.

hours
trace

conj

intro

A'gen·cy
writes

nc

intro

[Gregg shorthand outlines] (141)

124. **Transcription Quiz.**   For you to supply: 8 commas—1 comma nonrestrictive, 2 commas series, 2 commas parenthetical, 1 comma *if* clause, 1 comma apposition; 2 missing words.

[Gregg shorthand outlines] (107)

If she is wise and wishes to advance, a secretary will always offer to help other members of the staff whenever she can. — James M. Clark, Personnel Relations, American Telephone and Telegraph Company

LESSON 17

● **Warmup.**   Your warmup letter is on page 109. This time, instead of warming up on the entire letter, use only the first paragraph. Write the paragraph slowly at first, in your best penmanship. Write the paragraph again, writing as rapidly as you can. If time permits, write it a third time, striving for an even higher writing speed. Finally, write the paragraph slowly for control.

Developing Word-Building Power

125.   BRIEF-FORM CHART

Can you read the 30 brief forms and derivatives in this chart in 30 seconds or less?

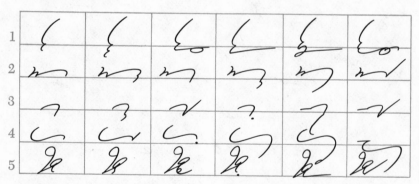

1. Business, businesses, businessman, businessmen, businesswomen, businesslike.
2. Suggest, suggests, suggestion, suggestions, suggestive, suggested.
3. Question, questions, questioned, questioning, unquestionable, unquestioned.
4. Progress, progressed, progressing, progressive, progressively, unprogressive.
5. Advertise, advertises, advertiser, advertising, advertisement, advertised.

126. GEOGRAPHICAL EXPRESSIONS

1. Wilmington, Baltimore, Richmond, Charleston, Columbus.
2. Delaware, Maryland, Virginia, West Virginia, South Carolina, North Carolina, Georgia.

Building Transcription Skills

127. PUNCTUATION PRACTICE

Hyphens

Hyphenated before noun
No noun, no hyphen
No hyphen after *ly*

You can quickly decide whether to use a hyphen in compound expressions like *past due* or *well trained* by observing these rules:

1. If a noun follows the expression, use a hyphen.

> We are concerned about your *past-due* account (*noun*).
> Our *well-trained* representative (*noun*) will call on you.

Whenever a hyphenated expression occurs in the Reading and Writing Practice, it will be called to your attention in the margin thus:

> past-due
> *hyphenated*
> *before noun*

2. If *no* noun follows the compound expression, do *not* use a hyphen.

> Your account is past due.
> Our representative is well trained.

Occasionally, these expressions in which a hyphen is not used will be called to your attention in the Reading and Writing Practice thus:

well trained

no noun,

no hyphen

3. No hyphen is used in a compound modifier where the first part of the expression is an adverb that ends in *ly*.

He was editor of a widely read magazine.

To be sure that you are not tempted to put a hyphen in expressions of this type, we will occasionally call attention to them in the Reading and Writing Practice thus:

widely read

no hyphen

after ly

128. BUSINESS VOCABULARY BUILDER

solicit To ask for.

testimonial A statement in favor of a product, service, or person.

evaluate To determine the value of.

cosmetics Beauty creams, rouge, face powder, etc.

Reading and Writing Practice

129.

128-page
*hyphenated
before noun*

ex·pens′es
prac′tice
so·lic′it

[Gregg shorthand outlines]

post'age-paid'
  hyphenated
  before noun

(120)

....

130. *[shorthand outline]* **as**

well'-planned'
  hyphenated
  before noun

bc

wide'ly read'
  no hyphen
  after ly

ap

par

[Gregg shorthand outlines]

nc

(173)

....

131.

ap

ma·te'ri·al
e·val'u·ate

intro

com·mer'cial
in·dus'tri·al

1961 intro

nc   intro   140

u·nique'
sup·plies'

cos·met'ics
wear'ing
ap·par'el

ser

[Gregg shorthand outlines]

if

ap

cr

330

42   36   (194)

132. Transcription Quiz.   For you to supply: 7 commas — 6 commas parenthetical, 1 comma nonrestrictive; two missing words.

[Gregg shorthand outlines]

(137)

LESSON 18

● **Warmup.** Once again, warm up on the phrase letter on page 109. This time warm up on the second paragraph in the same way you warmed up on the first paragraph of the letter.

Developing Word-Building Power

133. WORD FAMILIES

-tional

1

-book

2

-est

3

-side

4

---

1. National, additional, exceptional, professional, traditional, educational.
2. Book, handbook, textbook, notebook, bankbook, yearbook, passbook.
3. Latest, fullest, oldest, greatest, finest, widest.
4. Side, sides, aside, decide, reside, preside, inside, beside.

120

Building Transcription Skills

134. PUNCTUATION PRACTICE

The apostrophe

1. A noun that ends in an *s* sound and is followed by another noun is usually a possessive, calling for an apostrophe before the *s* when the word is singular.

> This company's advertising is designed for three colors.
> Mr. Green's job will be to look after our interests in television.

2. A plural noun ending in *s* calls for an apostrophe *after* the *s* to form the possessive.

> Their employees' wages have been raised.
> All students' marks will be issued Friday.

3. An irregular plural calls for an apostrophe *before* the *s* to form the possessive.

> We sell children's toys.
> He will open a men's clothing store soon.

4. The possessive forms of pronouns do not require an apostrophe.

> You will be wasting *your* time as well as *ours*.
> These papers are *theirs*, not *ours*.

135. BUSINESS VOCABULARY BUILDER

network   A chain of radio or television stations.

silver anniversary   The twenty-fifth anniversary.

appropriation   A sum of money set aside for a definite purpose.

merit   Deserve.

Reading and Writing Practice

136.

cli'ent
se'ri·ous

com'pa·ny's
col'ors

three'-col'or
*hyphenated
before noun*

(127)

•••••••••••••••••••••••••••••••

137.

buy'ing
Pitts'burgh

[Gregg shorthand outlines]

high'-grade'
low'-cost'
hyphenated
before noun

and o

chil'dren's
de·scrip'tion

par

bc

when

cr

of'fered
De·part'ment's

conj

if

(152)

....

138.

tel'e·vi'sion
Green's

pi'o·neers'
con·nect'ed

intro ⊙

su'per·vi'sion
well' known'
no noun,
no hyphen

bc ⊙

and o ⊙

(150)

....

139.

an'ni·ver'sa·ry
his'to·ry
suc·cess'

pause
pleas'ure

25

[Gregg shorthand outlines]

intro
⊙

ap·pre′ci·ate
growth

(163)

140.   Transcription Quiz.   For you to supply: 5 commas—1 comma conjunction, 4 commas parenthetical; two missing words.

[Gregg shorthand outlines]

(121)

LESSON 19

● **Warmup.**   Your warmup letter is on page 109. Practice the third paragraph as you practiced the first paragraph for your warmup when you were working on Lesson 17. Don't forget the final writing for control.

Developing Word-Building Power

141. WORD BEGINNINGS AND ENDINGS

Inter-

1 *(shorthand outlines)*

-ings

2 *(shorthand outlines)*

-ure

3 *(shorthand outlines)*

-ual

4 *(shorthand outlines)*

---

1. Interview, interest, international, interfere, internal, interpret, interruption.
2. Mailings, readings, billings, savings, greetings, clippings.
3. Furniture, feature, picture, nature, naturally, fracture, secure.
4. Annual, schedule, actual, actually, annually, perpetual.

126

Building Transcription Skills

142. **BUSINESS VOCABULARY BUILDER**

insight   A look into.

honorarium   A token payment for services on which no price can be set.

impetus   Push; encouragement.

expectations   Hopes.

143. **SIMILAR-WORDS DRILL**

Choose, chose

choose   To select.

[shorthand outlines]

We are sorry you did not choose us to do the job.

chose (past tense of *choose*)   Selected.

[shorthand outlines]

We chose the Tribune in which to advertise our products.

Reading and Writing Practice

144. *[shorthand outlines]*

ban'quet   *[shorthand outlines]*

and o

ac·cept′
in′sight′
fac′tors

ex·pens′es
hon′o·rar′i·um

par

(145)

·····························

145.

nat′u·ral·ly
wom′en

intro

par

how·ev′er
Jour′nal

intro

ap

cit′y's
write

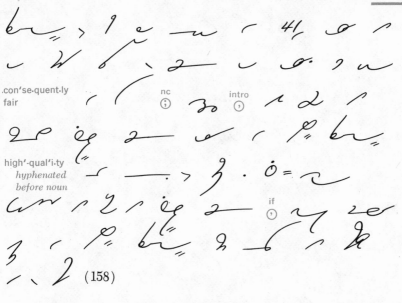

.con'se·quent·ly
fair

nc

intro

high'-qual'i·ty
hyphenated
before noun

if

(158)

····································

146.

two'-page'
hyphenated
before noun

conj

ac·com'plished
ac'tu·al·ly

when

bc

im'pe·tus
en·thu'si·asm

nonr

chose
ve'hi·cle

(111)

147.

Transcribe:
3141

a're·a
a·mazed'
re·sponse'

Transcribe:
3,000

as
3141
66
13
ser
14
15
conj
nc
3
ap
intro
par

(118)

148.

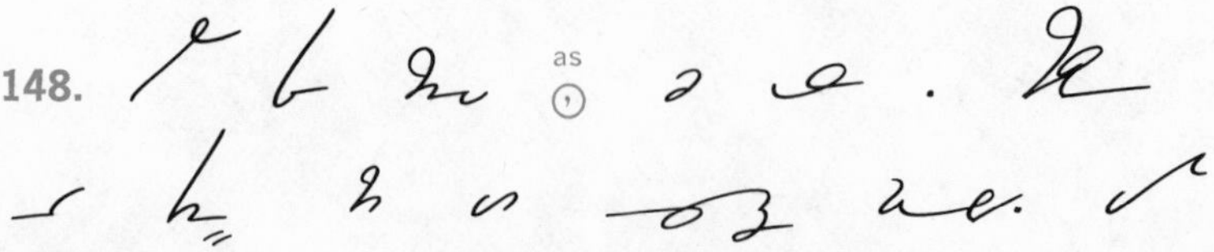
as

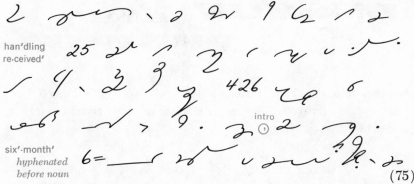

han'dling
re·ceived'

six'-month'
hyphenated
before noun

(75)

149. Transcription Quiz.   For you to supply: 6 commas—2 commas apposition, 1 comma introductory, 1 comma *as* clause, 2 commas series; two missing words.

(126)

LESSON 20

● **Warmup.** Your warmup letter, which you will use for the last time, appears on page 109. Copy the letter as many times as you can and as rapidly as you can.

Developing Word-Building Power

150. SHORTHAND VOCABULARY BUILDER

Oi

W Dash

Ū

Ow

1. Point, invoice, toil, enjoyed, boil, join, voice, avoid.
2. Quoted, quite, equipped, square, quick, quicker.
3. Few, view, unique, review, unit, unite, futile, utilize.
4. Down, brown, account, amount, flower, towel.

Building Transcription Skills

151. BUSINESS VOCABULARY BUILDER

currently At the present time.

132

assurance Certainty.

productive Bringing results.

Reading and Writing Practice

152.

in'voice
billed

[Gregg shorthand outlines]

re·call'
ef·fect'

(121)

....

153.

hap'pen·ing
cur'rent·ly
e'qual·ly

[Gregg shorthand outlines]

[Shorthand outlines]

up to the min'ute
no noun,
no hyphen

intro

ser

busi'ness·man's
of'fic·es

(141)

....

154.

en·joyed'
Com'pa·ny's

when

intro

quite
rea'son

bc

(Gregg shorthand outlines)

154.

em·ploy'ees
cus'tom·er's

intro

well e·quipped'
no noun,
no hyphen

if

cr

(120)

· ·

155.

ap

as

Transcribe:
90,000
110,000

par

nc   intro

cir'cu·la'tion
sub·scrib'ers

(120)

156. Pull or Push?

[shorthand outlines]

Was it pull *[shorthand outlines]*

[Gregg shorthand outlines]

Another *[Gregg shorthand outlines]*

[Gregg shorthand outlines] (297)

The Champion's Notes

When Martin J. Dupraw won the world's shorthand championship, he established some remarkable records for accuracy. On a speech dictated at 200 words a minute for five minutes, he made only one error. On court testimony dictated at 280 words a minute for five minutes, he made only two errors. These and many other records that he has established are due, in large measure, to the amazing legibility of his shorthand notes.

When you examine Mr. Dupraw's shorthand notes on the following page, which he wrote from dictation especially for *Gregg Dictation, Diamond Jubilee Series*, one thing will immediately impress you — the careful attention to proportion.

Notice for example how large he makes his *a* circles and how small he makes the *e* circles. There is never any question whether a circle represents *a* or *e*. Notice, too, how much larger his *l*'s are than his *r*'s. As you read Mr. Dupraw's notes, you will observe many other examples of good proportion.

Another thing that will strike you as you examine Mr. Dupraw's notes is the way he rounds off angles. He does not consciously do this; rounding angles comes naturally to him as a result of his high speed. As your speed increases, you, too, will find that you will naturally round off angles.

In the piece that Mr. Dupraw has written in his beautiful shorthand, he discusses the size of notes. You will notice that he has a fairly large shorthand style, just as he has a large longhand style.

Don't try to imitate Mr. Dupraw's style of writing; take the advice he gives in his article "How Big Should My Shorthand Be?"

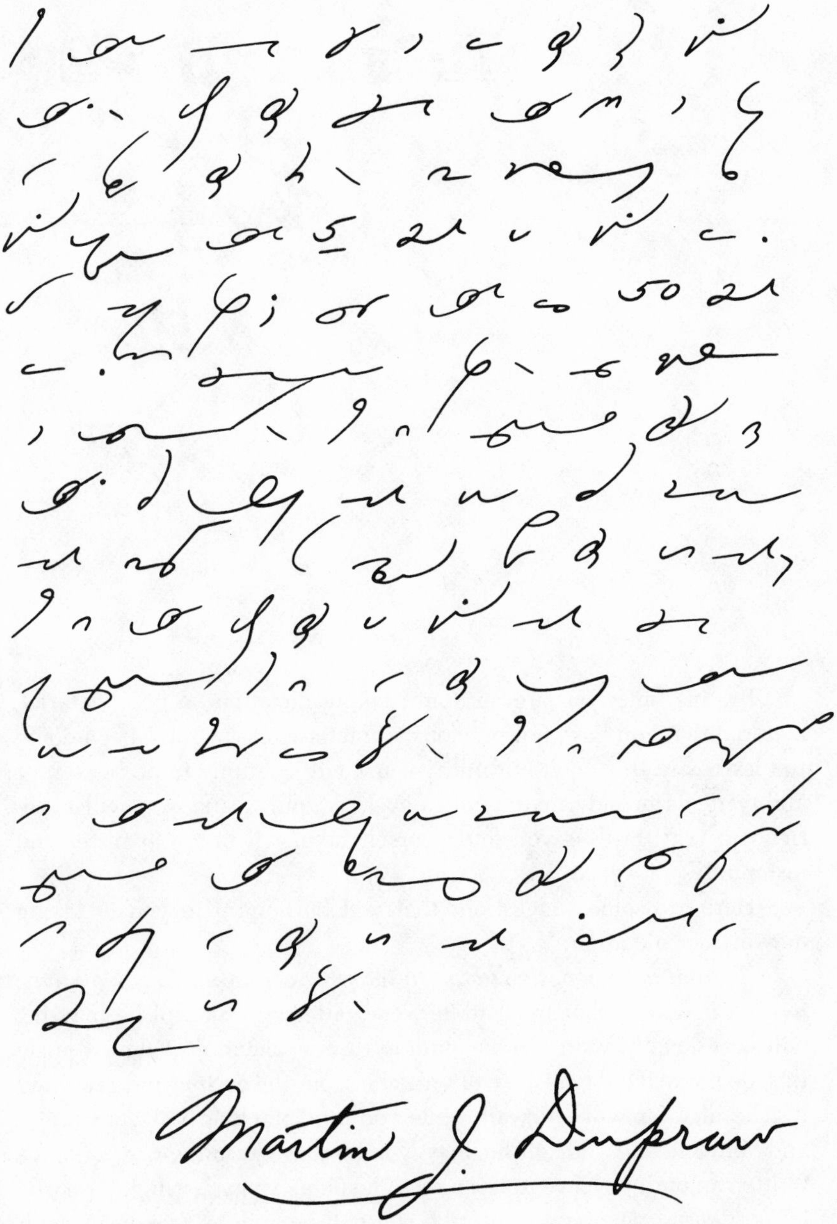

[Page of Gregg shorthand outlines — not transcribable as text]

Martin J. Dupraw (signature)

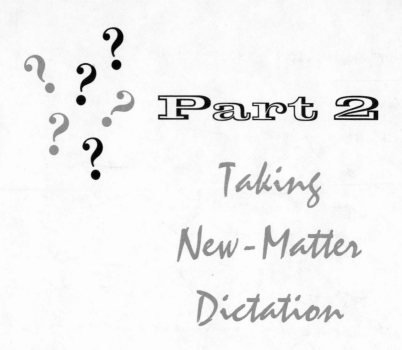

Part 2

Taking New-Matter Dictation

By this time, you are no doubt taking dictation on new material, material that you have not previously practiced. If you have been doing the lessons in this book faithfully — and will continue to do so — your ability to write new matter will develop rapidly, and you will experience a real thrill as you find yourself taking dictation at faster and faster rates of speed.

Here are some suggestions that will be helpful to you in taking new-matter dictation:

During dictation, don't stop to improve an outline once you have written it. Every shorthand writer, no matter how skillful he may be, will occasionally write a poor outline during dictation. When you do this, do not make the mistake of scratching out the outline and rewriting it. The dictator will not wait while you are "patching up" your notes, and you may find yourself hopelessly behind as a result. Once you have written an outline, leave it. Even though you may have written it poorly, in most cases when you transcribe you will be able to decipher it with the aid of the context.

When the dictator uses a word that is unfamiliar to you, write something down — don't stop writing. In your practice work and in your dictation on the job, you will constantly be encountering words that are unfamiliar to you. When one of these words comes along, try to write it in full; write all the sounds you hear. If you cannot do this, try to get down at least the beginning. Often this beginning, along with the context, will be sufficient to enable you to find the correct word in the dictionary.

There will be times when you are unable to write anything for an unfamiliar word. When that happens, leave a space in your notes and continue writing. Don't spend so much time trying to form an outline for the word that the dictation gets too far ahead of you. You will be surprised, when you transcribe, how often you will be able to fill in the word or supply an equally acceptable one — with the aid of the context.

Never stop writing. There will be times in your speed-development work when the dictation will be too fast for you and you will miss some of it. You must not let this worry you. If you always took dictation at speeds that you could write easily, you would make little progress. In order to build up your speed, you must practice at speeds beyond the rate that you are writing at the moment. When you find yourself getting behind the dictator, hang on as long as you can. Something may happen that will enable you to catch up — the dictator may stop to take a breath or there may be an easy spot in the dictation or a nice phrase may come to your rescue.

If, however, you are so far behind that you feel nothing will help you, drop the words that you have not yet written and pick up the dictation again. But don't decide to drop too soon — and never stop writing!

Don't try to phrase too much. Some writers have the feeling that the key to shorthand speed is phrasing. Phrases will help in gaining shorthand speed only if they can be written without hesitation.

Remember, too, that a dictator may not always say a phrase as one piece. He may say one word in a phrase and then pause before he says the remaining words. When that occurs, you will probably have the first word written before you hear the rest of the phrase. You should then write the remaining words of the phrase as though no phrase were involved. Under no circumstances should you scratch out the word that you have already written and then write the phrase.

141

Public Relations

Ray Farnsworth is a successful business executive. During the course of a day he writes many letters that pertain directly to the operation of his business. He writes sales letters that he hopes will convince prospects that it is to their advantage to buy his goods or services; he writes letters to suppliers ordering merchandise and equipment and following up on delivery schedules; he writes memos to his sales staff telling them about new products, guiding them to new prospects, and suggesting ways that they can better serve old customers.

In addition, however, he takes time to write another very important type of letter — the public relations letter. Though the public relations letter does not pertain to the day-to-day operation of a business, its value cannot be measured in dollars and cents. Most public relations letters fall into three categories — appreciation, congratulation, and sympathy.

Appreciation. Mr. Farnsworth has learned that it pays to say "Thank you" when someone does something nice for him. Whenever a customer sends in an especially large order, he writes him a note of appreciation. Whenever a business associate entertains him or goes out of his way to render some special service for him, he sends a note of appreciation.

Congratulation. Mr. Farnsworth never forgot the letters he received from his friends and business associates when he was promoted to his present position as vice-president. These letters convinced him that people were interested in his progress and wanted to share his happiness in his good fortune. Consequently, whenever a friend, customer, or business associate receives some special honor — is appointed to a higher position, is given a special recognition by his company or community, is elected to an office in a club or civic organization, or is commended for the new book he has written — Mr. Farnsworth is quick to write a note of congratulation. When one of his salesmen gets an order from a particularly difficult customer, he gives him a pat on the back by means of a letter. Whenever he learns that a business associate or customer has been married or that there has been a birth in his family, he writes a note. Anniversaries, retirements, new positions — all are events calling for letters of congratulation.

Sympathy. The most difficult letter Mr. Farnsworth has to write is a letter of sympathy. But that does not prevent him from writing to customers or business associates when they have experienced some misfortune or personal tragedy. He knows that people appreciate a sincere note of sympathy in their troubled hours.

No matter what type of business you may enter or for whom you may work, a good many of the letters you will take from dictation will fall in the category of public relations. The letters in this chapter are examples of public relations letters; they show that many business executives are thoughtful human beings who have a sincere interest in people.

LESSON 21

Building Phrasing Skill

157. PHRASE BUILDER

The following four groups of phrases contain 27 phrases. Can you read the entire list in 30 seconds?

Thank

1 *[shorthand outlines]*

Very

2 *[shorthand outlines]*

To

3 *[shorthand outlines]*

Let us

4 *[shorthand outlines]*

---

1. Thank you, thank you for, thank you for the, thank you for your, thank you for your order, thank you for this, to thank you for, to thank you for the.
2. Very important, very much, very well, very glad, very soon, very low.
3. To you, to the, to this, to us, to them, to these, to that, to time.
4. Let us, let us know, let us see, let us have, let us make.

158. WARMUP PHRASE LETTER

Your warmup phrase letter for this chapter contains 118 words.

144

There are 18 useful phrases in it. How fast can you read this letter?
How fast can you make a shorthand copy of it?

(118)

Building Transcription Skills

159. BUSINESS VOCABULARY BUILDER

> **complimentary** Expressing appreciation or admiration
> of.
>
> **format** The general makeup of a publication, such as
> a magazine, book, or newspaper.

participants Those who take part in something.

160. TYPING STYLE STUDY

Dates

1. If the name of the month precedes the day, do not use *th, st,* or *d* after the number. This is the most frequent way that dates are expressed in business letters.

On June 16, 1968, he will be sixty-five years old.

Notice that when a date is expressed in this way, there is a comma both *before* and *after* the year.

2. If the day precedes the month, *th, st,* or *d* should be included.

On the 25th of May he will be able to vote.

When dates appear in the Reading and Writing Practice, they will be called to your attention in the margin thus:

Transcribe:
June 15
July 15, 1968,
15th

Reading and Writing Practice

161.
Transcribe:
April 18
com'pli·men'ta·ry

vol'ume
in'di·cates

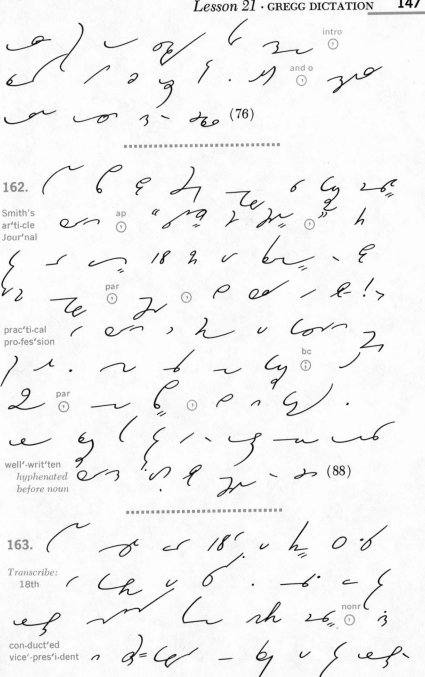

intro

(76)

162.

Smith's
ar'ti·cle
Jour'nal

ap

par

prac'ti·cal
pro·fes'sion

bc

par

well'-writ'ten
hyphenated
before noun

(88)

163.

Transcribe:
18th

nonr

con·duct'ed
vice'-pres'i·dent

[Shorthand outlines]

lis'ten·ers
edge
their

nonr

sense
hu'mor

nc

intro

par

par

(145)

···

164.

re·peat'
Transcribe:
June 16

conj

ap·pre'ci·ate
as·sign'ment

as

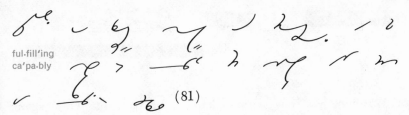

ful·fill'ing
ca'pa·bly

(81)

165. Transcription Quiz.　The transcription quizzes hereafter will be a greater challenge to you.

Thus far you have had to supply only commas to punctuate a letter correctly; hereafter, you will also have to supply semicolons. If you have paid close attention to the semicolons used in Chapters 3 and 4, this new feature will present no problem for you.

For you to supply: 3 commas—2 commas introductory, 1 comma *if* clause; 1 semicolon because of comma; 2 missing words.

(92)

LESSON 22

● **Warmup.** Your warmup letter is on page 145. Once again, practice it a paragraph at a time. Today, write the first paragraph slowly the first time, as rapidly as you can the second time, and in your best shorthand the third time.

Developing Word-Building Power

166. BRIEF-FORM CHART

Your reading goal: 30 seconds or less.

1. Manufacture, manufactures, manufactured, manufacturing, manufacturer, manufacturers.
2. Part, parts, parted, depart, department, apart.
3. Wish, wished, wishing, wishes, wishful, wishfully.
4. Correspond, corresponds, corresponded, corresponding, correspondent, correspondingly.
5. Organize, organized, organization, organizer, disorganized, reorganize.

167. GEOGRAPHICAL EXPRESSIONS

2 *[shorthand outline]*

1. Phoenix, Milwaukee, Providence, Birmingham, Lexington.
2. Alabama, Texas, New Mexico, Arizona, Wisconsin, Rhode Island.

Building Transcription Skills

168. BUSINESS VOCABULARY BUILDER

memorable Worthy of being remembered.

superb Splendid; fine.

hospitality The act of receiving people kindly and courteously.

169. TYPING STYLE STUDY

Addresses

1. Always use figures in house numbers.

   He lived at 600 (not *six hundred*) Market Street.
2. Spell out numbers in street addresses from one through ten.

   He worked at 330 Fourth Avenue.
3. Use numbers in street addresses over ten.

   His address is 18 East 67 Street.

Note 1: Always spell out *Street, Avenue, Road,* etc.

Note 2: Omit *th, st,* and *d* from numbered street names. The omission of these endings adds to the readability of the address.

When street addresses occur in the Reading and Writing Practice, they will occasionally be called to your attention in the margin of the shorthand thus:

Transcribe:
67 Street
Fourth Street

Reading and Writing Practice

170.

[shorthand outlines]

nat'u·ral·ly
rich'ly

intro
⊙

bc
⊙

intro
⊙

and o
⊙

par
⊙   ⊙

ac·com′plish·ments
trav′els

if
⊙

(134)

....

171.

Phoe′nix
mem′o·ra·ble
com′pa·ny's

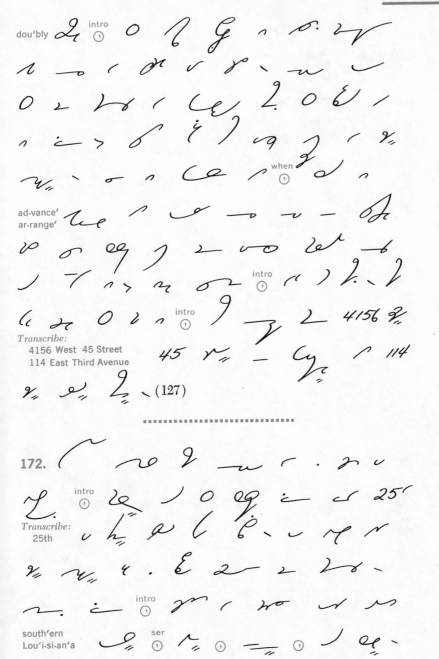

dou·bly

ad·vance'
ar·range'

Transcribe:
4156 West 45 Street
114 East Third Avenue

(127)

172.

Transcribe:
25th

south'ern
Lou'i·si·an'a

[shorthand outlines]

su·perb'
en'ter·tain'ing

ser

intro

(120)

173. **Transcription Quiz.** For you to supply: 3 commas—1 comma conjunction, 2 commas parenthetical; 1 semicolon because of comma; 1 missing word.

[shorthand outlines]

(82)

LESSON 23

Warmup.   Use the second paragraph of the phrase letter on page 145 today for your warmup. Remember, write the paragraph slowly on your first writing; then, as rapidly as you can without making your shorthand unreadable; and finally, in your best shorthand.

Developing Word-Building Power

174. WORD FAMILIES

-tend

-come

-ciate

-tain

1. Extend, pretend, contend, attend, intend, superintend.
2. Come, income, outcome, welcome, become.
3. Associate, appreciate, negotiate, substantiate, differentiate, depreciate, officiate.
4. Maintain, certain, contain, retain, attain, pertain, captain, detain.

155

Building Transcription Skills

175. BUSINESS VOCABULARY BUILDER

consignment A shipment of goods that do not have to be paid for by the agent until he sells them.

business associates Fellow workers.

pertain Relate to.

176. TYPING STYLE STUDY

Amounts of money

1. When transcribing even amounts of dollars in business letters, do not use a decimal point or zeros.

His check for $152 (not *$152.00*) was returned by the bank.

2. In business letters use the word *cents* in amounts under $1.

The book cost only 39 cents (not *$.39*).

When amounts such as the above appear in the Reading and Writing Practice, they will occasionally be called to your attention in the margin of the shorthand thus:

Transcribe:
$515
6 cents

Reading and Writing Practice

177.

sym'pa·thy
serv'ice

[Gregg shorthand outlines]

if

con·sign'ment
Transcribe:
  $5,000

conj

12

as·sist'ance
ap·pre'ci·ate

nc

(136)

....

178.

Transcribe:
  No. 1158

1158

best'-look'ing
  hyphenated
  before noun

(60)

179.

[shorthand outlines]

birth
re'al·ize

[shorthand outlines]

ser

[shorthand outlines]

Transcribe:
$10

[shorthand outlines]

Transcribe:
$1

[shorthand outlines]

cor'dial·ly
son's

[shorthand outlines] (126)

••••••••••••••••••••••••••••••••

180.

[shorthand outlines]

Transcribe:
15th
sur·prised'

[shorthand outlines]

as

[Gregg shorthand outlines]

bc

par

par

par

hap′pi·ness
re′al·ize
wheth′er

_ ! (107)

· ·

181.

80

for′ward
buy′ing

if

Guide
per′son·nel′

ap

nonr

phas′es
per′son·al·ly

[Gregg shorthand outlines] (121)

182. Transcription Quiz. For you to supply: 4 commas—2 commas introductory, 1 comma *and* omitted, 1 comma nonrestrictive; 1 semicolon no conjunction; 2 missing words.

[Gregg shorthand outlines] (108)

LESSON 24

● **Warmup.** For today's warmup, copy the phrase letter on page 145 as rapidly as you can.

Developing Word-Building Power

183. WORD BEGINNINGS AND ENDINGS

En-

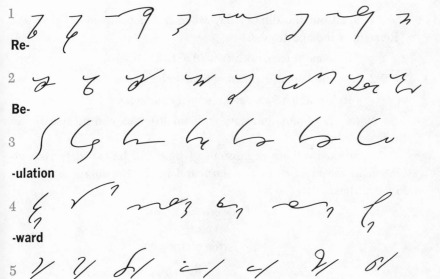

Re-

Be-

-ulation

-ward

---

1. Enjoy, enjoyable, engage, enforce, enroll, envy, enlarge, ensue.
2. Resign, repay, reside, result, revision, reproduction, reference, respect.
3. Before, believe, become, because, begin, began, below.
4. Population, stimulation, congratulations, circulation, calculation, tabulation.
5. Forward, upward, backward, homeward, onward, afterward, outward.

Building Transcription Skills

184.   BUSINESS VOCABULARY BUILDER

digest   To condense; to boil down.

environs   Surroundings.

residential   Pertaining to where people live.

185.   TYPING STYLE STUDY

Time

1. Spell out the time of day when it is accompanied by *o'clock*. (Remember the apostrophe!)

He came at ten o'clock (not *10 o'clock*).

2. Use numbers in expressing time with *a.m.* and *p.m.*

He left at 9:15 a.m. and returned at 9:30 p.m.

Note: Write a.m. and p.m. with small letters and no space after the first period.

Occasionally these expressions of time will be called to your attention in the margins of the shorthand in the Reading and Writing Practice thus:

Transcribe:
9 a.m.
ten o'clock

Reading and Writing Practice

186.

Transcribe:
ten o'clock
dis·turb'ing

par
conj
stim'u·la'tion
Di'gest
Transcribe:
4:30 p.m.
3:15
4:30
(122)

187.

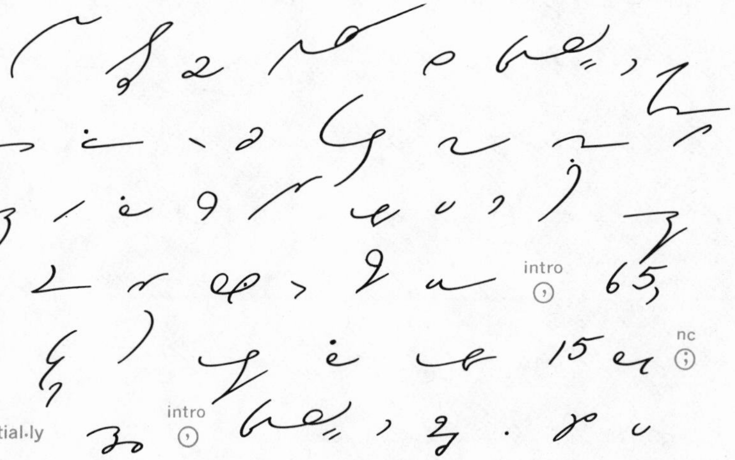

intro
65,
15
nc
es·sen'tial·ly
intro

new'com'ers
en·vi'rons

growth
rent'al
res'i·den'tial

Transcribe:
$50

Transcribe:
9 a.m.
5 p.m.

(141)

188.

shake
guests

one'-week'
 hyphenated
 before noun
guests'

[Gregg shorthand outlines]

en·joy′a·ble
com·mer′cial
trav′el·ers

nonr

(151)

189.   Transcription Quiz.   For you to supply: 4 commas—1 comma apposition, 1 comma *and* omitted, 2 commas parenthetical; 1 semicolon because of comma; 2 missing words.

[Gregg shorthand outlines]

(98)

LESSON 25

● **Warmup.** Your warmup for the last time is the phrase letter on page 145. Copy the entire letter as many times as you can and as rapidly as you can in the time available.

Developing Word-Building Power

190. SHORTHAND VOCABULARY BUILDER

Ĭa, Ēa

Īa

Ses

O on Its Side

---

1. Appreciate, area, associates, create, creation, brilliant, miniature.
2. Appliance, Miami, reliance, science, diet, trial.
3. Faces, paces, services, chances, courses, releases, presses, prices.
4. Home, own, tone, stone, owner, honorable, dome.

Building Transcription Skills

191. BUSINESS VOCABULARY BUILDER

duration   The time within which something lasts.

boredom   State of weariness resulting from dullness.

concrete evidence   Facts that cannot be denied.

fruitful   Producing results.

Reading and Writing Practice

192.

hos'pi·tal·i·za'tion
dis·com'fort
du·ra'tion conj

typ'i·cal
ma'jor

phys'i·cal
bore'dom

(111)

193. *[Gregg shorthand outlines]*

whole
ap·pli'anc·es

bc

ser

when

(78)

························

194. *[Gregg shorthand outlines]*

and o

as

bc

if

nc

par

fa·mil′iar
a′re·a

[Gregg shorthand outlines]

(141)

····························

195.

Transcribe:
April 16
an′ni·ver′sa·ry

or′gan·i·za′tion's
ap·pre′ci·a′tion

Transcribe:
$10,000
1960

e′qual·ly
fruit′ful′

(126)

196. Shh!

(shorthand content)

If she prepares

(shorthand content)

Many a secretary

Ask yourself

(366)

Personnel

When you have completed your stenographic training and have decided on the company for which you would like to work, your first contact with that company will probably be through someone in its personnel department. This department is usually under the direction of a personnel manager. If it is a large company, the personnel manager generally has a staff of assistants who are trained to recruit, interview, test, and place people in the jobs for which they are best fitted.

The personnel department serves three important functions in an organization:

1. It sees to it that the company is supplied with competent workers so that it can operate efficiently. It is to the personnel department that the executive turns when he needs a secretary, a clerk, a salesman, an assistant. A member of the personnel staff screens all the likely candidates for the position and refers to the executive those people who are best qualified for the position.

2. It looks after the interests, comfort, and welfare of the workers so that they are happy and productive employees. This includes recreation, health and life insurance programs, retirement benefits, salaries and wage incentives, vacations, and the like.

3. It provides opportunities to employees for further education through company-sponsored classes or on-the-job training.

After a worker has been hired, a member of the personnel department tries to make him feel at home immediately. He tells the employee about the business — the products it makes, the services it renders, the people who run it, and the part the new worker will play in the operation of the business. In some cases a representative of the personnel department will take the new worker on a tour of the company offices, perhaps even introduce him to the people with whom he will come in contact.

In addition, a member of the personnel department explains company policy to the new worker — policies regarding vacations, working hours, insurance programs, pay periods, and the various company rules and regulations that he will be expected to observe. The personnel department keeps all records concerning an employee — his application form; changes in pay status; insurance records; and records pertaining to his progress, promotions, and training.

The letters and memoranda on which you will practice in this chapter are representative types of material that pass through the hands of the stenographer who works in the personnel department of an organization.

LESSON 26

Building Phrasing Skill

197. PHRASE BUILDER

Can you read the 24 phrases in this phrase builder in 30 seconds or less?

Ago

(shorthand outlines)

Hope

(shorthand outlines)

One of

(shorthand outlines)

Some of

(shorthand outlines)

---

1. Years ago, days ago, months ago, hours ago, minutes ago.
2. I hope, I hope that, I hope you will, I hope you can, we hope, we hope that, we hope you will, we hope you can.
3. One of the, one of our, one of them, one of these, one of those, one of the most.
4. Some of the, some of them, some of these, some of our, some of those.

198. WARMUP PHRASE LETTER

Can you read this letter in 90 seconds? Can you copy it in 2 minutes?

(shorthand letter)

174

[Gregg shorthand outlines]

(120)

Building Transcription Skills

199. BUSINESS VOCABULARY BUILDER

business machines   Adding machines, typewriters, duplicators, etc.

editorial department   A division of a publishing company that works on the literary content of books, magazines, etc.

journalism   The business of writing or managing newspapers, magazines, and other publications.

Reading and Writing Practice

200. *[Gregg shorthand outlines]*

, intro *[Gregg shorthand outlines]*

[Gregg shorthand outlines]

might'y
dif'fer·ence

nc

per'son·nel'
di·rec'tor
as·sist'ants

when

ex·am'ple
be·gin'ners

par

ser

busi'ness-ma·chines'
hyphenated
before noun

Transcribe:
9 a.m.
5 p.m.

cr

(140)

....

201.

sub·mit'ting
Ed'i·to'ri·al

conj

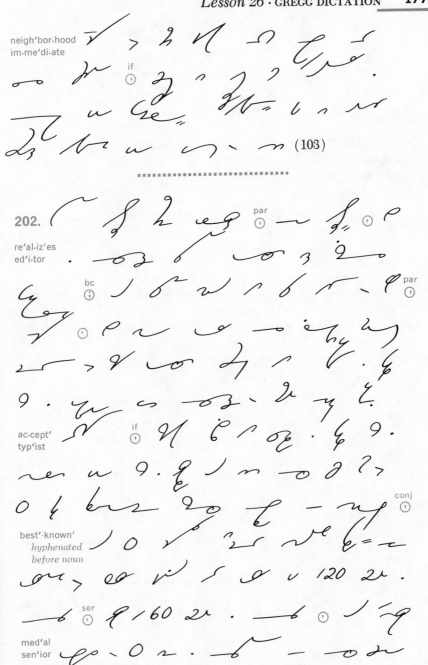

neigh'bor·hood
im·me'di·ate

if

(103)

202.

re'al·iz'es
ed'i·tor

bc

par

if

ac·cept'
typ'ist

conj

best'-known'
hyphenated
before noun

120

ser

60

med'al
sen'ior

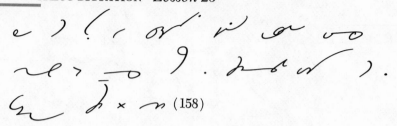

(158)

203. **Transcription Quiz.** For you to supply: 6 commas—4 commas parenthetical, 2 commas apposition; 1 semicolon because of commas, 1 semicolon no conjunction; 2 missing words.

(136)

LESSON 27

■■

● Warmup. Read the first paragraph of the phrase letter on page 174. Then copy that paragraph as many times as you can and as rapidly as you can before your teacher begins the regular classwork.

Developing Word-Building Power

204. BRIEF-FORM CHART

Your reading goal for the following 30 brief forms and derivatives: 35 seconds.

1. After, hereafter, thereafter, suggest, suggestion, suggestions.
2. Ever, whenever, wherever, whatever, whoever, whichever.
3. Satisfy, satisfying, satisfied, dissatisfied, unsatisfactory, satisfaction.
4. State, states, statement, reinstate, reinstatement, estate.
5. Regard, regarded, regarding, regards, regardless, disregard.

205. GEOGRAPHICAL EXPRESSIONS

2 

1. Pittsburgh, Harrisburg, Plattsburg, Greensburg, Newburgh, Fitchburg.
2. America, American, Canada, Canadian, England, English, United States.

Building Transcription Skills

206. BUSINESS VOCABULARY BUILDER

questionnaire A sheet of questions sent to a number of people to get opinions or information.

expanded Enlarged.

authorized Having permission.

assume To take upon oneself.

207. SIMILAR-WORDS DRILL

Formerly, formally

formerly Before; in the past.

He formerly worked in our Accounting Department.

formally According to established custom or form.

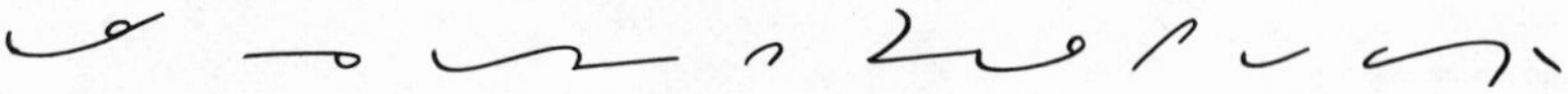

Let me welcome you formally to our organization.

Reading and Writing Practice

208. 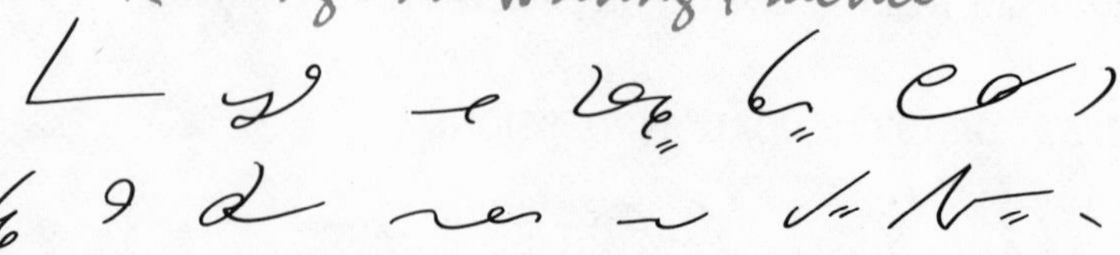

ap′pli·ca′tion
for′mer·ly

com′pa·ny′s
wheth′er

ques′tion·naire′
re·cip′ro·cate

if

if

(120)

209.

no′ti·fied
fa·cil′i·ties

par

intro

full′-time′
hyphenated
before noun

ser

Transcribe:
9 a.m.
5 p.m.

as

[Gregg shorthand outlines]

intro ⊙

phys'i·cal
au'thor·ized

[Gregg shorthand outlines]

③

intro ⊙

[Gregg shorthand outlines]

if ⊙

[Gregg shorthand outlines] (190)

································

210. *[Gregg shorthand outlines]*

for'mal·ly
em·ploy'ee

[Gregg shorthand outlines]

conj ⊙

[Gregg shorthand outlines]

ser ⊙

friend'li·ness
cour'te·sy

[Gregg shorthand outlines]

par ⊙

[Gregg shorthand outlines]

bc
⊙

par
⊙

anx'ious
suc·ceed'

par
⊙

(134)

211.

pub'lish·ers'
league

par
⊙

par
⊙

Transcribe:
five o'clock

ap
⊙

10   5

intro
⊙

(94)

212. Transcription Quiz. For you to supply: 8 commas—6 commas parenthetical, 2 commas nonrestrictive; 1 semicolon because of comma; 2 missing words.

[Gregg shorthand outlines]

(120)

LESSON 28

● **Warmup.** For your warmup use the second paragraph of the phrase letter on page 174. Copy it slowly, then rapidly, and finally in your best shorthand.

Developing Word-Building Power

213. WORD FAMILIES

-ally

1 

-cation

2 

-tive

3 

-prove

4 

1. Finally, totally, originally, personally, naturally.
2. Application, indication, communication, vacation, vocation, location.
3. Effective, active, creative, negative, positive, relative, alternative.
4. Prove, disprove, approve, approval, disapprove, disapproval, improve.

Building Transcription Skills

214. BUSINESS VOCABULARY BUILDER

leave of absence   Permission to be absent from employment.

assumed   Took responsibility for.

devised   Created; made up; originated.

215. SPELLING FAMILIES

Words in Which Y Is Changed to I in the Past Tense and in the S-Form

ap·ply'	ap·plied'	ap·plies'
re·ply'	re·plied'	re·plies'
im·ply'	im·plied'	im·plies'
sup·ply'	sup·plied'	sup·plies'
re·ly'	re·lied'	re·lies'
com·ply'	com·plied'	com·plies'
mul'ti·ply	mul'ti·plied	mul'ti·plies

Reading and Writing Practice

216.

re·signed'
ef·fec'tive

Transcribe:
September 1

ad·vice'
en·cour'age·ment

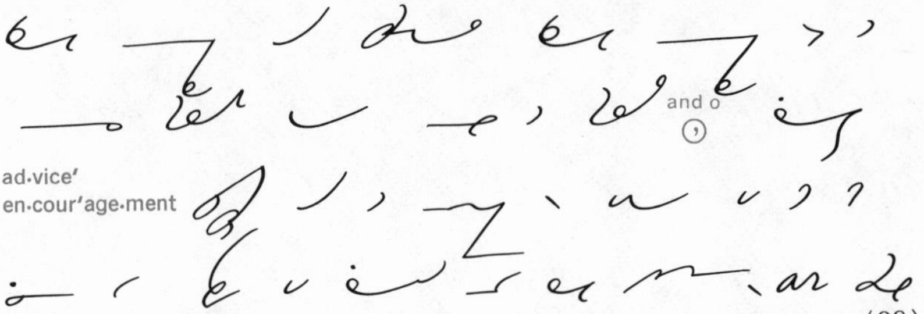
and o

(98)

217.

su'per·vi'sor
Sup·plies'

un·u'su·al·ly
re·or'gan·ized

mem'o·ran'dum
com·mu'ni·ca'tion

Transcribe:
$300

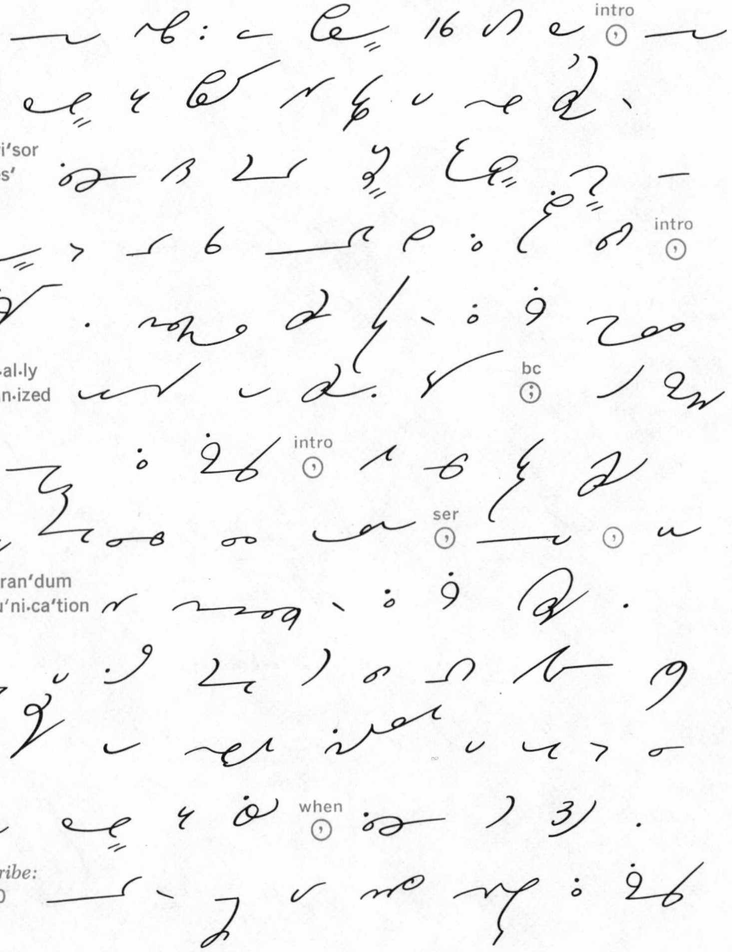
intro
intro
bc
intro
ser
when

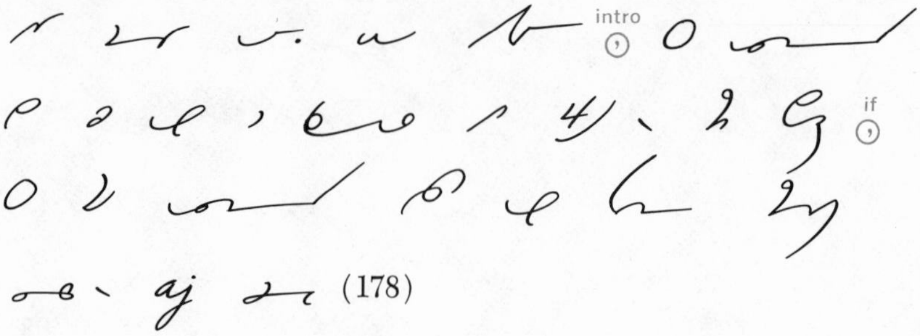
intro
if

(178)

218.

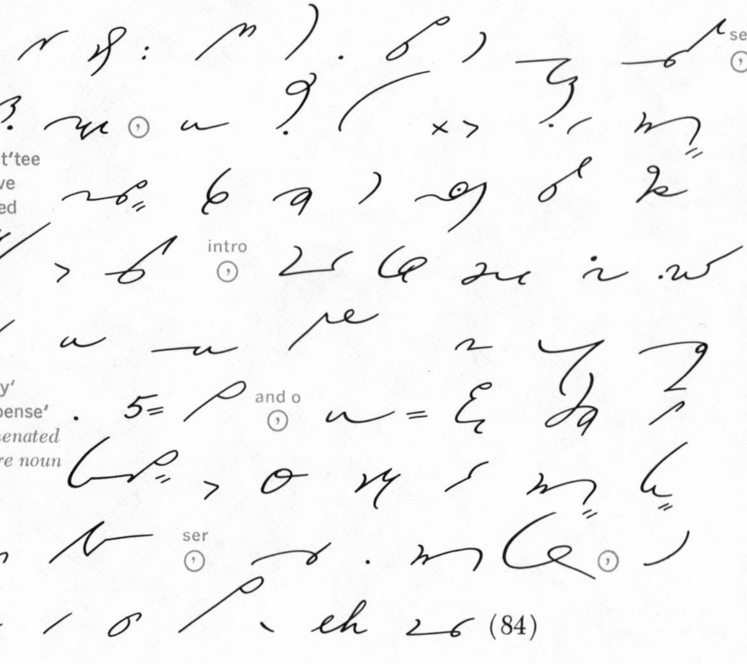
ser
intro
and o
ser

Com·mit'tee
cre·a'tive
a·dopt'ed

five'-day'
all'-ex·pense'
hyphenated before noun

(84)

219.

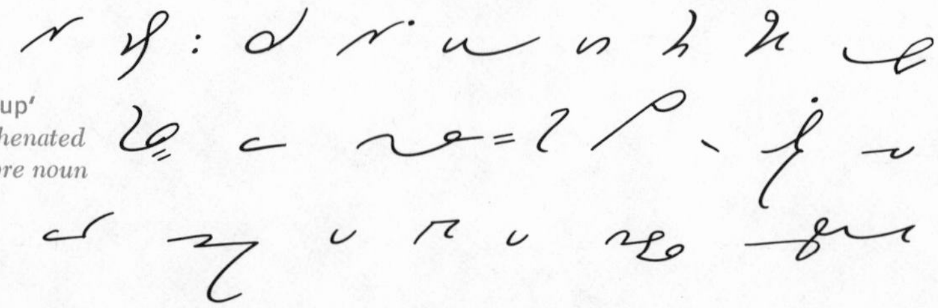

clean'-up'
hyphenated before noun

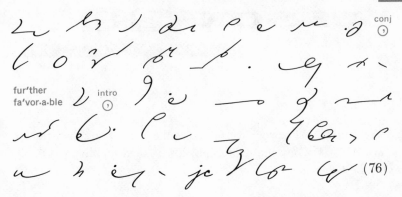

fur'ther
fa'vor·a·ble

(76)

220. **Transcription Quiz.** For you to supply: 5 commas—2 commas apposition, 1 comma conjunction, 2 commas parenthetical; 1 semicolon no conjunction; 2 missing words.

(102)

LESSON 29

● **Warmup.** For your warmup use the last paragraph of the letter on page 174. Copy the paragraph slowly, then rapidly, and finally in your best shorthand.

Developing Word-Building Power

221. WORD BEGINNINGS AND ENDINGS

-ingly

1

-lity

2

-ual

3

-ily

4

---

1. Accordingly, exceedingly, surprisingly, willingly, knowingly, sparingly, seemingly.
2. Ability, possibility, facility, probability, inability, reliability.
3. Schedule, annual, actual, factual, manual.
4. Family, customarily, necessarily, temporarily, speedily, readily.

Building Transcription Skills

222. BUSINESS VOCABULARY BUILDER

inducted   Installed, as into an office.

consecutive   Coming one after the other.

preceding   Before.

quite   Completely; entirely.

223. COMMON WORD ROOTS

A knowledge of the more common Greek and Latin word roots is of tremendous value in helping you increase your command of the English language.

In *Gregg Shorthand* you studied a number of the more common, simple word roots; in *Gregg Dictation* you will take up additional, somewhat more advanced word roots.

Read the definition of each word root carefully, and then study the illustrations that follow.

In-: The syllable *in* has several meanings. It is very frequently used as the prefix meaning *not*.

informal   Not formal; casual.

inconvenient   Not suitable.

incomplete   Not finished; partially finished.

incapable   Not able.

incompetent   Not proficient.

indisposed   Not well.

Reading and Writing Practice

224.

its
an'nu·al

28 ⟨shorthand outline⟩

in·duct′ed
en′ter·tain′ment

intro

bc

prompt
wheth′er

re·sponse′
guar′an·tee′

intro

intro

(144)

· ·

225. ⟨shorthand outline⟩

con·sec′u·tive
fam′i·ly
of·fi′cial·ly

intro

ap   24   ap   31

[Gregg shorthand outlines]

sched'ules
pre·ced'ing

(103)

....

226.

ex·ceed'ing·ly   nc
Transcribe: ⊙
December 24

        ap
        ⊙   24.   . 4=

four'-day'
hyphenated   22
before noun

            25,   par
                            ⊙

                                conj
                                ⊙

                                      4°

Transcribe:
four o'clock

[Gregg shorthand outlines] (122)

. . . .

227. *[Gregg shorthand outlines]*

Transcribe:
17 Street

[Gregg shorthand outlines] if

par

par

ap·prov'al
spe'cial

suit'a·ble
Smith's

as

[Gregg shorthand outlines] (141)

228. **Transcription Quiz.**   For you to supply: 6 commas—1 comma conjunction, 4 commas parenthetical, 1 comma introductory; 1 semicolon because of comma; 2 missing words.

(138)

LESSON 30

● **Warmup.** Copy the phrase letter on page 174 as rapidly as you can. If there is time, copy it a second time in your very best shorthand.

Developing Word-Building Power

229. SHORTHAND VOCABULARY BUILDER

Abbreviated Words

1 

Omission of Minor Vowel

2 

Ng

3 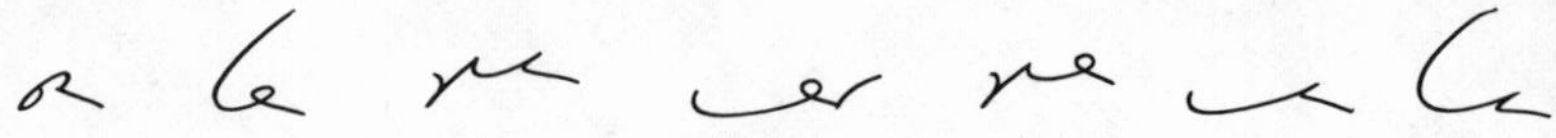

Nd

4 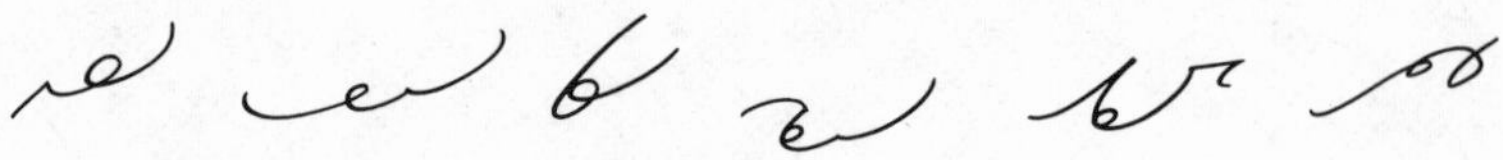

Ort

5 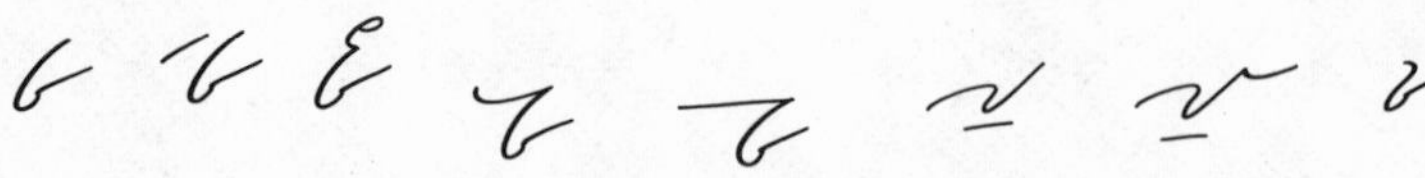

1. Anniversary, requirements, privilege, distribute, memoranda, conveniently.
2. Courteous, serious, various, tedious, studious, erroneous.
3. Young, bring, strong, length, string, long, belong.
4. Trained, learned, bind, concerned, independence, indicate.
5. Port, transport, export, report, import, quart, quarter, sort.

Building Transcription Skills

230.   BUSINESS VOCABULARY BUILDER

   golden anniversary   Fifty years.

   gratifying   Pleasing; satisfying.

   donate   To give.

   receptacles   Containers.

Reading and Writing Practice

231.

Smith's
an'ni·ver'sa·ry
lunch'eon

as·sem'ble
leath'er

(132)

232. *[shorthand]*

conj ⊙

well'-trained'
hyphenated
before noun

and o ⊙

be·gin'ning
sal'a·ry

nonr ⊙

(99)

....

233. *[shorthand]*

cour'te·ous
in'ter·view

intro ⊙

par ⊙

var'i·ous
ap'pli·cants

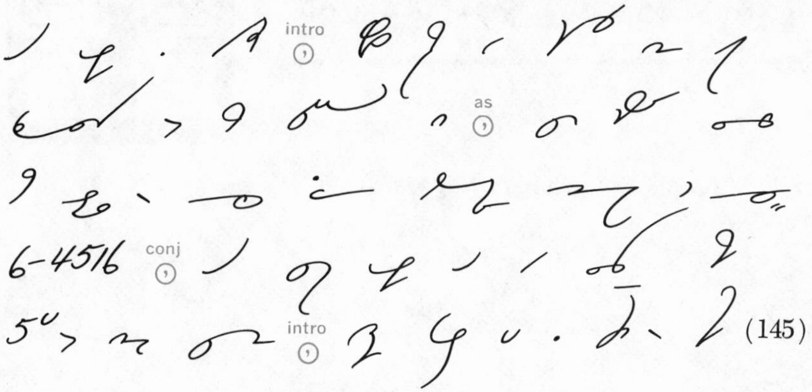

intro
⊙

as
⊙

6-4516 conj
⊙

5ᵘ intro
⊙

(145)

∙∙∙∙∙∙∙∙∙∙∙∙∙∙∙∙∙∙∙∙∙∙∙∙∙∙∙∙∙∙∙∙∙

234.

intro
⊙

Girls'
dis·trib'ute

in'sti·tu'tions
grat'i·fy'ing

intro
⊙

toys
col·lect'ed
do'nate

ap
⊙

33

3t

(114)

235. Chronic Complainers Not Welcome!

[shorthand text]

One day *[shorthand text]*

[shorthand text]

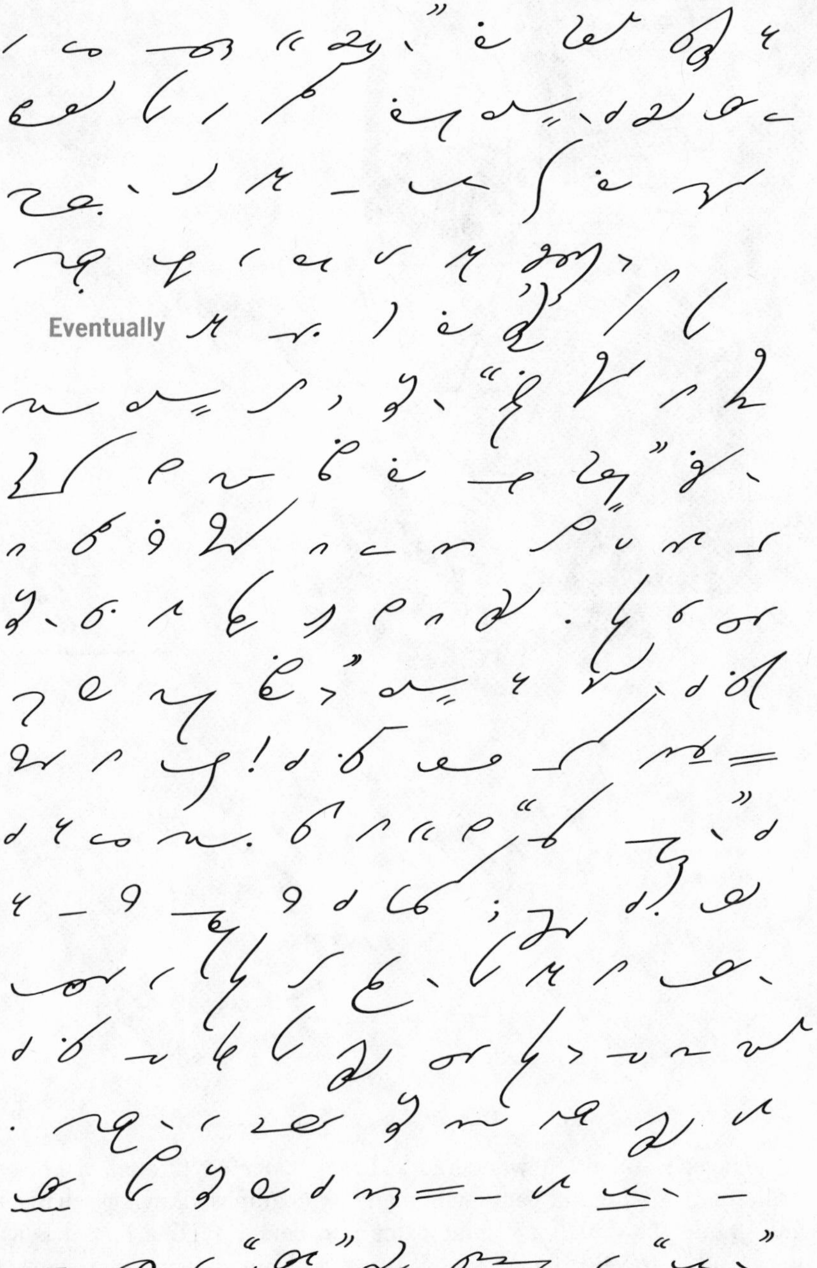

(337)

7

Publishing— Books

Haven't you often wondered, when you leafed through a book containing hundreds of pages with many photographs, drawings, charts, and graphs, how such a volume came into being? Well, a book has a long road to travel from the time it is just a gleam in an author's eye to the day it appears between two covers — a road that it would take many pages to describe fully. But briefly, this is how a book is born:

When an author gets an inspiration for a book, he develops it on paper; that is, he prepares a manuscript, which is usually in typewritten form. He submits this manuscript to a publisher with the fervent hope that the publisher will like it. If the publisher does like it and decides the public also will like it, he enters into a royalty agreement with the author, under which the author will receive a certain amount for each copy that is sold. Of course, the more copies that are sold, the greater the author's income — as well as the publisher's!

The author's manuscript is then assigned to an editor, who checks the accuracy of the author's facts and sees to it that his spelling, punctuation, and grammar are correct. Yes, even authors have trouble with the mechanics of our language!

The manuscript then goes to a book designer, who selects the type face to be used, decides on how the book will be illustrated — photographs, drawings, charts, etc. — and finally, designs a cover. In short, it is the designer's job to see that the book has eye appeal.

Then, the manuscript is sent to the printer, who sets it in type. Before he submits proofs to the publisher, however, he has the material proofread and corrected — just as you should proofread and correct everything you transcribe before you submit it to your employer.

After the material has been proofread by the publisher's proofreader and after the corrections have been made by the printer and the material has been organized into pages, the book is ready to be printed and bound.

You will see many of these steps in operation if you should decide on a career in book publishing; in fact, you will take part in some of them. You will experience a real thrill, when the book finally appears, in the knowledge that you had a part in its creation — especially if it turns out to be a best seller!

In this chapter you will have an opportunity to read and take from dictation material that pertains to publishing activities. Perhaps through these letters you can capture some of the flavor of this interesting work.

LESSON 31

Building Phrasing Skill

236. PHRASE BUILDER

The following list contains 33 useful business letter phrases. Can you read the entire list in 40 seconds?

Been

Able

To in Phrases

Want

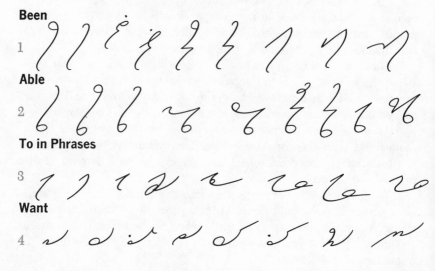

---

1. I have been, you have been, has been, it has been, I have not been, you have not been, would have been, should have been, could have been.
2. Have been able, I have been able, you have been able, you will be able, I will be able, we have not been able, you have not been able, to be able, I should be able.
3. To be, to have, to put, to find, to sell, to plan, to blame, to fly.
4. You want, I want, he wants, they want, I wanted, he wanted, if you want, do you want.

204

237. WARMUP PHRASE LETTER

The following 107-word letter is your warmup letter for Chapter 7. Can you read it in one minute? Can you write it in 90 seconds?

(107)

Building Transcription Skills

238. BUSINESS VOCABULARY BUILDER

proofread   Read over for errors.

anticipated   Expected.

scheduling   Planning work on a project to be done at a fixed time.

Reading and Writing Practice

239.

Transcribe:
April 10

[shorthand symbols]

proof'read'
dif'fer·ent
fi'nal

oc·ca'sion·al
through

(120)

··

240.

write
wives

[shorthand symbols]

ef·fect′
Christ′mas
won't

if

nc

nc

if

bc

(135)

241.

re′cent·ly
fig′ures
dis′ap·point′ed

when

Transcribe:
April 15, 1962,
6,000

15, 1962

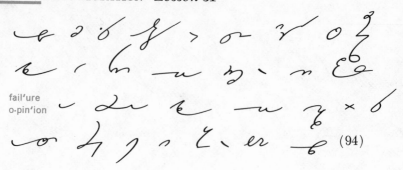

fail′ure
o·pin′ion

(94)

242. Transcription Quiz. In the Transcription Quizzes of earlier lessons, you have had to supply missing words that were obvious, as only one possible word made sense in the sentence; hereafter, any one of a number of words will make sense. It will be up to you to supply the word you think fits best in the sentence. To illustrate:

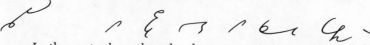

In the spot where there has been an omission, any one of the following words would be considered correct: *want, wish, like, care.* Assuming that you decide that the word *want* makes the sentence read most smoothly, you would write it in your shorthand notebook thus:

Whatever word you choose, be sure that it makes sense in the sentence.

For you to supply: 6 commas—2 commas apposition, 1 comma conjunction, 2 commas parenthetical, 1 comma *if* clause; 1 semicolon no conjunction; 2 missing words.

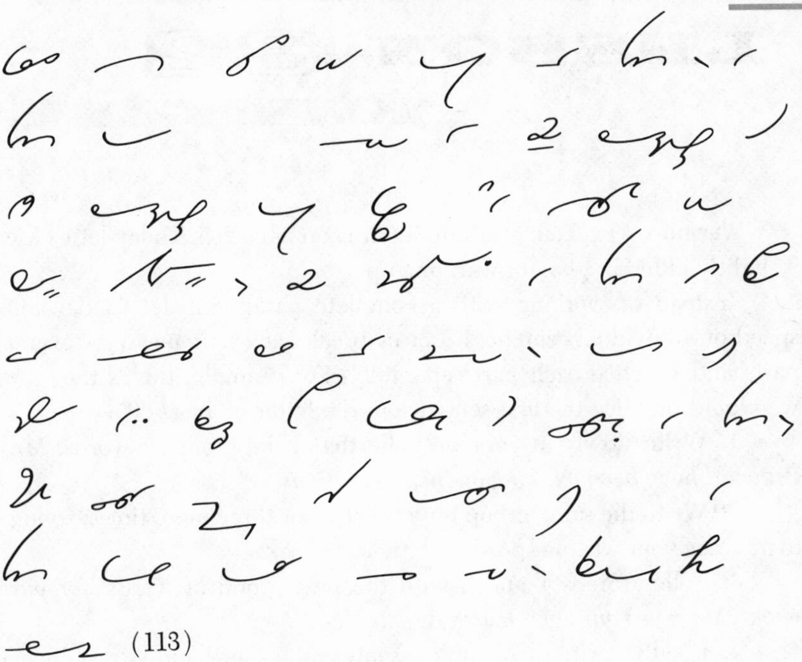

(113)

Don't be discouraged if your first invasion of the business world produces only a position that you feel is of a menial nature. No one starts at the top of a ladder. Hard work and an honest interest in your job are still the best aids to success that I know.—Tom Dodd, New York Regional Director, Manpower, Inc.

LESSON 32

● **Warmup.** Your warmup letter is on page 205. Today let us use a slightly different plan for warming up.

Instead of working with a complete paragraph, let us develop speed on individual sentences. Let us break each sentence into several parts and practice each part separately. For example, this is the way we would practice the first sentence in the letter on page 205.

1. Write slowly in your best shorthand the group of words, *Mr. Brown: I have been working on the illustrations.*

2. Write the same group of words two or three more times, trying to increase your writing speed each time.

3. Follow Steps 1 and 2 with the next group of words, *for our book, "Making Your Own Home Repairs."*

4. Finally, write the complete sentence in shorthand as rapidly as you can.

Follow this procedure with as many sentences in the letter as time permits.

Your warmup should look something like this in your shorthand notebook:

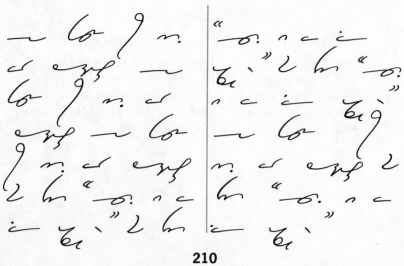

Developing Word-Building Power

243. BRIEF-FORM CHART

This chart contains 30 brief forms and derivatives. Can you read it in 30 seconds?

1. Morning, regarding, thinking, putting, being, using.
2. Out, outing, outlet, outline, outfit, outside.
3. Short, shortly, shorter, shorten, shorthand, shortest.
4. Enclose, enclosed, enclosing, encloses, enclosure, enclosures.
5. Advantage, advantages, disadvantage, disadvantages, advantageous, disadvantageous.

244. GEOGRAPHICAL EXPRESSIONS

1. Burlington, Nashua, Augusta, Worcester, New Haven, Providence.
2. Vermont, New Hampshire, Maine, Massachusetts, Connecticut, Rhode Island.

Building Transcription Skills

245. BUSINESS VOCABULARY BUILDER

facilitate To make easy.

derive Obtain.

manual A handbook.

246. SIMILAR-WORDS DRILL

Sometimes the simplest words give us the most difficulty—not because we do not understand them, but because we are likely to be a little careless in their use. *Hear* and *here* are examples.

Hear, here

hear To gain knowledge of by hearing; to be informed.

I hear that you are writing a book for us.

here In this place.

We are here to be of assistance to you.

here and there In one place or another.

We have been able to pick up interesting information here and there.

Reading and Writing Practice

247.

con·ven′tion
As·so′ci·a′tion

(Gregg shorthand outlines)

Transcribe:
10 a.m.
re·cep'tion

ap · *intro* · *nonr* · *intro* · *intro* · *conj* · *if*

(150)

248.

Transcribe:
5,000

intro · *as* · *par*

wheth'er
ma'jor

au'thor's

val'u·a·ble
in·clude'

[Gregg shorthand outlines]

ser

par

30

40

bc

(141)

249.

hear
man'u·script

intro

nc

par

intro

intro

(shorthand outlines) (134)

250. **Transcription Quiz.** For you to supply: 9 commas—1 comma *if* clause, 1 comma apposition, 6 commas series, 1 comma conjunction; 2 missing words.

(shorthand outlines) (107)

LESSON 33

Warmup. Your warmup letter is on page 205. Follow the same warmup procedure with the sentence in the second paragraph of the letter on page 205. Try to increase your writing speed with each repetition.

Developing Word-Building Power

251. WORD FAMILIES

-spect

1 

-gate

2 

-ic

3 

-bly

4 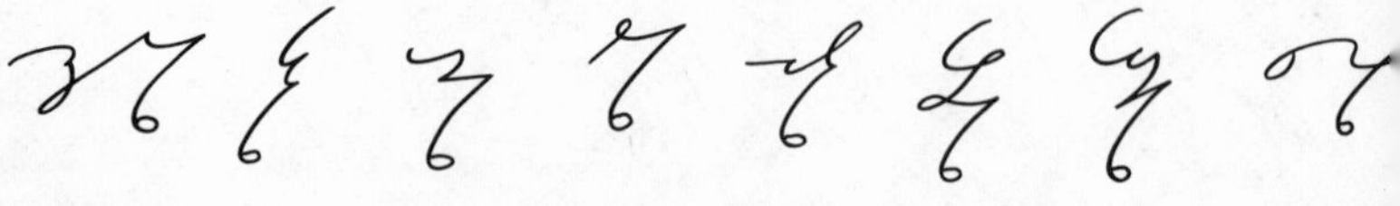

1. Prospect, inspect, respect, aspect, expect, suspect, self-respect.
2. Obligate, investigate, navigate, delegate, aggregate.
3. Classic, basic, topic, graphic, traffic, logic, magic.
4. Considerably, possibly, reasonably, terribly, noticeably, preferably, profitably, agreeably.

Building Transcription Skills

252. BUSINESS VOCABULARY BUILDER

classic   A work of the highest class.

reject   To refuse.

absorbed in   Thoughtfully occupied with.

253. SPELLING FAMILIES

Be very careful when you must transcribe a word ending with the sound of *shal;* sometimes it is spelled *cial;* at other times, *tial.*

Words Ending in -cial

spe'cial	of·fi'cial	ben'e·fi'cial
fi·nan'cial	so'cial	com·mer'cial
ar'ti·fi'cial	cru'cial	su'per·fi'cial

Words Ending in -tial

es·sen'tial	sub·stan'tial	po·ten'tial
con'fi·den'tial	res'i·den'tial	in'flu·en'tial
in·i'tial	cir'cum·stan'tial	par'tial

Reading and Writing Practice

254.

ge·og'ra·phy
pos'si·bly

con·sid'er·a'tions
man'u·script

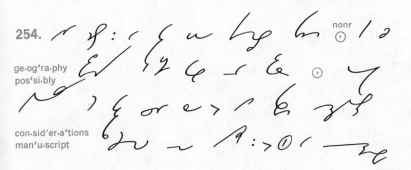

es·sen'tial
graphs

[shorthand outlines]

dis'ap·point'ment
de·ci'sion

[shorthand outlines]

(124)

∙∙∙∙∙∙∙∙∙∙∙∙∙∙∙∙∙∙∙∙∙∙∙∙∙∙∙∙∙∙

255.
past
ex·ceed'ing·ly
Es·sen'tials

[shorthand outlines]

Transcribe:
June 10

[shorthand outlines]

[Gregg shorthand outlines]

ser

up to date
no noun,
no hyphen

(134)

∙∙∙∙∙∙∙∙∙∙∙∙∙∙∙∙∙∙∙∙∙∙∙∙∙∙∙∙∙∙

256.

full'-length'
hyphenated
before noun

if

when

bc

pur'chase
can'cel

conj

bc

ac·cept'
vol'ume

intro

post'age-paid
hyphenated
before noun

conj

(143)

257.

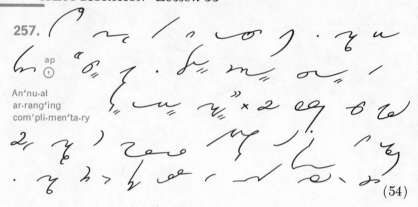

An'nu·al
ar·rang'ing
com'pli·men'ta·ry

(54)

258. Transcription Quiz. For you to supply: 4 commas parenthetical; 1 semicolon because of comma; 2 missing words.

(121)

LESSON 34

● **Warmup.** Your warmup letter is on page 205. For today practice the sentence in the third paragraph of the letter, following the steps outlined on page 210. Practice the sentence in three or four parts.

Developing Word-Building Power

259. WORD BEGINNINGS AND ENDINGS

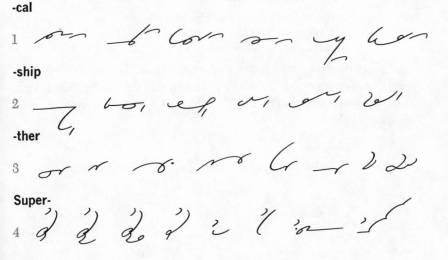

-cal

1

-ship

2

-ther

3

Super-

4

---

1. Technical, medical, practical, chemical, logical, political.
2. Membership, showmanship, relationship, authorship, readership, friendship.
3. Another, other, gathering, together, brother, mother, further, farther.
4. Supervise, supervisor, supervisory, supervision, superior, superb, superhuman, superintendent.

Building Transcription Skills

260. BUSINESS VOCABULARY BUILDER

hostile   Not friendly.

crammed   Filled with; stuffed.

sales training director   The person who instructs sales-men or those who will sell.

readership   The people who read a periodical or maga-zine.

261. GRAMMAR CHECKUP

Don't, doesn't

Use *doesn't* in the third person singular, not *don't*.

She doesn't (not *don't*) work here any longer.
He doesn't have an office at the present time.
That doesn't seem possible.

No one ever seems to use *doesn't* when he should use *don't*—you never hear anyone say, "I doesn't"; but you will frequently hear people incorrectly say, "he don't" and "that don't." Of course, *you* never make that mistake!

Reading and Writing Practice

262.

Col'lege
ex·haust'ed

de·vel'op·ment

and o

nonr

[Gregg shorthand outlines]

(113)

....

263.

tech'ni·cal
an·nounce'

conj

Transcribe:
  June 15, 1960,

15, 1960

ser

[Gregg shorthand outlines] ab (128)

264.

au'di·ence
hos'tile

cap'ture
lis'ten·ers'

when

ben'e·fit
years'

ap

nc

(134)

••••••••••••••••••••••••••••••••••

265.

as

20

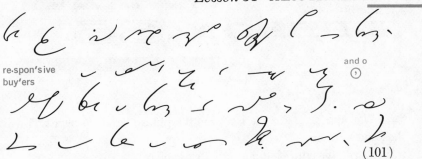

re·spon's·i·ve
buy'ers

and o

(101)

266. Transcription Quiz.   For you to supply: 5 commas—1 comma *when* clause, 1 comma *and* omitted, 1 comma parenthetical, 2 commas *if* clause; 1 semicolon because of comma, 1 semicolon no conjunction; 2 missing words.

(128)

LESSON 35

● **Warmup.** For the last time the phrase letter on page 205 will be your warmup.

Write the entire letter as rapidly as you can.

Developing Word-Building Power

267. SHORTHAND VOCABULARY BUILDER

Amounts

1

X

2

Tem

3

Omission of Vowel in -ition, -ation

4

---

1. 200; $200; 2,000; $2,000; $20,000; $300,000; $4,000,000.
2. Box, boxes, mix, mixes, text, textbook, indexes, relax.
3. Item, attempt, contemplate, customer, estimate, temple.
4. Edition, addition, admission, commission, information, station, determination.

Building Transcription Skills

268. BUSINESS VOCABULARY BUILDER

en route   On the way.

comprehend   To understand.

artwork   Pictures, drawings, cartoons, etc.

glossary   A collection of explanations of words or expressions.

Reading and Writing Practice

269.

Transcribe:
April 1
No. 1616

[shorthand outlines]

en route'
e·nough'

al·read'y
ap·pre'ci·ate

(103)

270.

[shorthand outlines]

[Gregg shorthand outlines]

en·joy′ment
ef·fi′cient·ly

well′-known′
  hyphenated
  before noun

par

nonr

ser

cr

Transcribe:
  $3
hours′

when

(136)

··············

271.

hand′book′
e·di′tion

and o

in′dex
glos′sa·ry

ser

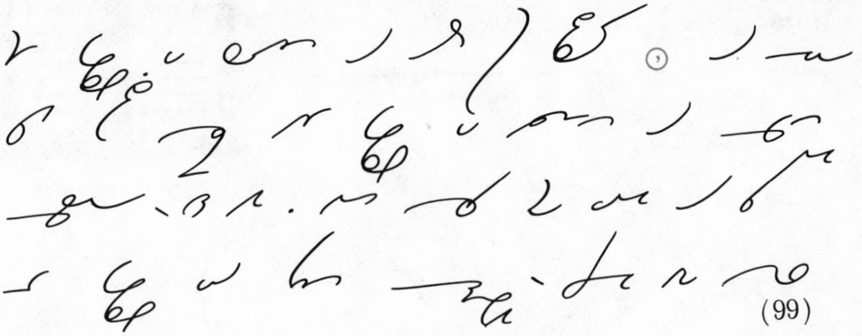

(99)

272.

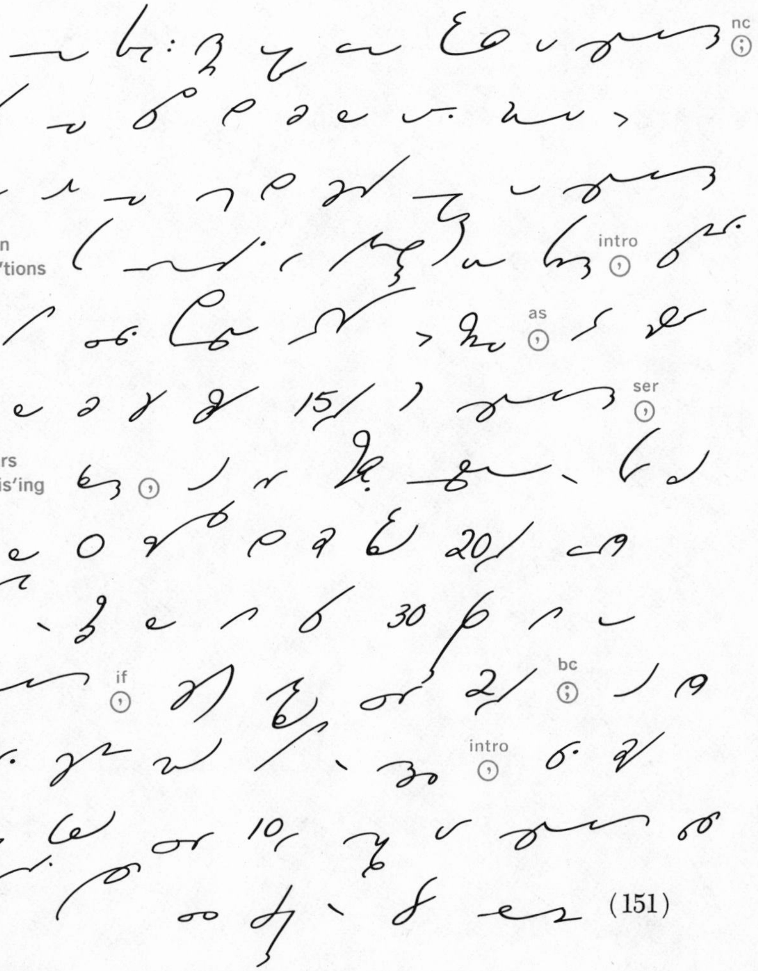

ques'tion
de·scrip'tions

cir'cu·lars
ad'ver·tis'ing

(151)

273. The Gadfly

[shorthand]

"This substitute *[shorthand]*

230

[Gregg shorthand outlines]

"While she [Gregg shorthand outlines]

(309)

8

Publishing—
Magazines

It takes only a glance at the number of magazines on sale at your local newsstand to realize that magazine publishing is an important industry in this country. Each year millions of copies of magazines of all types are printed and distributed to millions of subscribers.

Would you like to know how a magazine publishing company operates?

Most magazine publishing firms have three major divisions — editorial, circulation, and advertising.

The editorial staff is responsible for the content and appearance of the magazine — the articles, the stories, the features, the illustrations, etc. It is a big responsibility, too; if a subscriber doesn't like what he reads in a magazine, he will not long continue to subscribe.

Another responsibility of the editorial staff is to see that the magazine comes out on time — which means meeting deadlines. Editors burn much midnight oil to meet their deadlines!

The circulation department must sell the magazine to the reader and, once it has sold him, keep him sold, so that he will subscribe year after year. This is a very important function for two reasons: (1) Each paid subscription represents income; (2) Usually, the more paid subscribers the magazine has, the more it can charge for its advertising space. The greater its readership, the more valuable the advertising space in a magazine.

Then, there's the advertising department, whose job it is to convince prospective advertisers that advertising in the pages of its magazine will result in greater sales of their products or services. Most magazines must rely ultimately on income from advertising space to make a profit, because the cost of producing a copy of a magazine is greater than the price the subscriber pays for it.

The letters in this chapter will give you some idea of the type of material you would take from dictation if you worked in the circulation department of a magazine publisher.

LESSON 36

Building Phrasing Skill

274. PHRASE BUILDER

Can you read the following 38 phrases in 55 seconds?

Sure

Out of

About

Miscellaneous

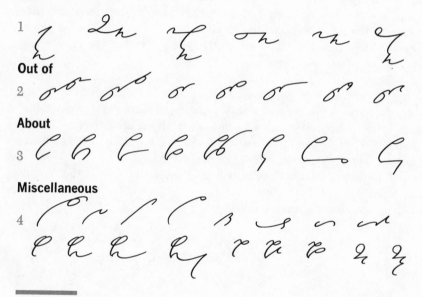

---

1. To be sure, I feel sure, you may be sure, I am sure, you are sure, I will be sure.
2. Out of town, out of date, out of the, out of that, out of them, out of these, out of those.
3. About it, about this, about them, about that, about that time, about which, about how many, about how much.
4. To make, to know, to do, to me, to us, let us, of course, of course it is, I hope, I hope you are, I hope you will, I hope you will be, we hope, we hope it is, we hope that, as soon as, as soon as possible.

275. WARMUP PHRASE LETTER

The following 138-word letter, which is your warmup letter for Chapter 8, contains 29 phrases. How fast can you read the letter? make a shorthand copy of it?

(138)

Building Transcription Skills

276. BUSINESS VOCABULARY BUILDER

interruption   A break.

go astray   To become lost.

lobby A large passage or hall often used as a waiting room.

Reading and Writing Practice

277.

[Gregg shorthand outlines]

re·ceived′
re·new′al

nonr

con′se·quent·ly
fur′ther
cop′ies

nc   intro

par

(131)

278.

when

Transcribe:
18 Street

lob'by
sub·scrib'ers'
con·ven'ience

bc ;

out'-of-town'
hyphenated before noun

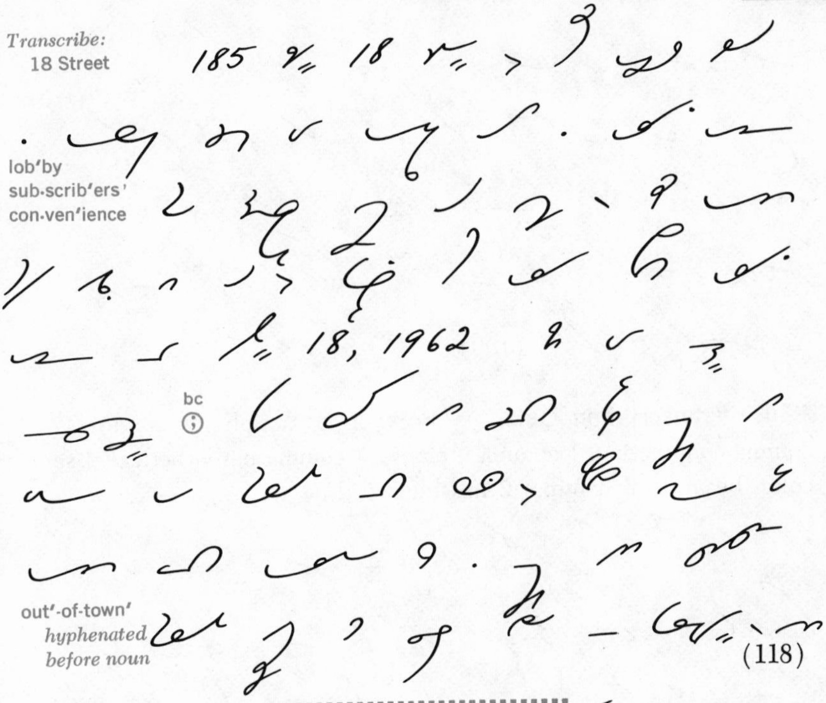

(118)

279.

ac'cu·rate
care'ful·ly ed'it·ed
no hyphen after ly

and o ,

as ,

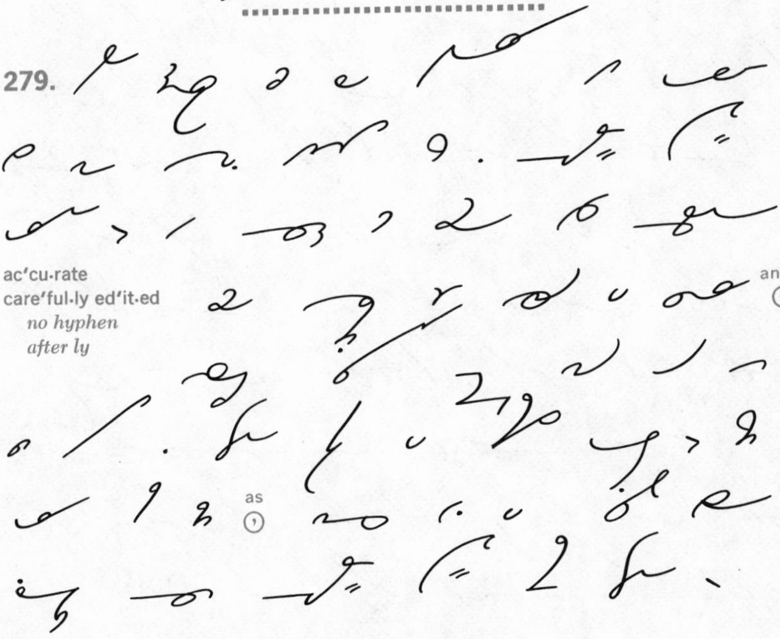

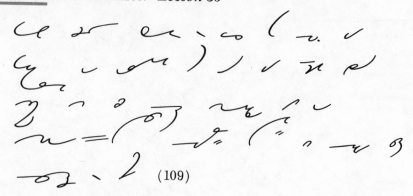

(109)

280. Transcription Quiz. For you to supply: 3 commas — 1 comma conjunction, 1 comma *if* clause, 1 comma parenthetical; 1 semicolon because of comma; 2 missing words.

(104)

LESSON 37

● **Warmup.** Your warmup letter is on page 235. Warm up on the sentence in the first paragraph, breaking down the sentence into two or three convenient parts. Write each part of the sentence three or four times, trying to write faster with each repetition. After you have practiced the sentence in this way, write the entire sentence once in your best shorthand, for control.

Developing Word-Building Power

281. BRIEF-FORM CHART

Can you read the brief forms and derivatives in this chart in 30 seconds or less?

1. Represent, represents, representative, request, requests, requested.
2. Year, years, yearly, send, sending, sender.
3. There, thereby, therefore, one, once, everyone.
4. Regular, regularly, irregular, great, greater, greatest.
5. Use, uses, used, useless, useful, usefully.

239

282. GEOGRAPHICAL EXPRESSIONS

[shorthand outlines]

1. Kansas City, Tulsa, Nashville, Knoxville, Omaha, Des Moines.
2. Missouri, North Dakota, South Dakota, Iowa, Tennessee, Nebraska, Oklahoma.

Building Transcription Skills

283. BUSINESS VOCABULARY BUILDER

> **commissions** The amounts paid to one person for transacting business for another.
>
> **supplementing** Adding to.
>
> **likelihood** Possibility; chance.

284. SIMILAR-WORDS DRILL

Advice, advise

> **advice** *(noun)* Recommendations; suggestions; guidance.

[shorthand outlines]

We want your advice on how to correct the errors.

> **advise** *(verb)* To guide; to suggest; to inform.

[shorthand outlines]

Every reader has an opportunity to advise us on the formation of our policies.

Reading and Writing Practice

285. *[shorthand outlines]*

sug·ges′tions
crit′i·cisms
ad·vice′

ser

dif′fer·ent
cor′re·spond′ence

if

(144)

....

286. *[shorthand outlines]*

if

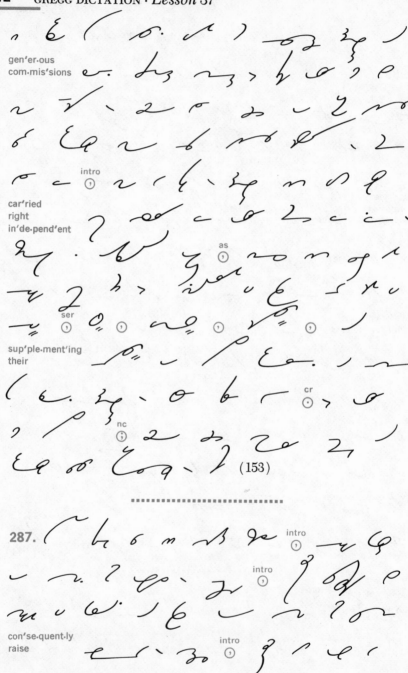

gen'er·ous
com·mis'sions

intro

car'ried
right
in'de·pend'ent

as

ser

sup'ple·ment'ing
their

cr

nc

(153)

287.

intro

intro

con'se·quent·ly
raise

intro

par

one year *no noun, no hyphen*

like'li·hood

spe'cial

im·me'di·ate·ly

mon'eysav'ing

(131)

288. Transcription Quiz. For you to supply: 4 commas – 1 comma conjunction, 2 commas parenthetical, 1 comma *and* omitted; 2 missing words.

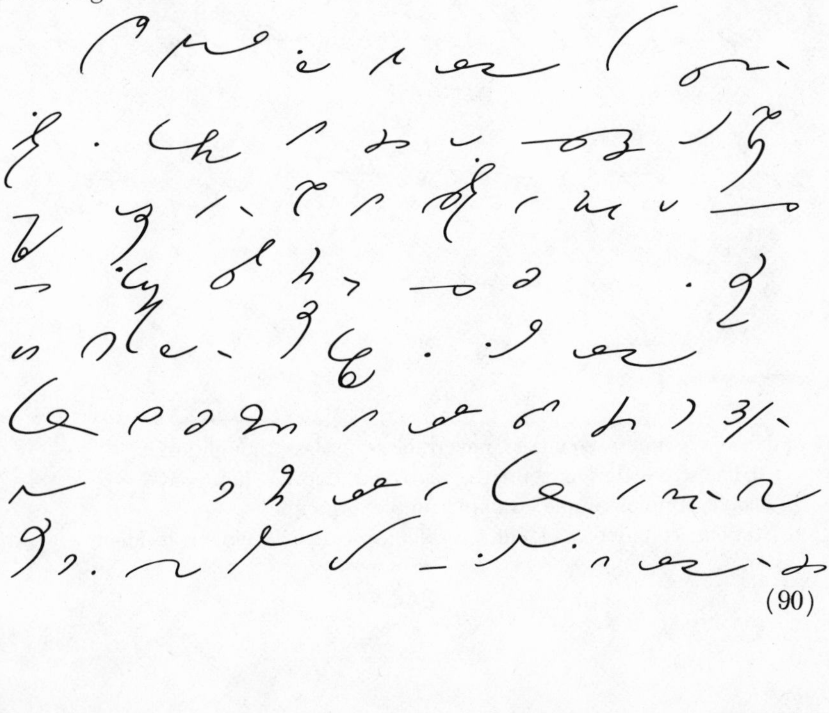

(90)

LESSON 38

● **Warmup.** For your warmup today, practice on the sentence in the second paragraph of the letter on page 235. Break the sentence down into as many parts as you feel desirable.

Developing Word-Building Power

289. WORD FAMILIES

-less

1 *[shorthand outlines]*

-rive

2 *[shorthand outlines]*

-ple

3 *[shorthand outlines]*

-dent

4 *[shorthand outlines]*

---

1. Needless, unless, countless, nevertheless, useless, thoughtless.
2. Arrive, strive, derive, contrive, contrived, deprive, deprived.
3. People, simple, sample, example, ample, principle.
4. Student, confident, evident, president, incident, accident, resident.

Building Transcription Skills

290. BUSINESS VOCABULARY BUILDER

outlook   Prospect for the future.

uninterruptedly   Without a break.

stirred   Excited; moved.

inflated   Expanded abnormally, as prices.

291. COMMON WORD ROOTS

-er: *one who*

reader   One who reads.

worker   One who works.

teacher   One who teaches.

banker   One who banks.

subscriber   One who enters his name for a book, a magazine, etc.

receiver   One who receives.

Reading and Writing Practice

292.

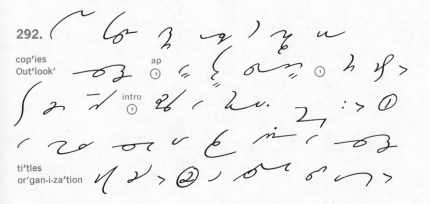

cop'ies
Out'look'

ap

intro

ti'tles
or'gan·i·za'tion

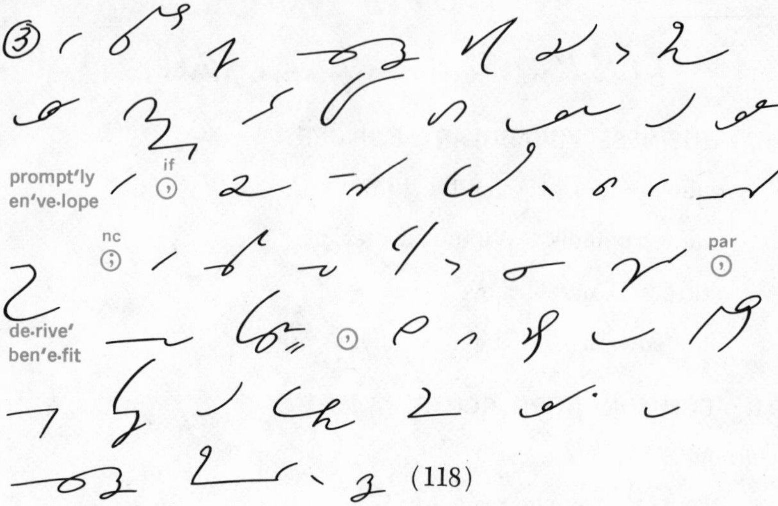
③
if
nc
par
(118)

prompt'ly
en've·lope

de·rive'
ben'e·fit

293.

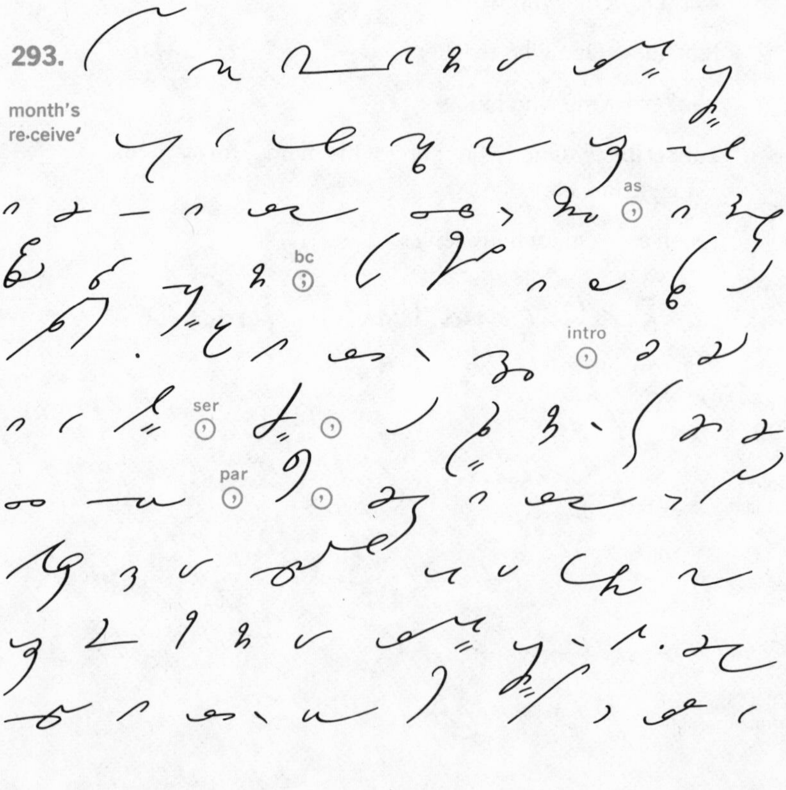
as
bc
intro
ser
par

month's
re·ceive'

Transcribe:
$10

[Gregg shorthand outlines] conj

[Gregg shorthand outlines]

[Gregg shorthand outlines] nonr

[Gregg shorthand outlines] cr   (154)

....

294. *[Gregg shorthand outlines]*

well′-known′
hyphenated
before noun
screen
[Gregg shorthand outlines] ser   /   *[Gregg shorthand outlines]*

[Gregg shorthand outlines]

[Gregg shorthand outlines]

re′lax·a′tion
stirred
[Gregg shorthand outlines]

[Gregg shorthand outlines] par

[Gregg shorthand outlines]

[Gregg shorthand outlines]

[Gregg shorthand outlines]

[Gregg shorthand outlines] intro

[Gregg shorthand outlines]

[Gregg shorthand outlines]

[Gregg shorthand outlines] (130)

295. **Transcription Quiz.** For you to supply: 4 commas — 1 comma conjunction, 2 commas introductory, 1 comma *and* omitted; 2 missing words.

[shorthand outlines]

(134)

LESSON 39

● **Warmup.** Today, warm up on the sentences in the third paragraph of the phrase letter on page 235. To be on the safe side, why not turn to page 210 and reread the instructions given there for warming up.

Developing Word-Building Power

296. WORD BEGINNINGS AND ENDINGS

Sub-

1 [shorthand outlines]

For-

2 [shorthand outlines]

Ex-

3 [shorthand outlines]

Con-

4 [shorthand outlines]

---

1. Subscribe, subscription, subscriber, subscribed, submit, substantial, subdivide.
2. Form, inform, information, forget, forgot, foremost, enforce.
3. Extra, extend, expire, extremely, expert, express, explained, excess.
4. Continue, consequently, consider, convinced, conveniently, conflict, confidence.

Building Transcription Skills

297.   BUSINESS VOCABULARY BUILDER

presumptuous   Overconfident; taking undue liberties.

apt   Likely.

ballot   Vote.

invaluable   Inestimable; priceless.

298.   GRAMMAR CHECKUP

Than, as

You can determine which pronoun to use after *than* or *as* by mentally adding the words that make a complete clause.

> I prefer to deal with you rather than him. (rather than *deal with* him)
> John can do the job as well as I. (*can do the job*)
> No one knows better than I that you are qualified. (better than I *know* that you are qualified)

Reading and Writing Practice

299.

[shorthand outlines]

sub·scrip′tion
sur·prise′

[shorthand outlines]

two′-year′
hyphenated
before noun

[shorthand outlines]

nc
①

intro
①

[shorthand outlines]

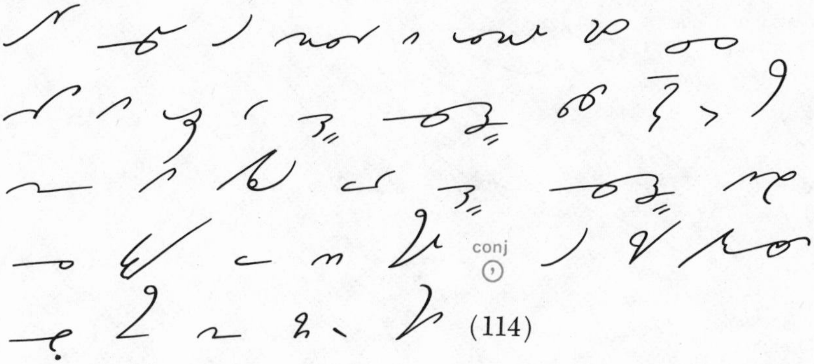

(114)

300.

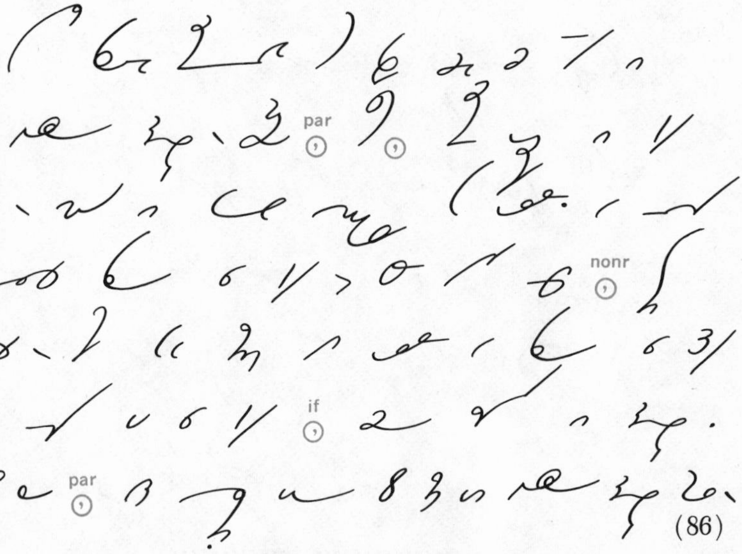

passed
tri'al

(86)

301.

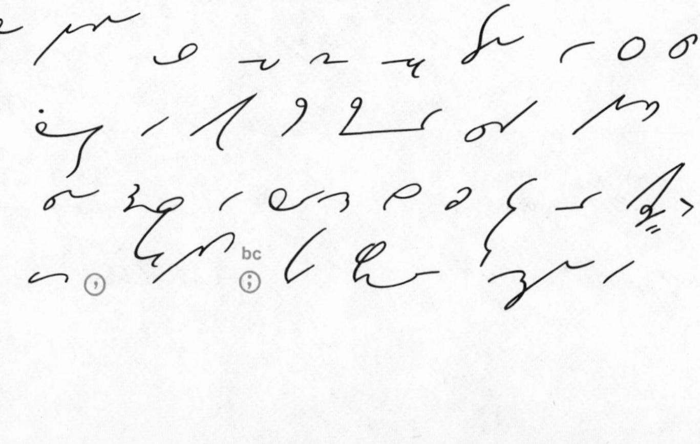

dis·cuss'
per'son·al·ly
ar'ti·cles

pre·sump'tu·ous
Ad·vi'so·ry
Board

[Gregg shorthand outlines]

en·joy'a·ble
brought

ser

be·lieve'
bal'lot

intro

intro

nc

(183)

....

302. *[Gregg shorthand outlines]*

par

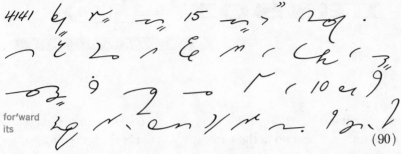

4141

for'ward
its

(90)

303. Transcription Quiz.   For you to supply: 4 commas — 1 comma *as* clause, 3 commas introductory; 1 semicolon because of comma; 2 missing words.

(148)

LESSON 40

● **Warmup.** For the last time you will use the letter on page 235 to warm up. Warm up in the same way you did in the preceding lessons of this chapter.

Developing Word-Building Power

304. SHORTHAND VOCABULARY BUILDER

Days of the Week

1

Months of the Year

2

Dit, Det

3

Omission of Ē in Ū

4

---

1. Friday, Monday, Tuesday, Wednesday, Saturday, Sunday, Thursday.
2. August, October, September, July, November, December, March, February.
3. Audit, auditor, credit, creditor, ditto, detailed, determine.
4. Issue, renew, suit, suited, music, continue, numerous, new.

Building Transcription Skills

305.   BUSINESS VOCABULARY BUILDER

remittance   Payment.

audit   A formal examination of accounts.

prepublication   Before the date a book or magazine appears on the market.

Reading and Writing Practice

306. *[shorthand outlines]*

one'-year'
hyphenated
before noun

ob'·vi·ous·ly
re·mit'tance
can'celed

ar'ti·cles
es·pe'cial·ly

(110)

· ·

307. *[shorthand outlines]*

con·tin'ued
be·yond'

for'ward
Bu'reau
Cir·cu·la'tion

[Gregg shorthand outlines]

nonr

anx'ious
pos'si·ble

intro

nc

intro

(94)

....

308.

sub·scrib'er
Mu'sic

ap

high'-fi·del'i·ty
*hyphenated
before noun*

ap

12

pleas'ure-filled'
down'-to-earth'
*hyphenated
before noun*

and o

lan'guage
suit'ed

intro

up to date
*no noun,
no hyphen*

pre'pub·li·ca'tion
sub·scrib'ing

intro
intro
intro
nc
25
4/

(206)

309.

Transcribe:
$3
$4
his'to·ry

op'por·tu'ni·ty
re·new'al

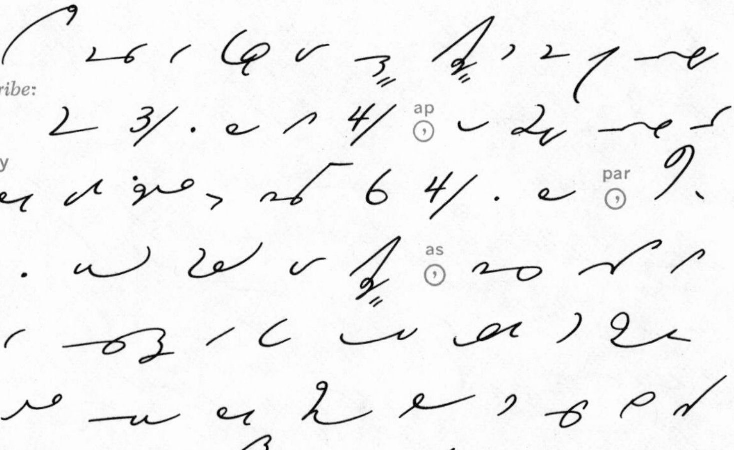
ap
par
as
nc
intro
35
3/
4/
6 4/

(95)

310. Office Housekeeping

[shorthand]

Upon arriving *[shorthand]*

[shorthand]

[Gregg shorthand outlines]

Of course [shorthand outlines]

(309)

Retailing

No doubt you have often shopped from the counters of a department store — perhaps for a pair of gloves, a box of stationery, a pound of candy, a tube of toothpaste — or for any of the other thousands upon thousands of items stocked by the store. Have you ever stopped to think how all those items found their way to those counters? They found their way there through the miracle of modern retailing.

What is retailing? Briefly, it is the process of buying goods in large quantities from producers, wholesalers, or jobbers and then selling those goods in small quantities direct to the consumer. Retailing has grown into one of the largest fields of business endeavor in the country. Today there are almost 2,000,000 retail stores of one type or another in the United States. Wherever people live, retail stores are there to serve them. These stores supply just about everything we need for our homes, the things we wear, and the things we eat. These stores range in size from tiny, one-man, "hole-in-the-wall" stores to tremendous department stores and shopping centers that employ thousands of people.

To assemble and sell the mounds of merchandise that consumers need, the retail industry employs almost 7,000,000 people in hundreds of different types of jobs. The retail industry employs buyers, sales-clerks, models, interior decorators, shoppers, commercial artists, copy writers, and many other persons in varying jobs. Obviously, a field as large and complex as retailing involves a great deal of office activity. And one of the most important people in retailing is the secretary.

If you are interested in some phase of retailing — perhaps buying or interior decorating or designing — you will find it is easy to get your "foot in the door" as a stenographer.

The letters in this chapter will give you a taste of the type of correspondence you would handle as a stenographer in a retailing establishment.

LESSON 41

Building Phrasing Skill

311. PHRASE BUILDER

Reading goal: 55 seconds.

Several

1 [shorthand outlines]

Us

2 [shorthand outlines]

Special Phrases

3 [shorthand outlines]

Omission of Words in Phrases

4 [shorthand outlines]

---

1. Several minutes, several months, several months ago, several days, several times, several other.
2. Send us, give us, for us, with us, between us, from us, by us, inform us.
3. Your order, your orders, as soon as, as soon as possible, of course, of course it is, let us, to us.
4. One or two, two or three, three or four, one of the, some of these, none of them, many of the, some of the, some of them, out of this, out of the, at a loss, as a result, by the way.

262

312. WARMUP PHRASE LETTER

The following 118-word letter, which is your warmup letter for this chapter, contains 26 phrases. How fast can you read it? How fast can you copy it?

(118)

Building Transcription Skills

313. BUSINESS VOCABULARY BUILDER

gross Twelve dozen (144).

established Firmly fixed.

phase Stage; interval.

Reading and Writing Practice

314.

birth'day'

[Gregg shorthand outlines]

as

one'-day'
hyphenated
before noun

ex·cept'
na'tion·al·ly

int

al·read'y
pur'chase
con·ven'ient

nc   intro

(134)

● ●

315.

Transcribe:
No. 11651

11651

nonr

conj

due
oc·ca'sion
fre'quent·ly

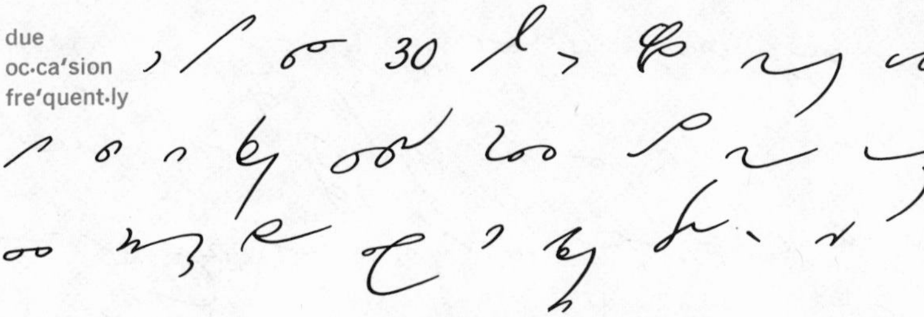

(98)

316.

in·quir'y
re·ferred'
hes'i·ta'tion
in'ex·pen'sive
de·vice'

and o
conj
if

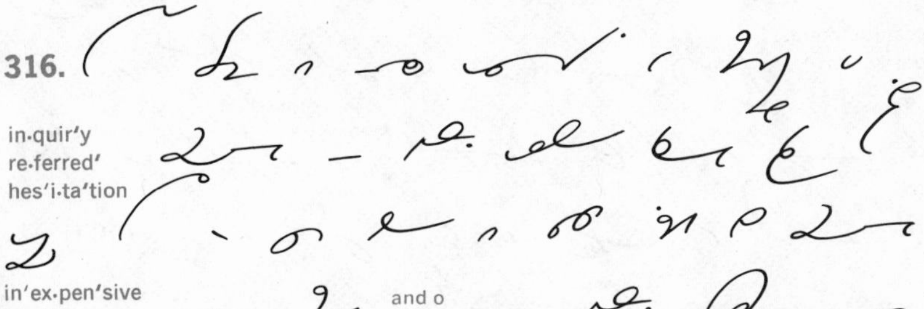

(104)

317.

Transcribe:
Fifth Avenue

[Gregg shorthand outlines]

wh

if

re·quire'ments
per'son·al

ap

conj

(109)

318. Transcription Quiz. For you to supply: 5 commas — 4
commas parenthetical, 1 comma *if* clause; 1 semicolon because of
comma; 1 missing word.

[Gregg shorthand outlines]

30

(101)

LESSON 42

● **Warmup.**   Your warmup letter today is on page 263. Continue to follow the warmup plan that you used in Chapter 8, breaking each sentence into parts, writing each part several times as rapidly as possible, and finally writing the complete sentence.

Developing Word-Building Power

319. BRIEF-FORM CHART

Read through the entire chart once, reading from left to right. Then read through it again, reading down each column.

1. Company, companies, accompany, accompanies, accompanied, accompaniment.
2. Every, everyday, everywhere, everyone, everybody, everything.
3. Soon, sooner, quantity, quantities, merchandise, merchandising.
4. Difficult, difficulty, difficulties, purpose, purposes, purposely.
5. General, generally, immediate, immediately, glad, gladly.

320. GEOGRAPHICAL EXPRESSIONS

267

2 [shorthand outlines]

1. Princeton, Evanston, Lewiston, Jamestown, Johnstown, Allentown.
2. Pennsylvania, Ohio, Virginia, West Virginia, Minnesota, Colorado, Mississippi, Oregon.

Building Transcription Skills

321. BUSINESS VOCABULARY BUILDER

crate A container, usually made of wood.

disposition Act of getting rid of; disposal.

make amends To correct; to make right.

remiss Negligent; careless.

racks Stands on which merchandise is displayed.

322. SIMILAR-WORDS DRILL

Some, sum

some A portion.

[shorthand outlines]

Have some of our services displeased you?

sum Amount; the total.

[shorthand outlines]

This check represents the difference between the total charges and the sum you sent us.

Stenographers very seldom mistranscribe *some;* but, through carelessness, they will occasionally transcribe *some* for *sum.* Be careful that you don't do this.

Reading and Writing Practice

323.

ap
3
4
when
sau'cers
crate
6
intro
intro
dis'po·si'tion
mer'chan·dise

(98)

324.

16
Transcribe:
4151 East 81 Street
4151
81
par
15
63
37
Transcribe:
37 cents
to'tal
nonr

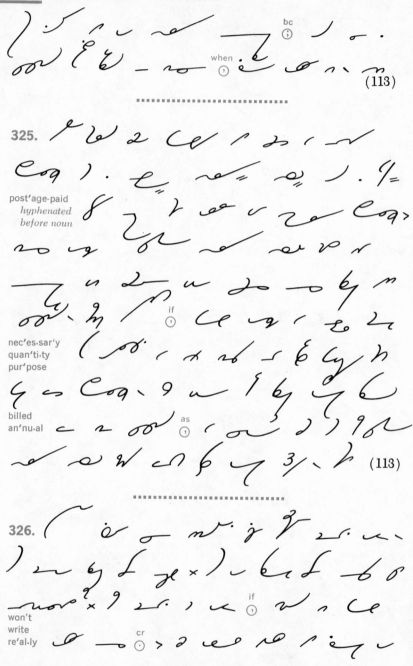

(113)

325.

post'age-paid
hyphenated
before noun

nec'es·sar'y
quan'ti·ty
pur'pose

billed
an'nu·al

(113)

326.

won't
write
re'al·ly

(shorthand outlines) (91)

327. Transcription Quiz.   For you to supply: 4 commas — 2 commas parenthetical, 1 comma *and* omitted, 1 comma introductory; 1 semicolon no conjunction; 2 missing words.

(shorthand outlines) (130)

LESSON 43

● **Warmup.** Your warmup letter today is on page 263. Warm up on the sentence in the second paragraph, breaking it down into convenient groups.

Developing Word-Building Power

328. WORD FAMILIES

-ply

1 [shorthand outlines]

-long

2 [shorthand outlines]

-serve

3 [shorthand outlines]

-tate

4 [shorthand outlines]

-sist

5 [shorthand outlines]

1. Supply, imply, comply, reply, replied, multiply.
2. Long, belong, along, prolong, oblong, furlong.
3. Serve, deserve, reserve, preserve, conserve, servant, service, services, serviced.
4. Hesitate, facilitate, rotate, dictate, imitate, irritate.
5. Resist, persist, consist, assist, insist, resistance, assistance, persistence, insistence.

Building Transcription Skills

329. BUSINESS VOCABULARY BUILDER

air-conditioned *(adjective)* Having equipment that cools a room or building in hot weather.

frankly Candidly; without reserve.

opportune Timely; fit.

330. SPELLING FAMILIES

Be very careful of words ending in the sound of *er*—they may be spelled *er, or,* or *ar*. When in doubt, look them up!

Words Ending in -er

of′fi·cer	**train′er**	**man′a·ger**
sub·scrib′er	**di·vid′er**	**reg′is·ter**
pro·duc′er	**read′er**	**cus′tom·er**

Words Ending in -ar

sug′ar	**col′lar**	**par·tic′u·lar**
gram′mar	**cel′lar**	**reg′u·lar**

Words Ending in -or

ma′jor	**gov′er·nor**	**el′e·va′tor**
pro·fes′sor	**su′per·vi′sor**	**sen′a·tor**
hu′mor	**dic′ta·tor**	**gen′er·a′tor**

Reading and Writing Practice

331. 

re·ceived'
re·quest'

es·pe'cial·ly
at·trac'tive

(132)

332.

charge'-ac·count'
*hyphenated
before noun*

be·gin'ning
pleas'ant
oc·ca'sion

and o

when

(137)

··

333.

bus'y
sum'mer's

if

guar'an·teed'
sat'is·fac'tion

bc

par

years'
e·quip'ment

(135)

334.

wel'come
al·read'y
dis·cov'ered

[Gregg shorthand outlines]

(91)

335. Transcription Quiz. For you to supply: 5 commas — 2 commas *if* clause, 2 commas parenthetical, 1 comma conjunction; 1 semicolon no conjunction; 1 missing word.

[Gregg shorthand outlines]

(98)

LESSON 44

● **Warmup.**   Your warmup letter is on page 263. Practice the sentence that makes up the third paragraph, breaking it down into three or four parts.

Developing Word-Building Power

336. WORD BEGINNINGS AND ENDINGS

Mis-

1 [shorthand outlines]

Trans-

2 [shorthand outlines]

-self

3 [shorthand outlines]

Com-

4 [shorthand outlines]

1. Mistake, mistaken, misplace, misrepresent, mislead.
2. Transaction, transfer, transferable, transit, translate, transport, transportation, transpire.
3. Yourself, herself, myself, himself, itself, ourselves, themselves, yourselves.
4. Comply, compute, combine, complete, complain, complained.

Building Transcription Skills

337. BUSINESS VOCABULARY BUILDER

computing   Calculating.

billhead   A blank with a business address at the top and
spaces beneath for billing purposes.

expedite   To hurry along.

transferable   Capable of being used by another.

338. GRAMMAR CHECKUP

Preposition at the End of a Sentence

Careful writers try, as a general rule, to avoid ending a sentence
with a preposition.

No

Can you give me the name of the store in Springfield that you
bought your hat in?

Yes

Can you give me the name of the store in Springfield in which
you bought your hat?

However, if the application of this general rule would result in
an unnatural or stilted construction, the sentence may end with a preposition.

He was an easy man to work with.
What is this good for?

Reading and Writing Practice

339.

[Gregg shorthand outlines]

mer'chant
cash'ier
cus'tom·er's

par

ser

intro

bc

when

re·ceipt'
to'tal

ser

cr

Transcribe:
18 Street

14 %, 18

(184)

340.   *nonr*

[Gregg shorthand outlines]

bill'head'
ex·pe·dite

nonr

[Gregg shorthand outlines] (80)

- -

341. *[Gregg shorthand outlines]*

intro

re·quest'
sig'na·ture

[Gregg shorthand outlines]

re·ceipt'
ar·range'ments
es·tab'lish

par

[Gregg shorthand outlines] (94)

- -

342. *[Gregg shorthand outlines]*

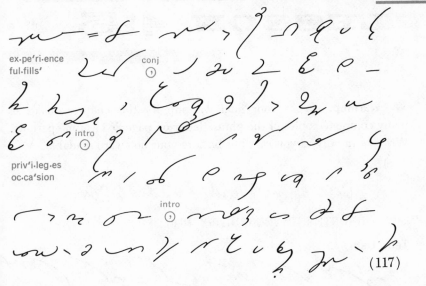

ex·pe′ri·ence
ful·fills′

conj

priv′i·leg·es
oc·ca′sion

intro

intro

(117)

343.   Transcription Quiz.   For you to supply: 4 commas—2 commas *as* clause, 2 commas parenthetical; 1 semicolon no conjunction; 2 missing words.

(98)

LESSON 45

● **Warmup.** As your final warmup for this chapter, make as many complete copies of the phrase letter on page 263 as time permits. Write as rapidly as you can, but be sure your notes are readable.

Developing Word-Building Power

344. SHORTHAND VOCABULARY BUILDER

Tem, Dem

Ort

Th

Ses

Abbreviation

1. Customer, automatically, system, seldom, random, demonstration.
2. Report, reporting, reported, supporting, import, export, mortal.
3. Earth, health, wealth, truth, month, these, teeth, bath.
4. Arises, realizes, services, addresses, releases, system, access.
5. Frequent, infrequent, infrequently, consequently, subsequent, delinquent.

Building Transcription Skills

345. BUSINESS VOCABULARY BUILDER

survive To exist; to last.

patronage Business.

mutually profitable Of value to both parties.

Reading and Writing Practice

346. *[shorthand outlines]*

15

Transcribe:
$8
book'keep'er

nec·es·sar'y
cor·rec'tion

if

up to date
no noun,
no hyphen

cr
(92)

....

347. *[shorthand outlines]*

[Gregg shorthand outlines]

fre'quent·ly
mer'chan·dise

if

par

bc

nonr

(110)

348.

as

year's
e·di'tion

conj

intro

nc

ser

il'lus·tra'tions
col'or

intro ⊙

high'·qual'i·ty
hyphenated
before noun

if ⊙

(113)

....

349.

stead'i·ly
prompt'ly

intro ⊙

pur'pose
ap·pre'ci·ate
pa'tron·age

(140)

350. Good Grooming Is Forever

[shorthand]

But after *[shorthand]*

[Shorthand outlines - Gregg shorthand characters fill the page]

Well

(333)

10

Banking

Most people look upon a bank merely as a safe place in which to keep their money. True, there is no safer place in which to keep your money. Not only is your money safe in a bank, but the money can also work for you while it is there — by earning interest.

A bank offers many services other than safekeeping — services without which business could not operate effectively. Here are a few ways in which banks serve you:

If you want to remodel your kitchen, build a garage, or repair your roof, your bank can arrange a home loan for you.

If you wish to travel, your bank will not only lend you money for the trip, help you plan your trip, and obtain your reservations, but it will also let you pay back the loan in convenient payments.

If you want to start in business for yourself, your bank may grant you a business loan.

If you want to buy a car but cannot pay cash for it, your bank may offer you a personal loan.

If you want a safe place in which to store valuable papers, such as insurance policies, government bonds, etc., the safe deposit department of your bank offers storage facilities.

Every person, no matter how modest his income, should have a banker — just as he has a doctor or a lawyer. The banker can be a real friend in need when financial problems arise.

Today's bank is a friendly place. Banks have only one thing to sell —service. Today's banks exert every effort to make banking convenient and pleasant. Some have added drive-in branches in which customers can make deposits, withdraw money, and transact routine banking business without leaving their cars. Others provide a "banking-by-mail" service, so that customers can take care of their banking needs without even setting foot in the bank.

If you were to talk to some of the people who work in the bank, you would find that their work is interesting and varied. Banks carry on a great deal of business by correspondence; therefore, the stenographer and the secretary play important roles in the daily affairs of the business. The letters in this chapter are typical of those that might be dictated to you in a banking office.

LESSON 46

Building Phrasing Skill

351. PHRASE BUILDER

Reading goal: 30 seconds.

Month

1 [shorthand outlines]

To Omitted in Phrases

2 [shorthand outlines]

As

3 [shorthand outlines]

Every

4 [shorthand outlines]

---

1. Each month, few months, this month, months ago, every month.
2. Glad to hear, able to say, in addition to the, in order to obtain, ought to be, seems to be, up to date.
3. As little, as much, as low, as long, as many, as you know.
4. Every day, every minute, every month, every time, every other, every one, every one of the.

352. WARMUP PHRASE LETTER

This is your warmup letter for Chapter 10. How fast can you read it? copy it?

[Gregg shorthand outlines] (144)

Building Transcription Skills

353.   BUSINESS VOCABULARY BUILDER

> **minimum balance**   The smallest amount a depositor can
> keep in his checking account without having to pay
> carrying charges.

> **accommodates**   Takes care of.

receipt   Written evidence of payment. (Do not confuse with *recipe,* which means a set of cooking instructions.)

Reading and Writing Practice

354.

[shorthand outlines]

min'i·mum
bal'ance

par
⊙

conj
⊙

con·ven'ient

if
⊙

(124)

· ·

355.

[shorthand outlines]

nc
⊙

intro
⊙

(Gregg shorthand outlines)

un·for'tu·nate
re'al·ly
wor'ried

out'-of-the-way'
hyphenated
before noun

de·pos'it
month's

can'celed
re·ceipts'

(142)

. . . .

356.

eas'i·er
con·ven'ient

Transcribe:
1146 West 63 Street

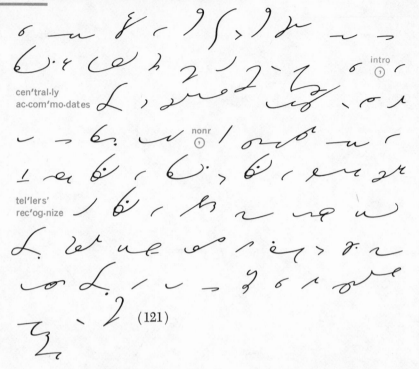

cen'tral·ly
ac·com'mo·dates

intro

nonr

tel'lers'
rec'og·nize

(121)

357. Transcription Quiz. For you to supply: 6 commas—1 comma apposition, 2 commas series, 1 comma *when* clause, 2 commas parenthetical; 2 missing words.

(107)

Loyalty

*The secretary doesn't divulge confidential infor-
mation about her employer's activities because she
knows that this can lead to complications. She doesn't
run down her boss when she's in a bad mood or when
things aren't going just the way they should, for this
only reflects on her own integrity. She doesn't take advantage of her boss by keeping late hours or overstay-
ing her lunch hour, for these are forms of disloyalty and
show a lack of responsibility.* —Ray Josephs, Author
and Public Relations Consultant

LESSON 47

● **Warmup.** Your warmup letter is on page 291. Copy as much of the letter as time permits. Write as rapidly as you can, but be sure that your shorthand is readable.

Developing Word-Building Power

358. BRIEF-FORM CHART

Reading goal: 30 seconds.

1					
2					
3					
4					
5					

1. Statement, advertisement, government, department, acknowledgment, accompaniment.
2. Enclosed, manufactured, governed, organized, questioned, advertised.
3. Value, values, valued, valuable, invaluable, valueless.
4. Experience, experiencing, public, publicly, world, worldly.
5. Where, wherever, elsewhere, speak, speaks, speaker.

359. GEOGRAPHICAL EXPRESSIONS

1

2 〔shorthand outline〕

1. Nashville, Danville, Knoxville, Jacksonville, Brownsville, Louisville, Crawfordsville.
2. Texas, Louisiana, Florida, Tennessee, Kentucky, Alabama, New Mexico.

Building Transcription Skills

360. BUSINESS VOCABULARY BUILDER

overdrawn   Checks have been written for an amount that is greater than that on deposit in the bank.

reputable   Enjoying a good reputation.

poll   The casting of votes by a body of persons.

361. SIMILAR-WORDS DRILL

Loss, lose, loose

loss *(noun)*   That which one is deprived of.

〔shorthand outline〕

Do not wait until you suffer a loss before renting a safe deposit box.

lose *(verb)*   To be deprived of.

〔shorthand outline〕

You cannot afford to lose your valuable papers.

loose   Unattached; not fastened.

〔shorthand outline〕

As a token of appreciation, I am sending you a convenient loose-leaf notebook.

Reading and Writing Practice

362.

[shorthand outlines]

o'ver·drawn'
suf·fi'cient

[shorthand outlines] nc ⊙

[shorthand outlines]   116

Transcribe:
  $30
September 16

[shorthand outlines]   as ⊙

bc ⊙

[shorthand outlines]

(72)

································

363.

[shorthand outlines]

cus'tom·ers
mu'tu·al·ly

[shorthand outlines] conj ⊙

sou've·nir'
loose'-leaf'
  hyphenated
  before noun

[shorthand outlines] intro ⊙

ser ⊙

⊙

as ⊙

rep'u·ta·ble
fi·nan'cial

[shorthand outlines]

(shorthand outline) if *(shorthand outline)* (127)

....

364. *(shorthand outline)*

los'ses
sen'si·ble   intro *(shorthand outline)*

(shorthand outline)

intro *(shorthand outline)*

pol'i·cies   ser
mort'gag·es *(shorthand outline)*
lose

intro *(shorthand outline)*

im·me'di·ate·ly   if *(shorthand outline)*
suf'fer

(shorthand outline) (113)

....

365. *(shorthand outline)*

(shorthand outline) 60, *(shorthand outline)*

(shorthand outline)

(shorthand outline)

sim'ply
an'swered   ser *(shorthand outline)*

[Gregg shorthand outlines]

(85)

366. **Transcription Quiz.** For you to supply: 6 commas—1 comma apposition, 4 commas parenthetical, 1 comma conjunction; 1 semicolon because of comma; 2 missing words.

[Gregg shorthand outlines]

(143)

LESSON 48

● **Warmup.** Your warmup letter is on page 291. This time, write as many copies of the first paragraph as time permits. Strive to increase your speed with each writing.

Developing Word-Building Power

367. WORD FAMILIES

Pro-

1 *[shorthand outlines]*

-ious

2 *[shorthand outlines]*

-ify

3 *[shorthand outlines]*

-rise, -rize

4 *[shorthand outlines]*

---

1. Propose, problems, providing, promote, produce, protect, protest.
2. Furious, various, serious, curious, studious, industrious, obvious, previous.
3. Notify, simplify, verify, justify, classify, amplify, qualify.
4. Rise, prize, enterprise, surprise, notarize, authorize, summarize.

301

Building Transcription Skills

368. BUSINESS VOCABULARY BUILDER

   arrears   That which is unpaid but due.

   habitual   Acting by force of habit.

   stave off   To keep at a distance, hold off.

369. SPELLING FAMILIES

   Always be cautious when you must transcribe a word that begins with the sound of *for*. Sometimes the word will be spelled *for*, sometimes, *fore*.

   Words Beginning with For-

for·bid'	for·get'	for'feit
for·gave'	for·give'	for'ward

   Words Beginning with Fore-

fore'cast	fore'ground'	fore'sight'
fore·close'	fore'most	fore·tell'

   Also, watch out for the number *four*

four	four'teen'	fourth
	BUT for'ty	

Reading and Writing Practice

370. *(shorthand outlines)*

tact'less
lan'guage

[Gregg shorthand outlines]

ha·bit'u·al
de·lin'quent

conj

if

ap

fur'ther
dealt
prompt'ly

if

intro

(130)

....

371.

en'ter·prise
de·ci'sive
stave

and o

com′pa·ny′s
then
ad·vise′

[Gregg shorthand outlines]

(109)

· ·

372.

[Gregg shorthand outlines]

fi·nance′
re·pairs

[Gregg shorthand outlines]

intro ①

② ③

(106)

· ·

373.

[Gregg shorthand outlines]

conj ①

[Gregg shorthand outlines]

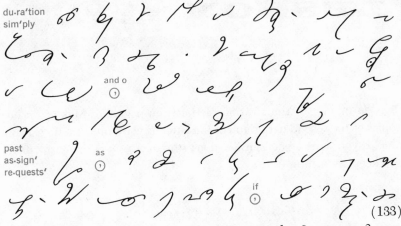

du·ra′tion
sim′ply

and o

past
as·sign′
re·quests′

as

if

(133)

374. Transcription Quiz. For you to supply: 6 commas—3 commas *if* clause, 1 comma *when* clause, 2 commas apposition; 2 missing words.

(113)

LESSON 49

● **Warmup.** Your warmup letter is on page 291. Make as many copies of the second paragraph of the letter as you can in the time available. If you write a poor outline, don't stop to cross it out and rewrite it; just keep on writing.

Developing Word-Building Power

375. WORD BEGINNINGS AND ENDINGS

Ul

1

Fur-

2

Enter-, Entr-

3

De-

4

---

1. Result, consult, insult, adult, multiply, ultimate, ultimately.
2. Furnish, furnishes, furnished, furniture, further, furthermore, furnace, furnaces.
3. Entered, entertain, enterprise, enterprises, entertained, entertainment, entrance, entrances.
4. Delay, delayed, deposit, depositor, department, decide, decision.

Building Transcription Skills

376.   BUSINESS VOCABULARY BUILDER

restraint   Control over one's thoughts and their expression.

tactless   Giving offense.

tellers   Bank employees who take and pay out money.

377.   COMMON WORD ROOTS

Tri-: *three*

triple   *v.* To make three times as many or as great or as much.   *n.* A three-base hit.

triplicate   Made in three identical copies.

tricycle   A three-wheeled vehicle.

tripod   A three-legged stand used to support an instrument, as a camera.

triangle   A three-sided figure.

Reading and Writing Practice

378.

[shorthand outlines]

tact'less
a·pol'o·gies

intro ⊙

and o ⊙

par ⊙

[Gregg shorthand outlines]

cour'te·ous
slight

re·straint'
ir'ri·tat'ing

par

(150)

379.

de·pos'it
trip'li·cate
cop'ies

nonr

ex·am'ple
en·a'ble

intro

[Gregg shorthand outlines]

de·pos′i·tor′s
i′tem·ized
re·ceipt′

intro
⊙

intro
⊙

(148)

380.

mem′o·ries
shiv′er

if
⊙

in′su·lat′ed
roof

ser
⊙

if
⊙

max′i·mum
fur′ther

intro
⊙

as
⊙

bc
⊙

long′-term′
hyphenated
before noun

[Gregg shorthand outline] (123)

381. Transcription Quiz. For you to supply: 5 commas—2 commas parenthetical, 3 commas *if* clause; 1 semicolon no conjunction; 2 missing words.

[Gregg shorthand outline] (118)

LESSON 50

● **Warmup.** Your warmup letter is on page 291. Write the third paragraph as rapidly as you can; then make a copy of the entire letter in your best shorthand.

Developing Word-Building Power

382. SHORTHAND VOCABULARY BUILDER

Compound Words

X

OO Hook on Its Side

O Hook on Its Side

1. However, someone, worthwhile, within, notwithstanding, anyhow, anywhere.
2. Tax, taxes, relax, relaxation, flexible, box, mix.
3. None, number, enough, numerous, manuscript, news.
4. On, home, loan, stone, omit, nominate, tone.

Building Transcription Skills

383. **BUSINESS VOCABULARY BUILDER**

withdrawal Taking money out of a bank.

verified Determined the accuracy of.

flexible Capable of being modified or adapted to changing conditions.

Reading and Writing Practice

384.

re′cent·ly
with·draw′al

not′with·stand′ing
ver′i·fied
cour′te·sy

(120)

385.

cur'rent
flex'i·ble
de·vised'

(105)

386.

Transcribe:
October 15
No. 3131
$1,000

wheth'er
pos·ses'sion

(64)

387. Dial "S" for Secretary

"Hello."

"May I ask who is speaking, please?"

"This is Sarah Johnson."

"Is this Mr. Hoffman's office?"

"Yes, it is."

"May I speak to him, please? This is J. W. Jackson, of the Arnold Products Corporation."

"Just a moment, Mr. Jackson. I'll see if he is in."

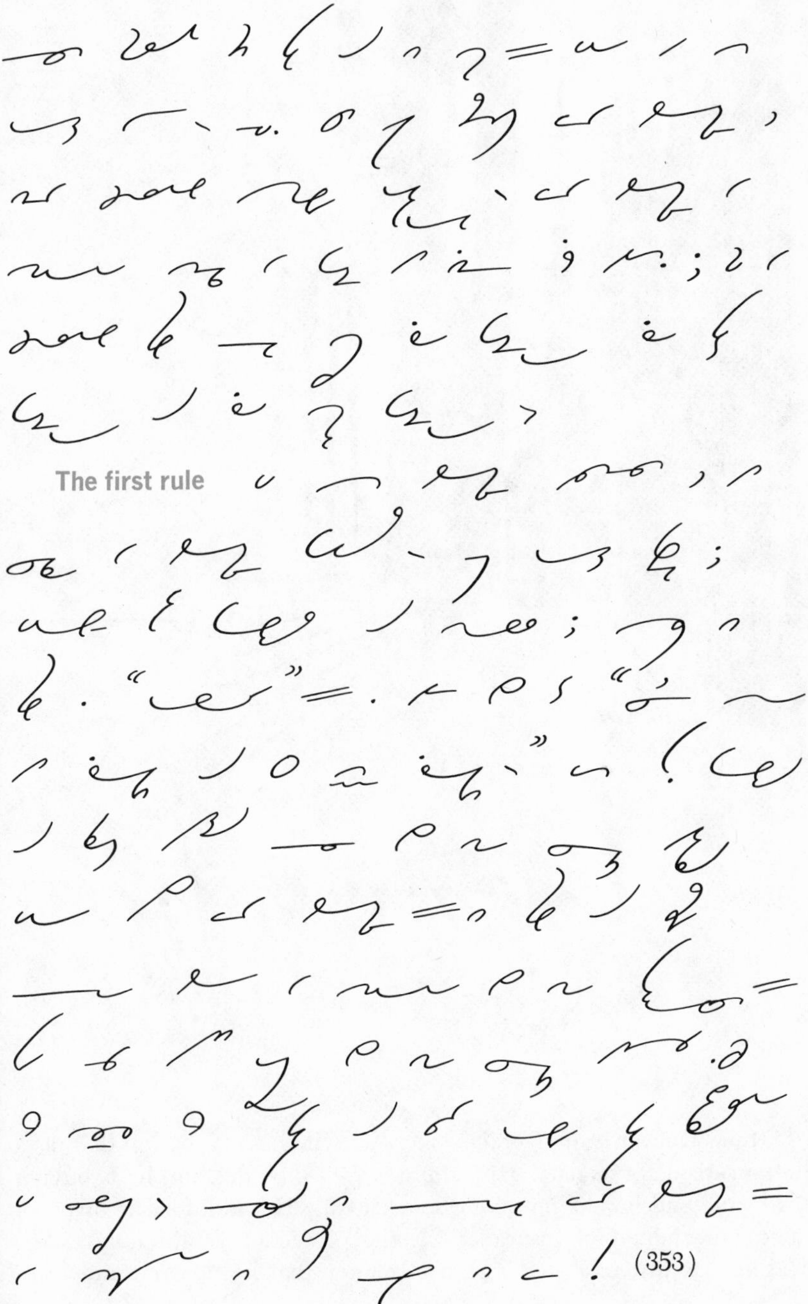

The first rule

(353)

11

Investments

John Harper is an average American who has a good job that pays him a satisfactory salary. His family is well provided for, he is buying his home, and he has put away some savings. In addition, he owns an adequate amount of insurance for the protection of his family. Mr. Harper has just inherited a sum of money that he does not need immediately for his daily living. He decides to invest it by buying a "share of business." He knows that if he buys stock in a good, strong company, he has an opportunity to earn money on his investment — in the form of dividends — in addition to having a relatively safe place for his investment. Also, if this company has intelligent, progressive management, it will grow; and as it grows, his investment will increase in value.

Of course, if he buys stock in a business about which he knows very little, expecting to make a large amount of money on his investments, he stands a risk of losing everything. The investor who buys stocks relying on "tips on the market" from people who are "in the know" may one day wake up a wiser but poorer person!

How can Mr. Harper tell which company is safe and is most likely to give him a fair return on his investment? If he is wise, he will obtain all the information he can about the company — its products, its management, its earnings in the past, and its plans for the future. There are various ways to obtain this information, but perhaps the best way is to consult a broker or an investment counselor.

Millions of Americans like Mr. Harper invest money every day in business. In addition, many businesses invest in other businesses by buying stocks and bonds. Such investments are a necessary part of our system of business. Without the money of investors, many large businesses simply could not bring to us the products and services we enjoy. For example, your telephone company, the company that manufactures the automobile your family drives, the company that publishes your favorite magazine — all depend on the investor's money for carrying on their business and expanding it for better production. Thus, the investment counselor is an important person in American business.

The main offices of investment counselors are usually situated in larger cities and are generally near the financial district—such as LaSalle Street in Chicago, Montgomery Street in San Francisco, and Wall Street in New York. Some investment counselors maintain smaller offices in outlying suburban areas. In addition, many banks are happy to offer free investment advice to their customers.

If you were to work in the office of an investment counselor, you might take from dictation letters similar to those in this chapter.

LESSON 51

Building Phrasing Skill

388. PHRASE BUILDER

Can you read the following four groups of phrases in 40 seconds or less?

If

Able

Hope

Which

1. If there is, if you, if you have, if you have not, if you can, if you will, if you get, if you could.
2. To be able, should be able, you should be able, would be able, may be able, may not be able, might be able.
3. We hope, we hope you are, we hope you will, we hope that, I hope, I hope you are, I hope you will, I hope you can.
4. In which, by which, for which, to which, which you can, which you will, which you may, which is.

389. WARMUP PHRASE LETTER

Your warmup phrase letter is very short this time. Your reading goal, 45 seconds; your copying goal, 1 minute.

[shorthand outlines]

(90)

Building Transcription Skills

390. BUSINESS VOCABULARY BUILDER

proxy   A written form that authorizes one person to cast a vote for another.

impaired   Harmed.

primary   First; main.

preclude   To prevent; to bar.

Reading and Writing Practice

391. *[shorthand outlines]*

re·quest′ed
in·ves′ti·gat′ed

debts
man′age·ment

in·tel′li·gent
com·mend′a·ble

full′-time′
hyphenated before noun

hes′i·ta′tion
rec′om·mend′ing

(174)

392.

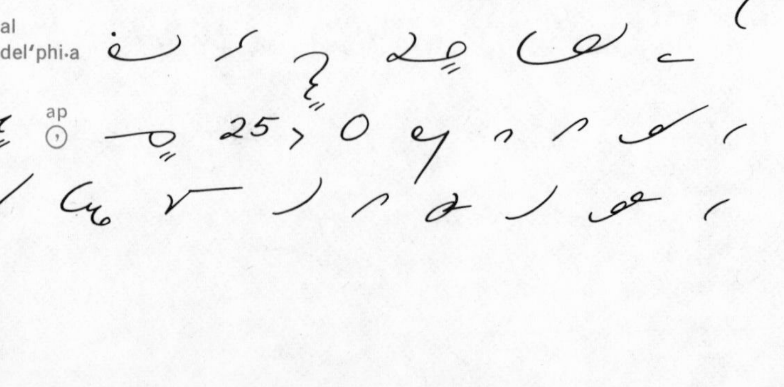

an′nu·al
Phil′a·del′phi·a

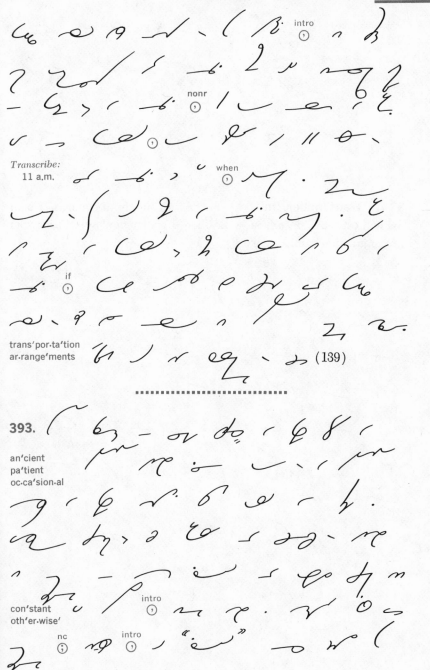

Transcribe:
11 a.m.

trans′por·ta′tion
ar·range′ments

(139)

393.

an′cient
pa′tient
oc·ca′sion·al

con′stant
oth′er·wise′

or'gan·i·za'tion's
fi·nan'cial

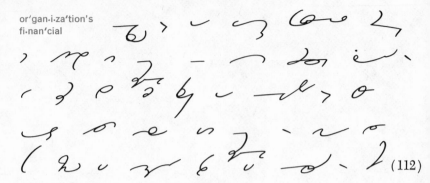

(112)

394.   Transcription Quiz.   For you to supply: 4 commas—1 comma nonrestrictive, 2 commas apposition, 1 comma *if* clause; 1 semicolon no conjunction; 2 missing words.

(97)

LESSON 52

● **Warmup.** Your warmup letter is on page 319. Practice the sentences in the first paragraph, breaking down each sentence into several parts and writing each part as rapidly as you can.

Developing Word-Building Power

395. BRIEF-FORM CHART

On your first reading of the following brief forms, read from left to right. On your second reading, read *down* each column. Do you read the brief forms and derivatives as rapidly when you read down as when you read from left to right?

1					
2					
3					
4					
5					

1. Particular, particularly, opinion, opinions, question, questions.
2. Dissatisfied, dissatisfaction, opportunity, opportunities, advertise, advertised.
3. Organize, organizer, envelope, envelopes, work, worked.
4. Experience, experiences, experienced, wish, wished, wishful.
5. Govern, governor, government, business, businesses, businessmen.

396. GEOGRAPHICAL EXPRESSIONS

1 *[shorthand outlines]*

2 *[shorthand outlines]*

1. Detroit, Chicago, St. Louis, Milwaukee, Buffalo, Syracuse, Boston.
2. Illinois, Michigan, Indiana, Missouri, New York, New Jersey, United States, Puerto Rico.

Building Transcription Skills

397. BUSINESS VOCABULARY BUILDER

"tips on the market"   Hints, usually based on inside information, as to which stocks will probably rise in value.

expansion   Enlargement; growth.

silent partner   A person who has no voice in the running of a partnership.

capital   A stock of accumulated wealth.

398. SIMILAR-WORDS DRILL

Purpose, propose

purpose *(noun)*   Aim; intention.

[shorthand outlines]

It is our purpose to help our clients.

propose   To offer for consideration.

[shorthand outlines]

You need not accept any plan that we may propose.

Reading and Writing Practice

399.

[Gregg shorthand outlines]

in·flu'enced
pur'pose

bc

dis'sat·is·fac'tion
pol'i·cies

par

pleas'ure
wel'com·ing

(140)

400.

conj

wheth'er
suf·fi'cient

ser

e·mer′gen·cies
Transcribe:
$5,000

par

and o

firm's
ad′ver·tis′ing

nc

(135)

401.

in·ves′tors
av′er·age

conj

intro

par

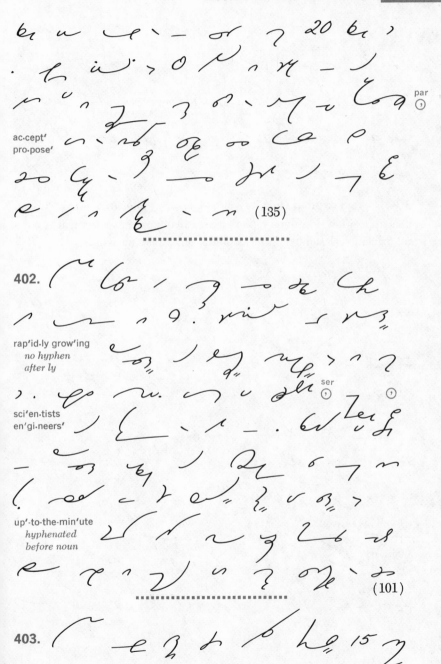

ac·cept'
pro·pose'

(135)

402.

rap'id·ly grow'ing
no hyphen
after ly

sci'en·tists
en'gi·neers'

up'-to-the-min'ute
hyphenated
before noun

(101)

403.

[Gregg shorthand outlines]

(70)

404. Transcription Quiz. For you to supply: 6 commas—2 commas apposition, 1 comma *when* clause, 2 commas parenthetical, 1 comma *if* clause; 1 semicolon no conjunction; 2 missing words.

[Gregg shorthand outlines]

(137)

LESSON 53

● **Warmup.** Your warmup letter is on page 319. Take the sentence in the second paragraph for your warmup today. Break it down into convenient parts. Practice writing each part several times as rapidly as you can.

Developing Word-Building Power

405. WORD FAMILIES

-tment

1 [shorthand outlines]

-olve

2 [shorthand outlines]

-cially

3 [shorthand outlines]

-son

4 [shorthand outlines]

---

1. Investment, department, apartment, allotment, adjustment, treatment.
2. Solve, resolve, evolve, involve, involved, absolve.
3. Especially, specially, socially, financially, substantially, partially, officially, essentially.
4. Son, reason, season, person, comparison, personal, reasonable.

Building Transcription Skills

406. BUSINESS VOCABULARY BUILDER

inheritance   That which is left to an heir by someone who has died.

tailored   Made especially to fit a specific situation.

unbiased   Impartial; fair to all sides.

forged   Moved forward steadily.

resolve   To find a solution for.

407. COMMON WORD ROOTS

Mis-: *wrong; incorrect; erroneous*

mistaken   In error.

misunderstand   To interpret incorrectly.

misspell   To spell incorrectly.

miscount   To count incorrectly.

misinform   To give incorrect information.

Reading and Writing Practice

408.

mod′ern
pop′u·lar

of′ten
oc′cu·pied
stud′y·ing

[Gregg shorthand outlines]

cr

conj

ser

nonr

(167)

409.

[Gregg shorthand outlines]

re·tire′ment
young′er
in·her′it·ance

dif′fer·ent
tai′lored

conj

if

(124)

410.

intro

when

de·spite′
in·fla′tion
e′co·nom′ic

intro

re′al·ize
nec′es·sar′y

as

bc

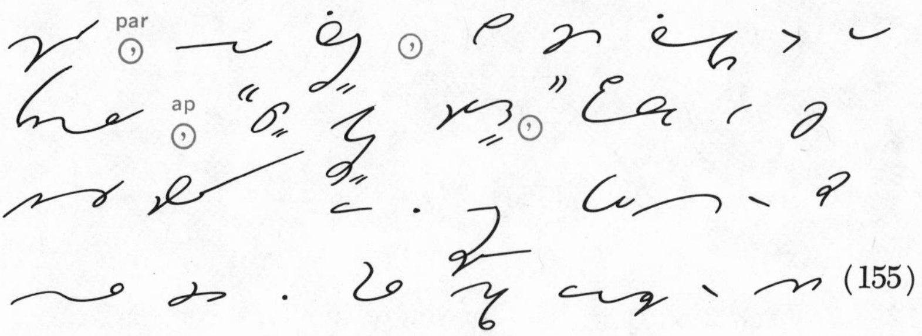

[Gregg shorthand outlines] (155)

....

411. *[Gregg shorthand outlines]*

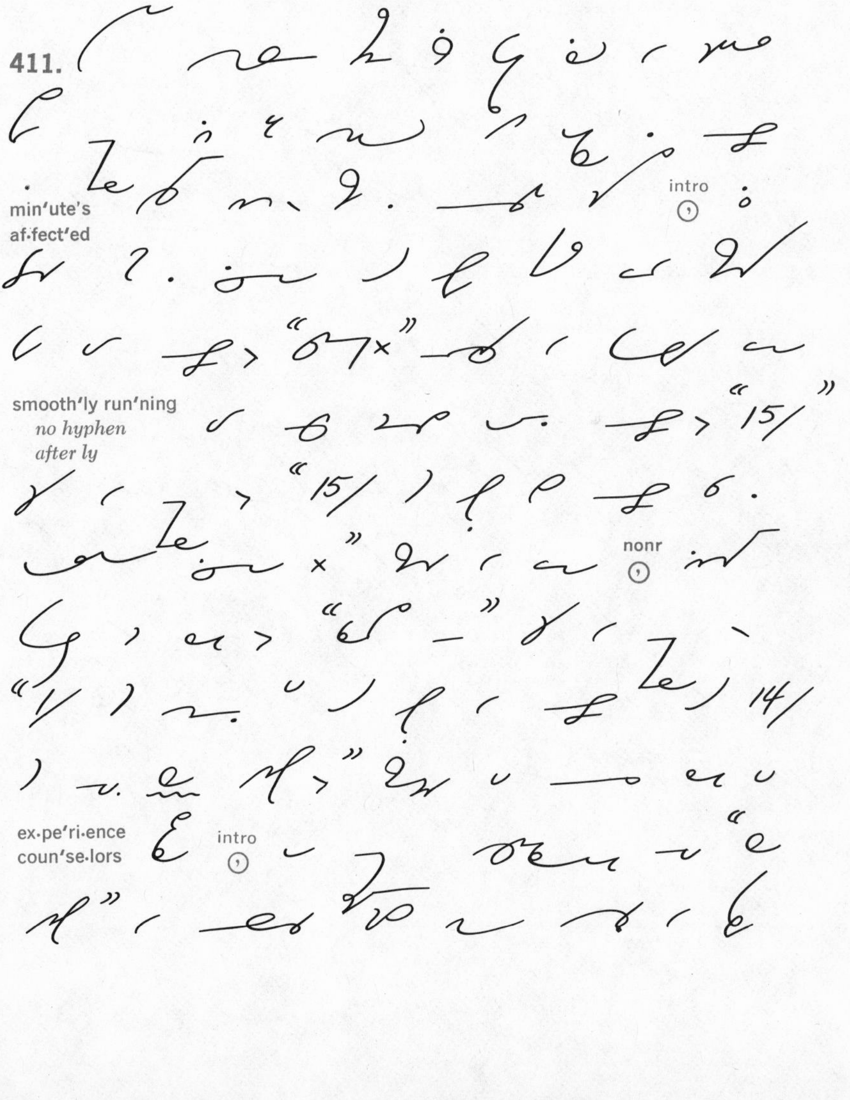

min'ute's
af·fect'ed

intro

smooth'ly run'ning
no hyphen
after ly

"15/"

"15/"

nonr

"14/"

ex·pe'ri·ence
coun'se·lors

intro

(shorthand outline) when *(shorthand outline)*

(153)

412. **Transcription Quiz.** For you to supply: 4 commas—2 commas series, 1 comma apposition, 1 comma *if* clause; 2 missing words.

(shorthand outline)

(113)

LESSON 54

● **Warmup.**   Your warmup letter is on page 319. Practice the sentences in the last paragraph. Remember, when you write an outline that is not to your liking, don't stop to scratch it out—keep on writing.

Developing Word-Building Power

413. **WORD BEGINNINGS AND ENDINGS**

-gram

1 [shorthand outlines]

-ulate

2 [shorthand outlines]

Post-

3 [shorthand outlines]

In-

4 [shorthand outlines]

---

1. Program, radiogram, telegram, cablegram, diagram.
2. Accumulate, formulate, congratulate, circulate, calculate.
3. Postal, postage, postman, post office, post card, postpone, postponement.
4. Invest, investor, investment, information, inquire, intend, income, inside.

Building Transcription Skills

414. BUSINESS VOCABULARY BUILDER

similarly   In the same way.

interim   Covering the time in between.

bristled   Took on an angry attitude.

415. GRAMMAR CHECKUP

May, can

may   Implies *permission* or *possibility*.

You may leave at four o'clock if your work is finished. (*You have permission.*)

I may go to the ball game if the weather is nice. (*There is a possibility.*)

can   Implies *ability* or *power*.

I can read very rapidly. (*Am able to.*)

He can leave any time he desires. (*He has the power to.*)

Reading and Writing Practice

416.

crit'i·cize
writ'ing

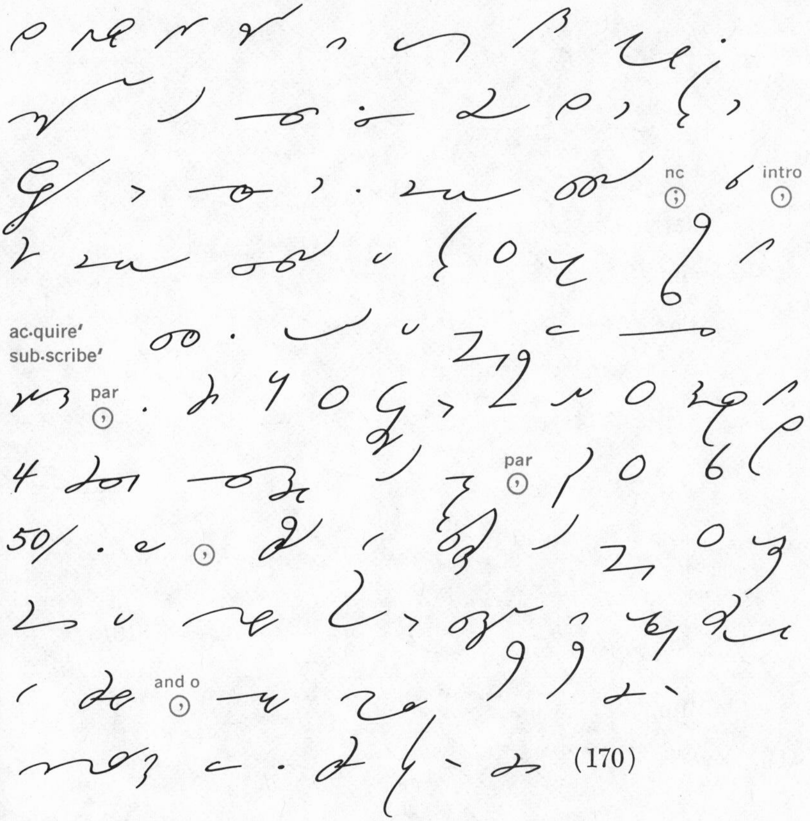
nc
intro
ac·quire'
sub·scribe'
par
par
and o
(170)

417.

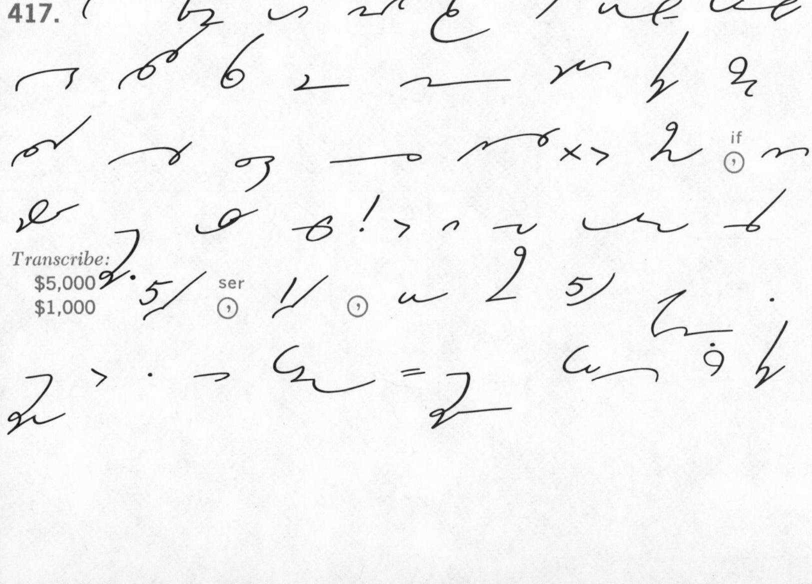
if
Transcribe:
$5,000
$1,000
ser

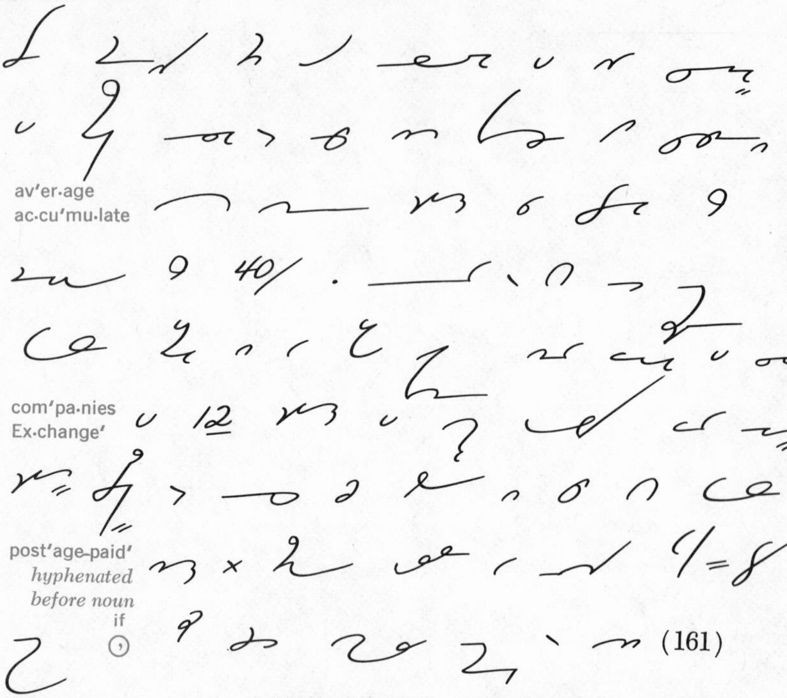

av'er·age
ac·cu'mu·late

com'pa·nies
Ex·change'

post'age-paid'
hyphenated before noun

if

(161)

418.

as

plan'ning
sim'i·lar·ly

bc

par

conj

in·quir'y
post'al

[Gregg shorthand outlines] (112)

•••••••••••••••••••••••••••••

419. *[Gregg shorthand outlines]*

nat'u·ral·ly
con'fi·dence
grat'i·fy'ing

an'nu·al
fis'cal

par·tic'i·pa'tion
source

[Gregg shorthand outlines] (169)

420. Transcription Quiz.   For you to supply: 4 commas—1 comma nonrestrictive, 1 comma *when* clause, 2 commas series; 2 missing words.

(154)

LESSON 55

● **Warmup.** Your warmup letter is on page 319. Write one complete copy of the letter. Write it in your best style of shorthand.

Developing Word-Building Power

421. SHORTHAND VOCABULARY BUILDER

Ow

1

OO-S

2

ī

3

Oi

4

Past Tense

5

1. Now, thousands, sound, found, brown, town, down, vouch.
2. Us, just, discuss, continuous, customer, bus, conscious, gracious.
3. Type, right, vital, striving, mile, line, mind.
4. Royal, join, enjoy, boy, boil, point, appoint, appointment.
5. Missed, stamped, attached, purchased, enclosed, arranged, approved.

341

Building Transcription Skills

422.   BUSINESS VOCABULARY BUILDER

Monthly Investment Plan   A plan whereby a person sets aside a definite amount each month for the purchase of stocks.

lapse   To run out; to terminate.

insatiable curiosity *(ĭn·sā'shĭ·à·b'l)*   Curiosity that can never be satisfied or fulfilled.

Reading and Writing Practice

423.

writ'ing
se'ri·ous
be·lief'

ob·jec'tives
con·tin'u·ous

(117)

424.

[Gregg shorthand outlines]

ef·fect'
re·mote'

par

intro

cus'tom·ers
De·part'ment's

e·val'u·ates
af·fects'
se·cu'ri·ties

ser

up'-to-the-min'ute
*hyphenated
before noun*

(144)

· ·

425.

[Gregg shorthand outlines]

if

(47)

The Secretary on the Job

426. Harry's Insatiable Curiosity

[shorthand notation]

When Harry *[shorthand notation]*

[Gregg shorthand outlines]

A few years *[Gregg shorthand outlines]*

[Gregg shorthand outlines] (331)

12

Insurance

Imagine for a moment that you lived in an age in which insurance was unknown. What would happen if you, the sole breadwinner for the family, should suddenly die; if you should become disabled or sick and required prolonged hospitalization or treatment; if you should grow too old or feeble to work and had no source of income; if your house should burn down with all your possessions; if someone should steal all your money? Without insurance, the financial problems these events would create would be staggering — too staggering for all but the wealthy to solve.

Fortunately, we do not live in that kind of age. We can buy insurance to soften the blow of losses such as these and many others. With insurance, we shall, of course, still suffer losses from events that are beyond our control; but the losses will be bearable because many others will share them with us — through insurance.

Today the average family man carries many types of insurance to protect him against many different types of losses. He probably has a life insurance policy to take care of his family if he should die. If he owns the house in which he lives, he probably carries liability insurance in case some visitor injures himself while on the premises; fire insurance in case the house or furnishings are damaged by fire; theft insurance in case someone breaks into the house and steals valuable possessions; automobile insurance to protect him against risk of injury or damage. He may have a health insurance policy that provides for monthly payments in the event that he is unable to work. If the family owns a dog, he may have a policy that pays the bills if the dog bites the mailman or the deliveryman!

Insurance also provides a means of saving. Most people recognize the importance of saving regularly, but they will not save unless they are forced to do so. Insurance forces a person to save. Once he has purchased an insurance policy, he makes every effort to pay his premiums; he knows that if he misses a payment he may lose his entire investment.

The insurance business, touching as it does the lives of all of us, employs many thousands of office workers. Probably no other business carries on more correspondence than the insurance business; therefore, stenographers and secretaries are highly valued employees in the insurance business.

If you were a stenographer in an insurance executive's office, your dictation might be similar to that of the letters in this chapter.

LESSON 56

Building Phrasing Skill

427. PHRASE BUILDER

Your reading goal: 25 seconds.

Many

To in Phrases

This

Few

1. Many other, many days, many times, many of the, many of them.
2. To purchase, to borrow, to preserve, to pay, to spend, to be, to have, to plan.
3. This information, this month, this time, this minute, this morning, this is.
4. Few days, few days ago, in a few days, few months, few moments, few thousand dollars.

428. WARMUP PHRASE LETTER

The following letter contains 20 useful phrases. Can you read it in one minute? Can you copy it in 90 seconds?

[Gregg shorthand outlines]

15/15/

(111)

Building Transcription Skills

429. BUSINESS VOCABULARY BUILDER

sunset years Usually the years after a person has retired from active work.

premium The amount paid at regular intervals to keep insurance in force.

conflicting Clashing.

Reading and Writing Practice

430.

nat'u·ral·ly
fam'i·ly's

[Gregg shorthand outlines with annotations: intro, par, bc]

[shorthand outlines]

intro ⟨,⟩

intro ⟨,⟩

low'-cost'
hyphenated
before noun

if ⟨,⟩

sun'set'
a're·a

ap ⟨,⟩

(107)

....

431.

per·mit'ted
pol'i·cy
lapse

par ⟨,⟩

re'al·ize
per'son·al

nc ⟨;⟩

intro ⟨,⟩

(Gregg shorthand outlines)

low'-cost'
eas'y-pay'ment
hyphenated
before noun

conj

if

and o

(146)

432.

as

par

sur·prise'
tenth

20

10

25

fam'i·lies

[Gregg shorthand outlines]

intro

bc

(141)

433. Transcription Quiz. For you to supply: 4 commas—1 comma *when* clause, 2 commas series, 1 comma introductory; 1 semicolon because of comma; 2 missing words.

[Gregg shorthand outlines]

(125)

LESSON 57

● **Warmup.** The letter on page 349 is your warmup letter for today. Write rapidly as much of the letter as time permits.

Developing Word-Building Power

434. BRIEF-FORM CHART

Read the brief forms and derivatives in the following chart from left to right; then, down each column. Can you read them down as rapidly as you can read them across?

1. Responsible, responsibility, responsibilities, big, bigger, biggest.
2. Worth, worthy, worthwhile, recognize, recognizes, recognition.
3. Situation, situations, short, shortly, glad, gladly.
4. Gentlemen, businessmen, newspapermen, ordinary, extraordinary, extraordinarily.
5. Willingly, unwillingly, correspondingly, object, objects, objective.

435. GEOGRAPHICAL EXPRESSIONS

2 

1. Birmingham, Buckingham, Framingham, Washington, Lexington, Arlington.
2. Hawaii, Alaska, Oklahoma, Texas, Louisiana, Michigan.

Building Transcription Skills

436. BUSINESS VOCABULARY BUILDER

totally disabled Completely incapable of working.

partially disabled Partly capable of working.

extraordinarily Remarkably.

layman One not belonging to some particular profession.

437. SIMILAR-WORDS DRILL

Scene, seen

scene A setting; a place.

He drove to the scene of the accident.

seen Past participle of *see*.

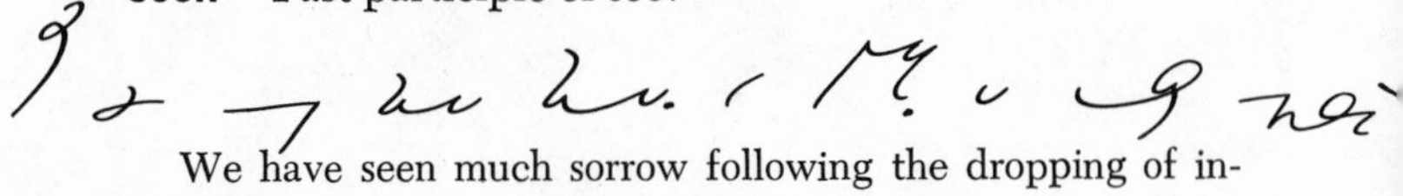

We have seen much sorrow following the dropping of insurance.

Reading and Writing Practice

438. 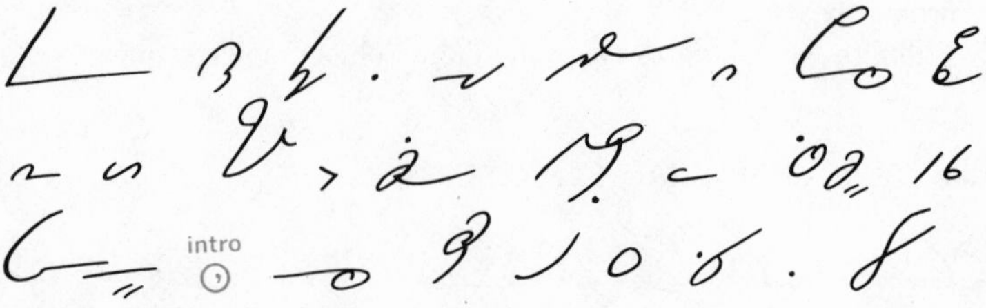

[Gregg shorthand outlines]

trav'eled
scene

intro

65

and o

wit'ness·es
re·spon'si·bil'i·ty

ser

tru'ly
grate'ful

(157)

439.

conj

20,

20,

20,

pol'i·cy·hold'ers
re·new'al
lo'cal

intro

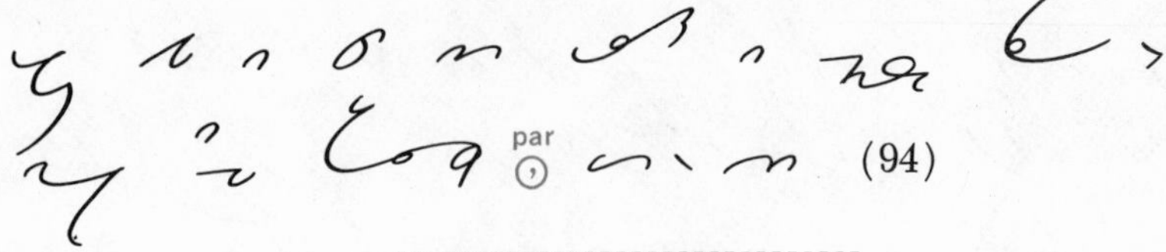

(94)

440.

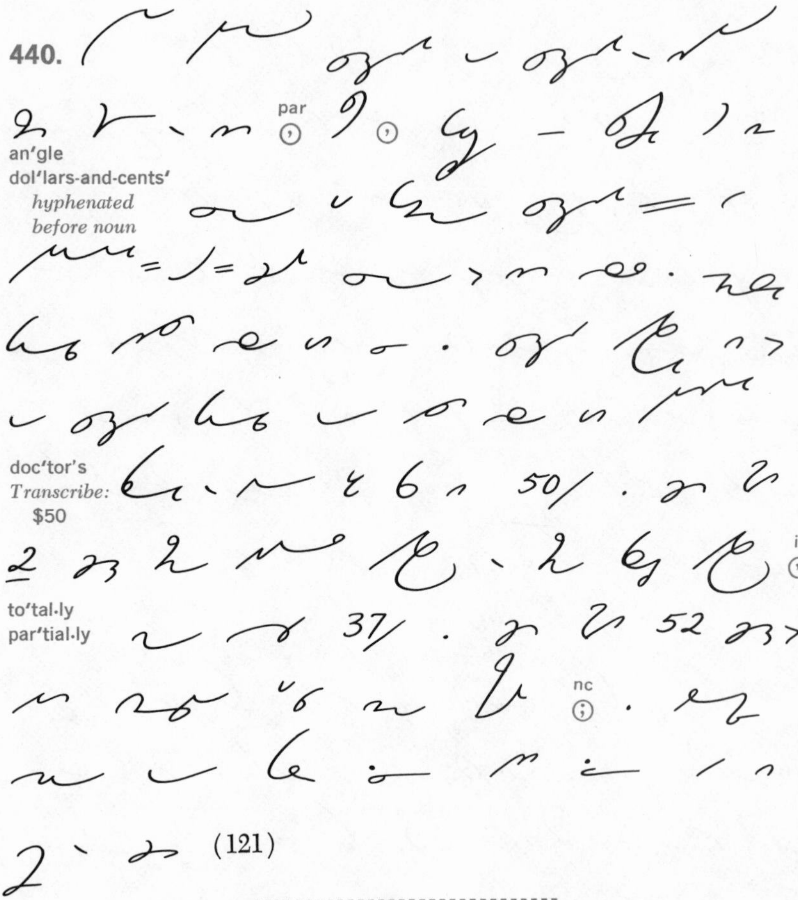

an'gle
dol'lars-and-cents'
hyphenated before noun

doc'tor's
Transcribe: $50

to'tal·ly
par'tial·ly

(121)

441.

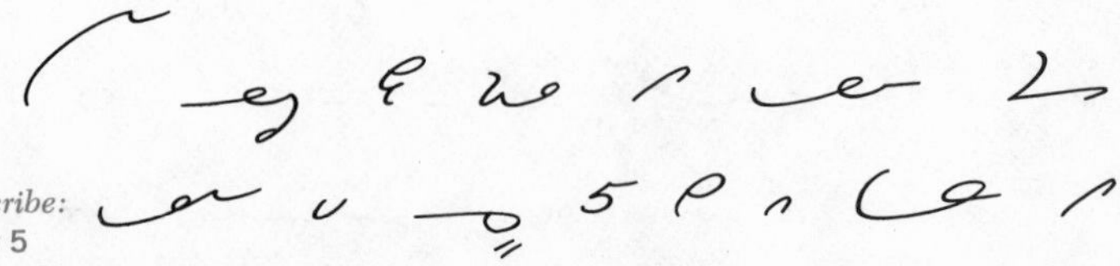

Transcribe: May 5

Gregg shorthand outlines.

11581 ~

Transcribe:
No. 11581
ex·traor′di·nar′i·ly

conj

vi′tal
fam′i·ly′s
re′al·ly

bc

par

if

ap

(144)

··

442.

intro

le′gal
lay′man

conj

nonr · dis·cuss'es · its · par · piece · in·creas'ing·ly · bc · as

(153)

443. Transcription Quiz. For you to supply: 6 commas—1 comma introductory, 2 commas series, 1 comma *as* clause, 2 commas parenthetical; 2 missing words.

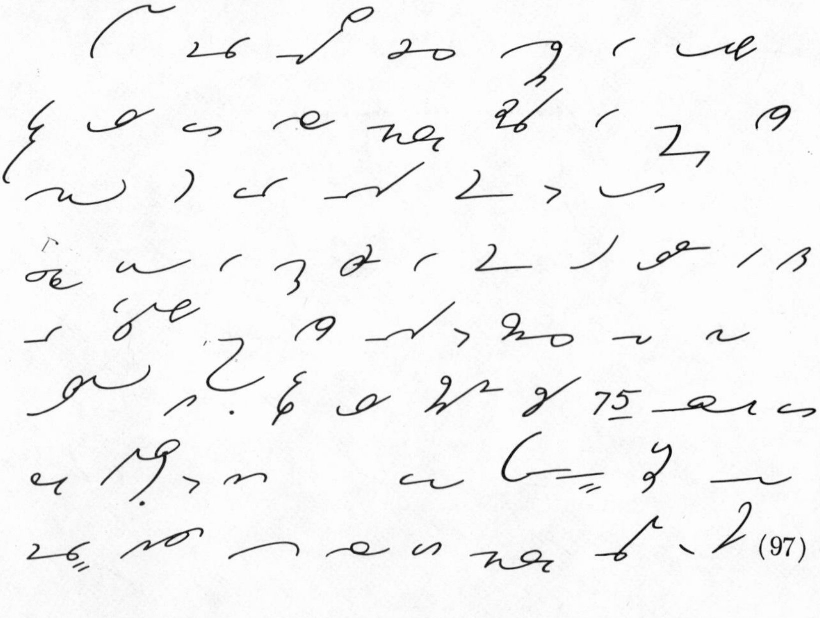

(97)

LESSON 58

● **Warmup.**   Your warmup letter is on page 349. Break up the sentences in the first paragraph into convenient groups, and write each group several times as rapidly as possible.

Developing Word-Building Power

444. WORD FAMILIES

-vent

1 [shorthand outlines]

-sist

2 [shorthand outlines]

-fer

3 [shorthand outlines]

-ness

4 [shorthand outlines]

-point

5 [shorthand outlines]

1. Prevent, invent, event, solvent, insolvent, circumvent, convent.
2. Assist, resist, insist, consist, persist, assistance, insistent, consistent.
3. Prefer, confer, infer, defer, transfer, preference, conference, reference.
4. Illness, thoughtfulness, willingness, helpfulness, goodness, greatness.
5. Point, pointless, appoint, appointed, appointment, disappoint, disappointment.

Building Transcription Skills

445. BUSINESS VOCABULARY BUILDER

grace period   A period (usually 30 days) during which a policy continues to remain in force even though the premium has not been paid.

dependents   Those relying upon someone else for support.

mature   Run the limit of its time; become due.

446. SPELLING FAMILIES

Whenever you hear the ending that is pronounced "kle," be careful; it may be spelled *cal* or *cle*. Here are examples of each ending.

Words Ending in -cal

med′i·cal	rad′i·cal	po·lit′i·cal
log′i·cal	phys′i·cal	crit′i·cal
sur′gi·cal	mu′si·cal	chem′i·cal

Words Ending in -cle

ve′hi·cle	mir′a·cle	bi′cy·cle
par′ti·cle	ar′ti·cle	spec′ta·cle

Reading and Writing Practice

447.
pre′mi·um
Transcribe:
$60
June 16

[shorthand outlines]

[Gregg shorthand outlines]

intro ①

conj ①

im·me'di·ate
laps'ing

(112)

448.
em·ploy'ees
med'i·cal
sur'gi·cal

their
de·pend'ents
ma'jor

cope
day'-to-day'
*hyphenated
before noun*

pi'o·neer'
e·quipped'

intro ①

40

lo'cal
ref'er·ence

[shorthand outlines] (137)

· ·

449.

20-pay'ment
hyphenated
before noun

[shorthand outlines]

de'scribed
leaf'let

[shorthand outlines] (110)

· ·

450.

crit'i·cal·ly
bi'cy·cle

[shorthand outlines]

(Gregg shorthand outlines) (100)

451.   Transcription Quiz.   For you to supply: 5 commas—1 comma introductory, 2 commas parenthetical, 2 commas *when* clause; 2 missing words.

(Gregg shorthand outlines) (130)

LESSON 59

● **Warmup.** Your warmup letter is on page 349. Break up the sentences in the second paragraph into convenient groups, and write each group several times as rapidly as possible.

Developing Word-Building Power

452. WORD BEGINNINGS AND ENDINGS

Inter

-ingly

-ward

-sume, -sumption

---

1. Interview, interested, interests, intervene, interfere, international, interstate, intermission.
2. Willingly, exceedingly, surprisingly, unflaggingly, knowingly, astonishingly.
3. Forward, backward, homeward, onward, reward, rewarded, outward.
4. Assume, assumption, consume, consumption, presume, resumed.

Building Transcription Skills

453. BUSINESS VOCABULARY BUILDER

estate The sum total of one's property.

decades Periods of ten years.

unflaggingly Tirelessly.

454. GRAMMAR CHECKUP

Either, or; neither, nor

The correlative conjunctions *either-or, neither-nor* are usually used in pairs. Do not mix the members of the pairs; that is, do not use *or* with *neither, nor* with *either.*

> He said he *either* would send the package by express *or* would deliver it himself.
> He *neither* would help him *nor* (not *or*) would he hinder his progress.

Reading and Writing Practice

455.

ap·pre'ci·ate
cour'te·sy
nat'u·ral·ly

prompt'ed
fur'ther

[Gregg shorthand outlines] (138)

456.

proud
dec'ades

un·flag'ging·ly
lo'cal

nonr

af·fect'ing
re·tire'ment

ser

par

[Gregg shorthand outlines] (110)

457.

nc

[Gregg shorthand outlines]

stu'dent's
ex·pens'es
pre'mi·um

sur·pris'ing·ly

pam'phlet
ad·di'tion·al

(139)

• •

458.

passed
re·quir'ing
oc·curred'

24-page *hyphenated before noun*

nc ;

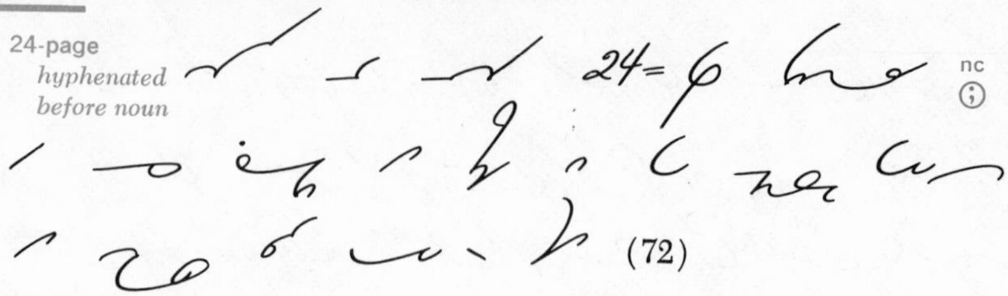

(72)

459. Transcription Quiz. For you to supply: 7 commas—4 commas parenthetical, 2 commas introductory, 1 comma *if* clause; 1 semicolon because of comma; 2 missing words.

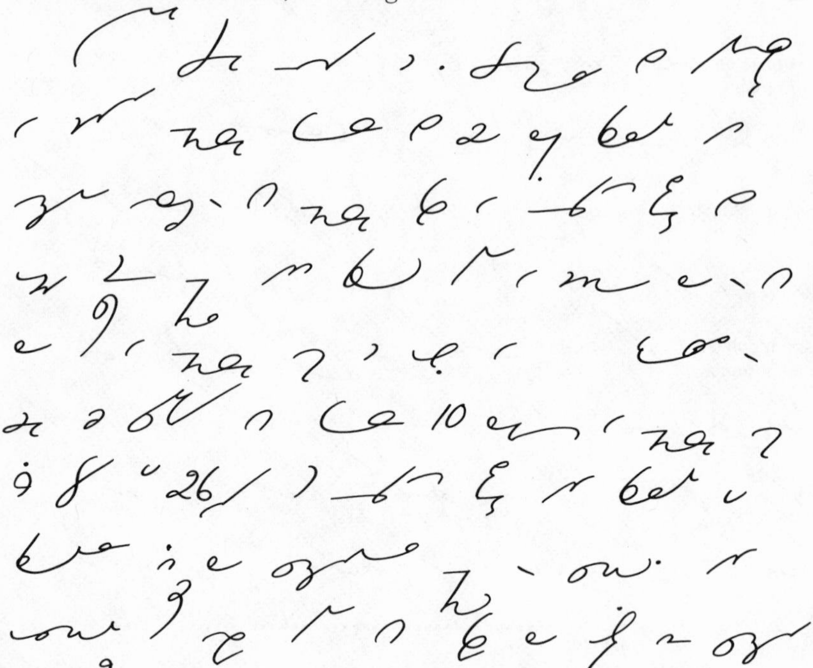

(159)

LESSON 60

● **Warmup.** Your warmup letter is on page 349. In your best shorthand, make a shorthand copy of the entire letter.

Developing Word-Building Power

460. SHORTHAND VOCABULARY BUILDER

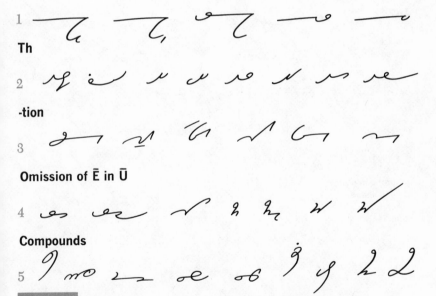

Mem-

Th

-tion

Omission of Ē in Ū

Compounds

1. Members, membership, remember, memory, memorandum.
2. Thrift, health, though, although, three, thought, through, thrill.
3. Examination, quotation, transportation, condition, permission, commission.
4. Renew, renewal, continue, issue, issuance, suit, suited.
5. However, worthwhile, someone, anywhere, anyhow, whoever, whatever, everyone, everywhere.

Building Transcription Skills

461. **BUSINESS VOCABULARY BUILDER**

commit To pledge; to bind.

Board of Directors A group of people who formulate policies under which a corporation is run.

benefits Amounts paid to an insured in time of sickness, old age, and the like.

Reading and Writing Practice

462.

re′al·ize
un·u′su·al

up′-to-the-min′ute
*hyphenated
before noun*
fa·mil′iar

[shorthand notations: conj, and o, cr]

(136)

463.
Board
Di·rec'tors
of'fi·cers

[Gregg shorthand outlines]

par

1950   bc

ap

if

(98)

464.

pur'pose
doc'tor's

[Gregg shorthand outlines]

intro

fi·nanc'es
raise
be·gin'ning

ap

(103)

465. Good Work Habits Win Promotion

[shorthand notation]

Frank soon *[shorthand notation]*

[Gregg shorthand outlines]

After nine *[Gregg shorthand outlines]*

(326)

Part 3

Taking Dictation in a Business Office

Could you take a letter from a businessman if you were called upon to do so? If you have been reading and copying each day's lesson each day, you probably could, provided the letter was not too difficult or was not dictated too fast.

You would, however, find the dictation of a businessman a little different from the dictation that you have probably been taking in class. In class, your teacher's main task has been to develop your shorthand speed as rapidly as possible. Your teacher knows that the best way to do this is to have you practice under the most favorable conditions. That is why his dictation has been smooth and even, with every word spoken clearly and distinctly.

Your teacher knows that, when you are striving to increase your speed, your attention should be completely occupied with writing and should not be distracted by problems of hearing. Furthermore, your teacher has probably timed most of your dictation, as that is the only way your skill development can be determined.

374

Office-Style Dictation

The businessman, however, is not concerned with developing your speed; he assumes that you have the necessary skill to take down what he says. His dictation will not always be smooth; in fact, it may on occasion be choppy — sometimes fast, sometimes slow. Occasionally, his mind will be so occupied with the thought he is trying to express that he may slur some of his words. What is more, he may sometimes change his mind about a word or phrase and substitute another that he thinks expresses more clearly what he wants to say. He may delete, insert, or even transpose words.

You will quickly become accustomed to this type of office-style dictation if you have sufficient shorthand speed. The more speed you possess, the easier office-style dictation will be for you. Therefore, strive to build your shorthand speed to the highest point possible; you will always be glad that you did!

In the following lessons you will become familiar with some of the problems you will meet when you take office-style dictation. You will be given suggestions on how to handle each problem and shown how to handle it in your shorthand notes.

Instructions During Dictation

A businessman will not only make deletions, insertions, and transpositions during dictation, but he also may ask you, right in the middle of a sentence, to check a date or an amount or the spelling of a name.

When he does this, the easiest way to indicate his instructions in your notes is to write in shorthand the word *check* in parentheses, close to the item to be checked. The businessman may say:

> We had a call from your representative, Mr. May,
> or was his name Gray? Please check that.

This will appear in your notes as follows:

Then, before you transcribe, you will go to previous correspondence, the files, or any other source from which you can obtain the necessary information and "check."

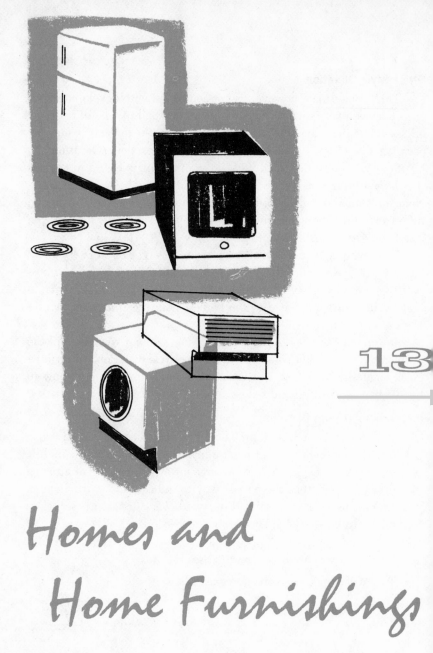

13

Homes and Home Furnishings

Today's modern home is a far cry from the home that our great-grandparents knew. They would rub their eyes in disbelief and awe if they could see the conveniences available even in today's most modest homes.

In great-grandmother's day, Monday was always washday. Every Monday she would gather up the soiled clothes, wash them on the scrubbing board, hang them on clothesline, and collect them when they were dry. If it rained on Monday, it was just too bad! Then the ironing began! Monday was indeed a long, long day for great-grand-mother.

In today's modern home, Monday may still be washday — but it is no longer a day to dread. Mother simply gathers up the clothes to be washed, places them in an automatic washing machine, and presses a button. She doesn't care whether the sun is shining or whether it is pouring rain because she doesn't have to worry about hanging the clothes on a clothesline — an automatic dryer does the drying.

Preparing a meal in great-grandmother's day was no small matter. Peas had to be shelled, potatoes peeled, poultry dressed — and everything had to be watched carefully as it cooked.

Today Mother simply reaches into the refrigerator or freezer and selects from a wide variety the vegetables and meats she wants — all of them ready for cooking. She places everything on the stove, sets a few knobs, and the stove does the rest — it even turns itself off when everything is cooked.

After great-grandmother's family finished eating, there were mounds and mounds of dishes to wash and dry. Washing and drying dishes is no problem for today's mother; she simply scrapes the dishes, places them in the dishwasher, and presto, there are the dishes, sparkling clean and thoroughly dry.

When summer came and the weather was hot and humid, great-grandmother's family simply suffered. Not today's family! Many homes are air-conditioned so that the house is comfortable regardless of the weather outside.

Today, manufacturing, selling, and servicing home appliances is big business; and as the population increases and more and more homes are built and more and more home conveniences are developed, it will become even bigger.

The letters in this chapter are concerned with the business of selling and servicing the homeowner.

LESSON 61

Building Phrasing Skill

466. PHRASE BUILDER

Reading goal: 45 seconds.

One of

1 *(shorthand outlines)*

Want

2 *(shorthand outlines)*

You

3 *(shorthand outlines)*

Upon

4 *(shorthand outlines)*

Each

5 *(shorthand outlines)*

---

1. One of our, one of them, one of the most, one of the best, one of these, one of those, one of the.
2. You want, I want, they want, who want, they wanted, he wanted, if you want, do you want.
3. On you, from you, send you, give you, inform you, can you, will you.
4. Upon the, upon this, upon that, upon them, upon the subject, upon these, upon those, upon request.
5. Each month, each day, each one, each other, each time, each morning, each night, each case.

467. WARMUP PHRASE LETTER

Can you read this letter—your warmup letter for Chapter 13—in one minute? Can you copy it in 90 seconds?

[Gregg shorthand outlines]

(106)

Building Transcription Skills

468. BUSINESS VOCABULARY BUILDER

craftsmen   People who are skilled in their line of work.

durable   Long lasting; strong.

buckle   Crumple up.

Reading and Writing Practice

469.   *[Gregg shorthand outlines]*

de·signed'
crafts'men   nonr
                          ①

[Gregg shorthand outlines]

ap·prov′al
fac′to·ry

ser ⊙

if ⊙

(104)

....

470.

up′-to-date′
hyphenated
before noun

par ⊙

bc ⊙

[Gregg shorthand outlines with annotations]

as ① (131)

if ①   nc ①

471.

fig'ure
scrap'ing
a·mazed'

ser ①   ①

if ①   5

for·ev'er
thank'less

nc ①   par ①   ①

intro ①

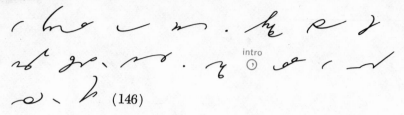

(146)

472. Transcription Quiz. Supply the necessary punctuation and the missing words.

(131)

Office-Style Dictation, 1

It is a very simple matter, in office-style dictation, to indicate in your notes that the dictator wishes to take out a word or a phrase. He may say:

> He bought a large but comfortable house in Springfield
> — no, take out *comfortable*.

Sometimes he may go back and repeat the sentence without the word or the phrase that he wishes to omit. He may say:

> He bought a large but comfortable house in Springfield —
> no, *he bought a large house in Springfield*.

To indicate this deletion, you would mark out in your notes not only the word *comfortable* but also the word *but*.

If only a word or two is to be taken out, use a long, heavy backward stroke; if several words are to be taken out, a wavy line is preferable.

473. ILLUSTRATION OF OFFICE-STYLE DICTATION

LESSON 62

● **Warmup.** Your warmup letter is on page 379. Write the first paragraph as rapidly as you can and as often as you can in the time you have available.

Developing Word-Building Power

474. **BRIEF-FORM CHART**

Reading goal: 25 seconds.

1. Use, uses, used, represent, represents, representative.
2. Accompany, accompanies, accompanied, question, questions, questionable.
3. Value, values, valuable, every, everyone, everybody.
4. Work, worker, workable, understand, understands, understanding.
5. Regular, regularly, irregular, where, somewhere, anywhere.

475. **GEOGRAPHICAL EXPRESSIONS**

1. Minneapolis, Billings, Boise, Pierre, Helena, Salem.
2. Minnesota, Montana, North Dakota, South Dakota, Idaho, Washington, Oregon.

Building Transcription Skills

476. BUSINESS VOCABULARY BUILDER

vitality Liveliness; vigor.

resist To withstand.

unique Only one of its kind.

477. SIMILAR-WORDS DRILL

Hole, whole

hole An opening.

[shorthand outlines]

We will repair all holes that may have developed in your rugs.

whole Entire.

[shorthand outlines]

The whole booklet will take you only a few minutes to read.

Reading and Writing Practice

478. *[shorthand outlines]*

Transcribe:
April 10
sup·pli′er

[shorthand outlines]

pro·duc'tion
dif'fi·cul·ties

[Gregg shorthand outlines]   (107)

479.

Ap·pli'ance
re'cent·ly

health
ill'ness

ac·com'pan·ied
whole

[Gregg shorthand outlines]   (133)

480.

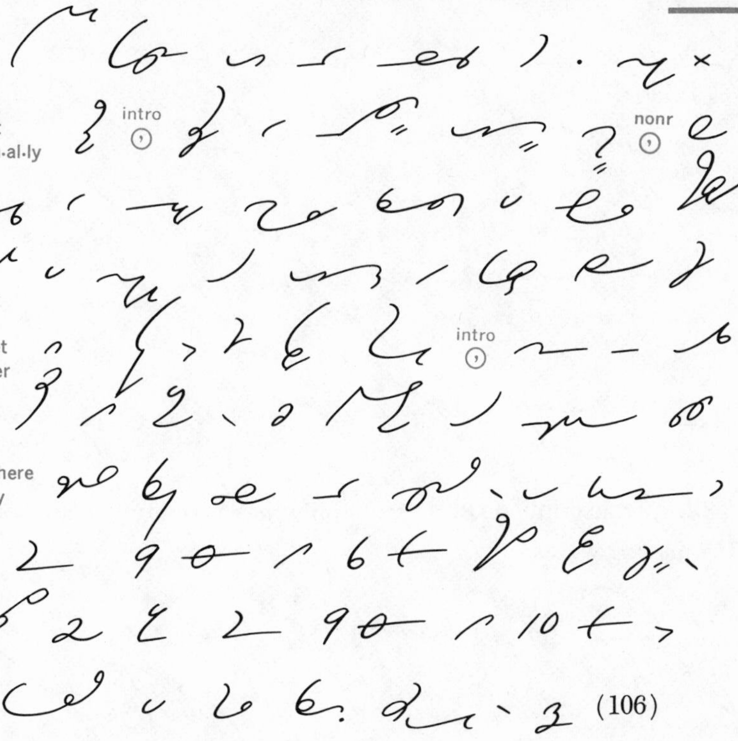

car'pet
na'tion·al·ly

budg'et
de·liv'er

an'y·where
coun'ty

intro
nonr
intro

(106)

481.

fur'nish·ings
con·sid'er·a·ble

choos'ing
holes

when
nonr
intro

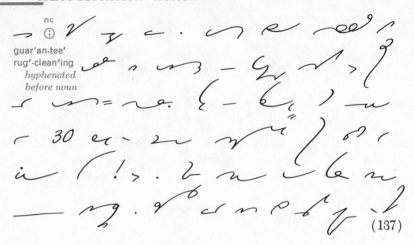

guar'an·tee'
rug'-clean'ing
hyphenated
before noun

(137)

482. Transcription Quiz. Supply the necessary punctuation and the missing words.

(107)

LESSON 63

● **Warmup.**   Your warmup letter is on page 379. Copy the second paragraph as rapidly as you can and as many times as you can in the few minutes that you have available.

Developing Word-Building Power

483.   WORD FAMILIES

-tract

1

-lt

2

-rt

3

-sive

4

1. Contract, attract, distract, detract, protract, abstract.
2. Built, rebuilt, felt, melt, dealt, fault.
3. Expert, insert, assert, exert, dessert, concert, alert.
4. Expensive, comprehensive, extensive, defensive, offensive, impressive, oppressive, pensive.

Building Transcription Skills

484.   BUSINESS VOCABULARY BUILDER

thermostat   An automatic device for regulating temperature.

comprehensive   Including much.

hollow   Empty.

frigid   Cold.

485.   SPELLING FAMILIES

Another spelling trap is the ending that is pronounced "e-ous." In most words in the English language, this combination of sounds is spelled *ious;* but there are just enough words in which it is spelled *eous* that you should stop to think each time you must transcribe a word containing that ending.

Words Ending in -ious

se′ri·ous	gra′cious	in·dus′tri·ous
ob′vi·ous	pre′cious	cu′ri·ous
pre′vi·ous	con′scious	cau′tious

Words Ending in -eous

cou·ra′geous	ad′van·ta′geous	mis′cel·la′ne·ous
cour′te·ous	spon·ta′ne·ous	si′mul·ta′ne·ous

Reading and Writing Practice

486.

con'tract
third

conj

ob'vi·ous·ly
o'ver·sight'

[Gregg shorthand outlines with annotations: intro, par]

(72)

....

487.

[Gregg shorthand outlines with annotation: if]

[Gregg shorthand outlines with annotation: nc]

ap·pear'ance
at·trac'tive

[Gregg shorthand outlines with annotation: par]

[Gregg shorthand outlines with annotation: if]

ther'mo·stat
tem'per·a·ture

[Gregg shorthand outlines with annotation: conj]

[Gregg shorthand outlines with annotation: if]

com'pre·hen'sive
yours

[shorthand outline] (173)

....

488. *[shorthand outline]*   intro ⊙

Transcribe:
   $475
brick'work'

[shorthand outlines] 475/

① ② ③

if ⊙

[shorthand outline] (72)

....

489. *[shorthand outline]*   as ⊙

64-page
hyphenated
before noun

[shorthand outline] 64= ⊙   ap "

" 1930

as ⊙

26 ser 27 ⊙ 28

[shorthand outlines]

[Gregg shorthand outlines]

Transcribe:
1216 West 14 Street

[Gregg shorthand outlines] if

[Gregg shorthand outlines] ap

[Gregg shorthand outlines] / 1216 *[outline]* 14 *[outline]* 16

conj

years'
ex·pe'ri·ence *[Gregg shorthand outlines]* 20 *[outlines]* (157)

....

490. *[Gregg shorthand outlines]*

cost'-con'scious
hyphenated
before noun

[Gregg shorthand outlines] par

[Gregg shorthand outlines]

[Gregg shorthand outlines]

[Gregg shorthand outlines]

[Gregg shorthand outlines]

ex·ten'sive
re·mod'el·ing *[Gregg shorthand outlines]*

[Gregg shorthand outlines] bc

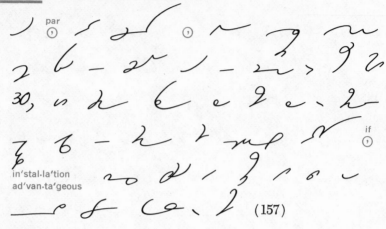

par ⊙

in'stal·la'tion
ad'van·ta'geous

if ⊙

(157)

491. **Transcription Quiz.** Supply the necessary punctuation and the missing words.

(116)

LESSON 64

● **Warmup.** Your warmup letter is on page 379. Write the last paragraph of the letter as rapidly and as often as time permits.

Developing Word-Building Power

492. WORD BEGINNINGS AND ENDINGS

Pur-, Per-

1 [shorthand outlines]

Des-, Dis-

2 [shorthand outlines]

-self

3 [shorthand outlines]

De-

4 [shorthand outlines]

Com-

5 [shorthand outlines]

---

1. Purchase, perhaps, personal, perform, permit, permission, perfect.
2. Describe, description, district, display, dismiss, disgrace.
3. Itself, yourself, oneself, myself, himself, herself, yourselves, ourselves, themselves.
4. Delight, deliver, delay, desirable, deprive, depart, depend.
5. Complete, competition, combine, competent, complaint, comment.

Building Transcription Skills

493. BUSINESS VOCABULARY BUILDER

prospect   A possible customer.

wholesalers   Those who sell only to dealers, not to the public.

hardware   Such items as locks, doorknobs, hinges, light fixtures, etc.

494. COMMON WORD ROOTS

Im-: *not*

impossible   Not capable of occurring.

improper   Not appropriate.

immature   Not fully developed.

immaterial   Not essential.

impolite   Not polite; rude.

Reading and Writing Practice

495.

Transcribe:
Model 1001

re·fer′ring
stopped
prof′it·a·bly

[Gregg shorthand outlines] (98)

....

496.

pur'chas·ing
liv'ing
whole'sal'ers

[Gregg shorthand outlines] intro

rec'om·mend'
Il'li·nois'

[Gregg shorthand outlines] par

nonr

col'or
scheme
per'son·al

and o

life'time'
for'ward·ing

ap   bc

un·doubt'ed·ly
short'ly

[Gregg shorthand outlines] (146)

497.

dried

when

clothes
au'to·mat'i·cal·ly

ser

conj

as

(117)

498.

hard'ware'
gen'er·al

nc

intro

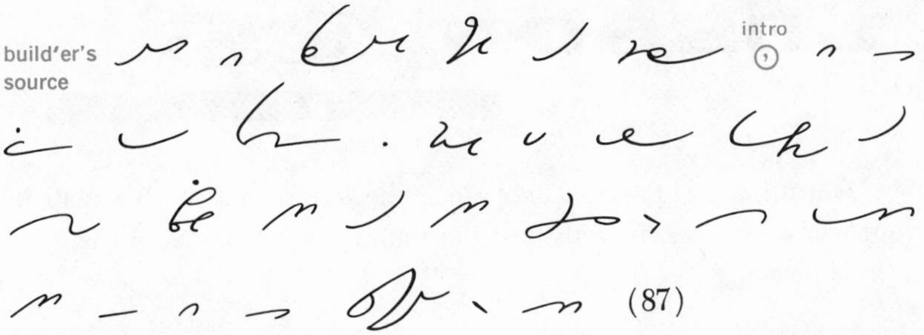
build'er's
source
intro

(87)

499. Transcription Quiz. Supply the necessary punctuation and the missing words.

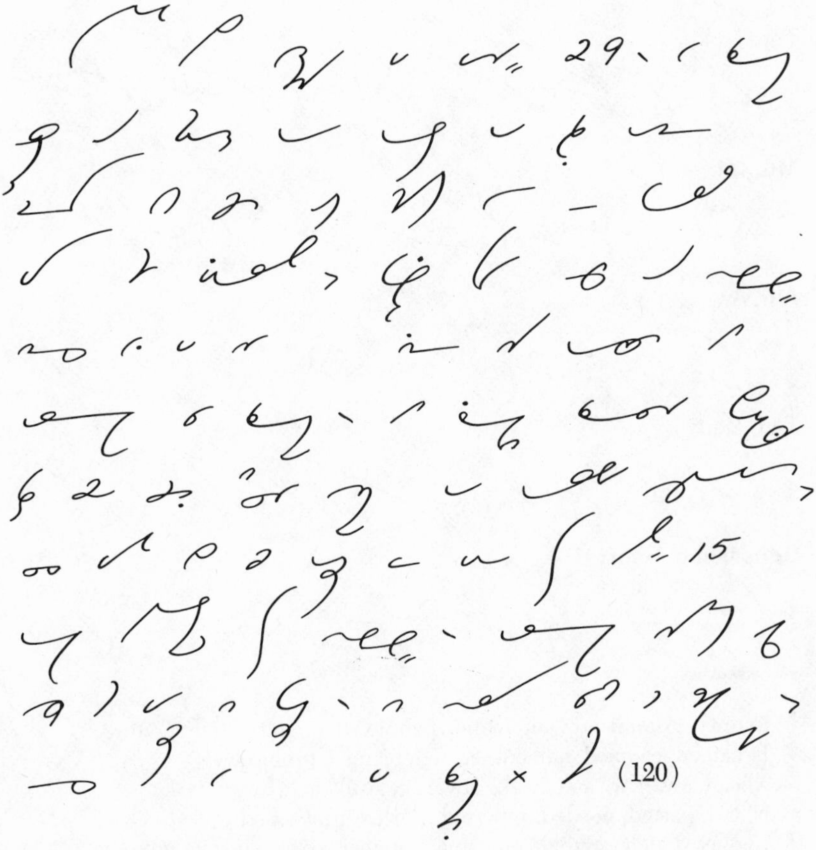

(120)

LESSON 65

● **Warmup.**   For the final time, the letter on page 379 will be your warmup letter. In your best shorthand, copy as much of the letter as time permits.

Developing Word-Building Power

500.   SHORTHAND VOCABULARY BUILDER

Tem

1

Md, Mt

2

Ah-, Aw-

3

Ted, Ded

4

Omission of Short Ū

5

1. Estimate, itemized, automatic, temple, temporary, temperature.
2. Dreamed, claimed, named, seemed, blamed, promptly.
3. Ahead, await, aware, awake, awaken, awakened, away.
4. Noted, parted, needed, reported, started, proceeded.
5. Budget, much, sunlight, coming, summer, done, fun, judge.

Building Transcription Skills

501. BUSINESS VOCABULARY BUILDER

itemized   Stated in terms of the items that make up the whole.

economically   Thriftily.

inventory *(noun)*   Goods or stock on hand.

drastically   Harshly; violently.

Reading and Writing Practice

502.

[shorthand outlines]

first'-class'
hyphenated
before noun

if

(82)

....

503.

[shorthand outlines]

yours
en·tire'ly

[Gregg shorthand outlines]

intro

se

au·to·mat'ic
e·co·nom'i·cal·ly

if

con·ven'ient
budg'et

and o

(105)

504.

when

ap·pear'ance
con'fi·dent
ap·plied'

when

(107)

505.

bar'gains
a·ware'   *if*

                           as

re·duce'
in'ven·to'ry   *par*
a·wait'ing

suite
dras'ti·cal·ly

(133)

....

506.   *as*

                          intro

(57)

507. The Importance of Shorthand Speed

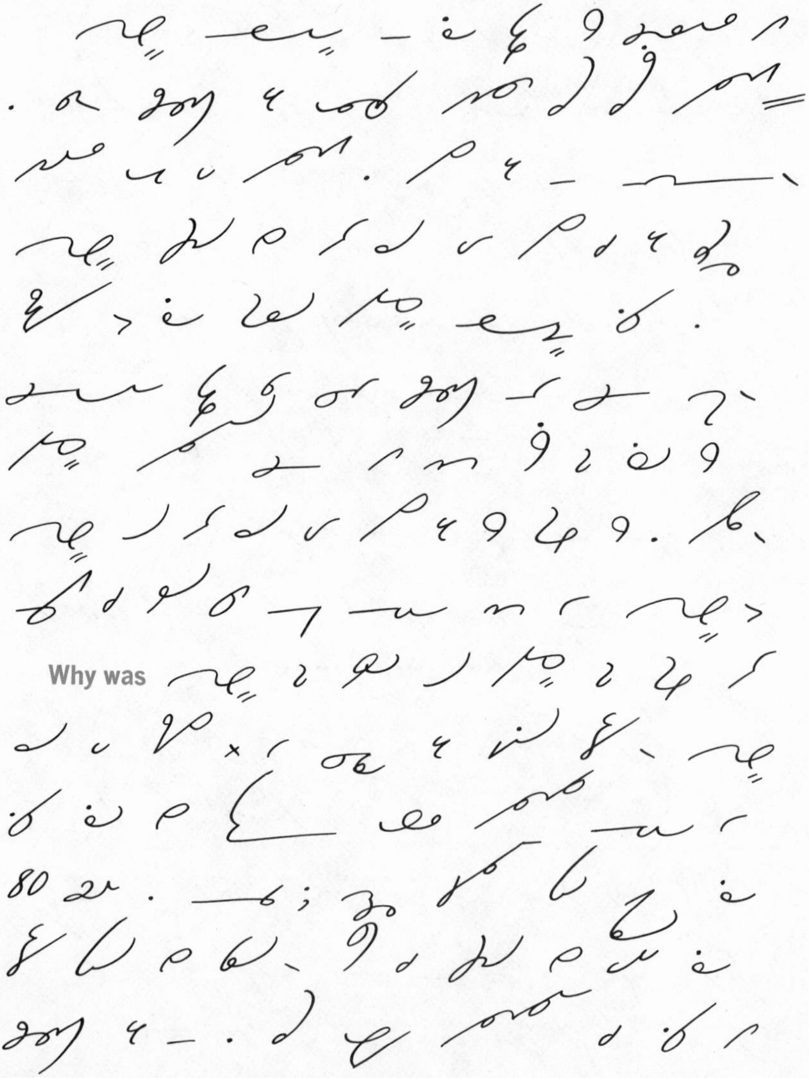

[shorthand outlines]

[shorthand outlines]

[shorthand outlines]

[shorthand outlines]

[shorthand outlines]

[shorthand outlines]

[shorthand outlines]

[shorthand outlines]

Why was *[shorthand outlines]*

[shorthand outlines]

[shorthand outlines]

80 *[shorthand outlines]*

[shorthand outlines]

[shorthand outlines]

[shorthand outlines]

[Gregg shorthand outlines]

She had

(338)

14

Office Supplies and Equipment

Let's take an imaginary tour of the office of a modern business firm. After we pass the reception room, we immediately get two impressions of the office: it is an efficient place to work; it is an attractive place to work.

The first thing that strikes you is the quiet atmosphere that prevails, an atmosphere that enables everyone to concentrate on his work and to put forth his best efforts. This quiet atmosphere is helped by the fact that there is a rug on the floor and a soundproof ceiling, which absorb 75 per cent of the noise from typewriters, telephones, and human voices.

You then notice that the office furniture is designed for efficiency and comfort. The desks have plenty of work space and easy-to-reach, spacious drawers for papers, stationery, supplies, and reference books.

No two chairs seem to be alike. That is because each chair is especially designed for a particular type of work and is adjusted to the height of the individual so that he can work without fatigue and discomfort.

And the office machines! For one thing, most are electric — typewriters, photocopiers, adding machines, calculators, and mail meters. For another, the machines are no longer finished in traditional black— they are blue or red or green or some other color, depending on the color scheme of the office.

The private office of the firm's top executive has several comfortable chairs so that he can hold conferences with his business associates and customers in a relaxed atmosphere. It has an intercommunications system that enables him to get in touch instantly with other executives or assistants simply by pressing a button.

The modern office would certainly provide many surprises to the roll-top-desk executive of fifty or sixty years ago!

The letters in this chapter will give you some idea of the type of dictation you would take if you worked for an organization that manufactures or sells office equipment such as that seen on your imaginary trip.

LESSON 66

Building Phrasing Skill

508. PHRASE BUILDER

Reading goal: 40 seconds.

Done

Do Not

Which

You Will

1. Could be done, may be done, should be done, to be done, can be done, will be done.
2. Do not, we do not, I do not, you do not, who do not, I do not see, I do not say.
3. In which, in which the, in which you, in which you can, in which you are, in which you will, by which, from which, to which.
4. You will, you will be, you will not, you will find, you will see, you will be able.

509. WARMUP PHRASE LETTER

This is your warmup phrase letter for Chapter 14. Read it and copy it as rapidly as you can.

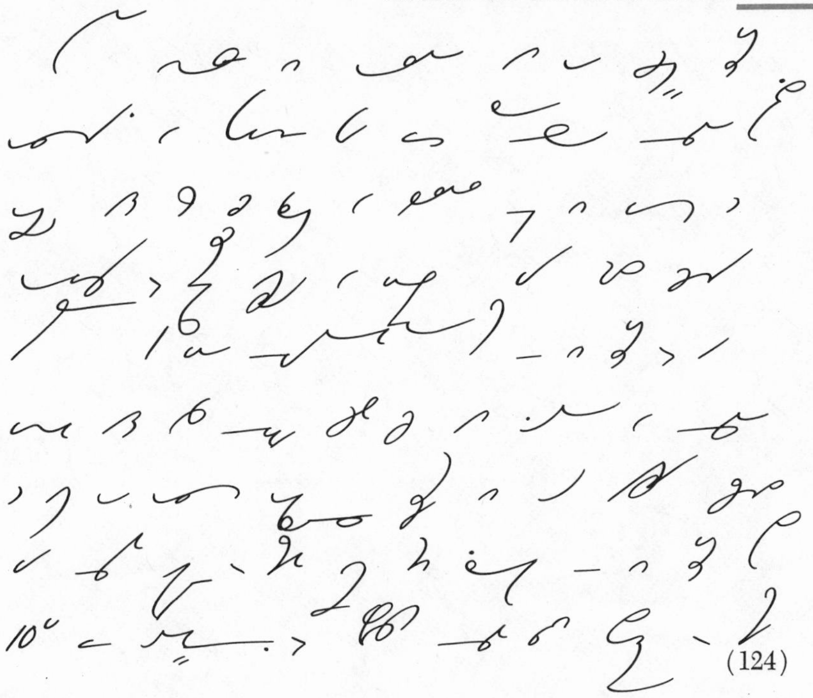

(124)

Building Transcription Skills

510. BUSINESS VOCABULARY BUILDER

versatile Having many uses.

devastating Ruinous; destructive.

irreparable Not able to be repaired.

Reading and Writing Practice

511.

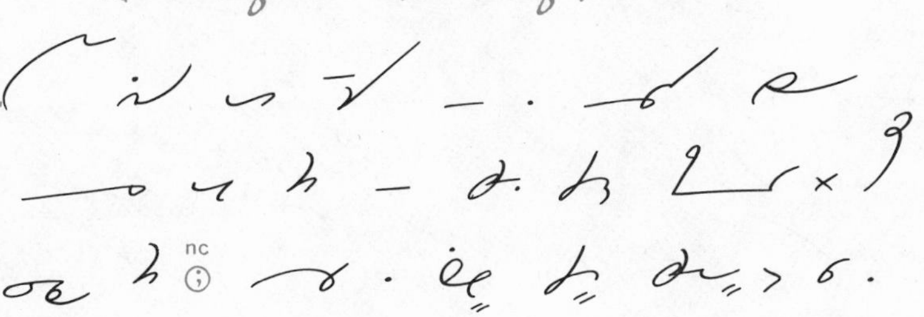

[Gregg shorthand outlines]

re·ceive'
de·scribes'
sat'is·fac'to·ry

when

(101)

....

512.

re'cent·ly
un·for'tu·nate·ly

intro

bc

bc

par

par

par

Transcribe:
$18
il'lus·tra'tion

10,

nonr

and o

ver'sa·tile

(134)

513.

[Gregg shorthand outlines]

pic'tured
beau'ti·ful

en·gi·neer'ing
u'su·al·ly
em·ploy'ees

ef·fi'cien·cy
tel'e·phone

(121)

....

514.

max'i·mum
per·form'ance
man'pow'er

ef·fi'cient
e·quip'ment
en·gi·neered'

[Gregg shorthand outlines] ser ① ②

(114)

515. **Transcription Quiz.** Supply the necessary punctuation and the missing words.

[Gregg shorthand outlines]

(118)

Office-Style Dictation, 2

Occasionally a businessman will dictate a word or a phrase and then change his mind and substitute another word or phrase. He may say:

> I want to purchase a cheap–no, *inexpensive* air-conditioning unit.

When that happens, the writer would simply place a line through the word *cheap* and write *inexpensive* right next to it.

Sometimes the dictator may change his mind about a word or a phrase after he has completed a sentence. He may say:

> I want to purchase a cheap air-conditioning unit – change that to *inexpensive*.

In this case the writer would place a line through the word *cheap* and would write *inexpensive* above it.

If several words are to be deleted, it is usually better to use a wavy line to indicate the deletion.

516. ILLUSTRATION OF OFFICE-STYLE DICTATION

LESSON 67

● **Warmup.** Your warmup letter is on page 409. Write the first paragraph of that letter as rapidly as you can and as often as you can in the time available.

Developing Word-Building Power

517. BRIEF-FORM CHART

Your reading goal: 25 seconds.

1						
2						
3						
4						
5						

1. Manufacture, manufacturer, manufactured, experience, experiences, experienced.
2. Worth, worthless, worthwhile, success, successful, successfully.
3. Enclose, enclosed, enclosure, use, useful, usefulness.
4. Represent, representation, representative, over, overcome, overdo.
5. Send, sends, sender, out, outside, outcome.

518. GEOGRAPHICAL EXPRESSIONS

1

2

414

1. Greenville, Nashville, Knoxville, Jacksonville, Ashville, Rushville, Danville, Crawfordsville.
2. America, American, Canada, Canadian, Mexico, Puerto Rico, Great Britain.

Building Transcription Skills

519.   BUSINESS VOCABULARY BUILDER

> **trepidation**   Fear.
>
> **intact**   Untouched; uninjured.
>
> **diminish**   To lessen.
>
> **manually**   By hand.

520.   SIMILAR-WORDS DRILL

Ceiling, sealing

> **ceiling**   The overhead covering of a room.

> They put a soundproof ceiling in each room.
>
> **sealing**   Fastening, as an envelope, with glue or paste.

> The machine is capable of sealing more than 6,000 envelopes an hour.

Reading and Writing Practice

521.

Transcribe:
January 22
de·stroyed'

through
ceil'ing
vi'tal
trep'i·da'tion
in·tact'
re·o'pen

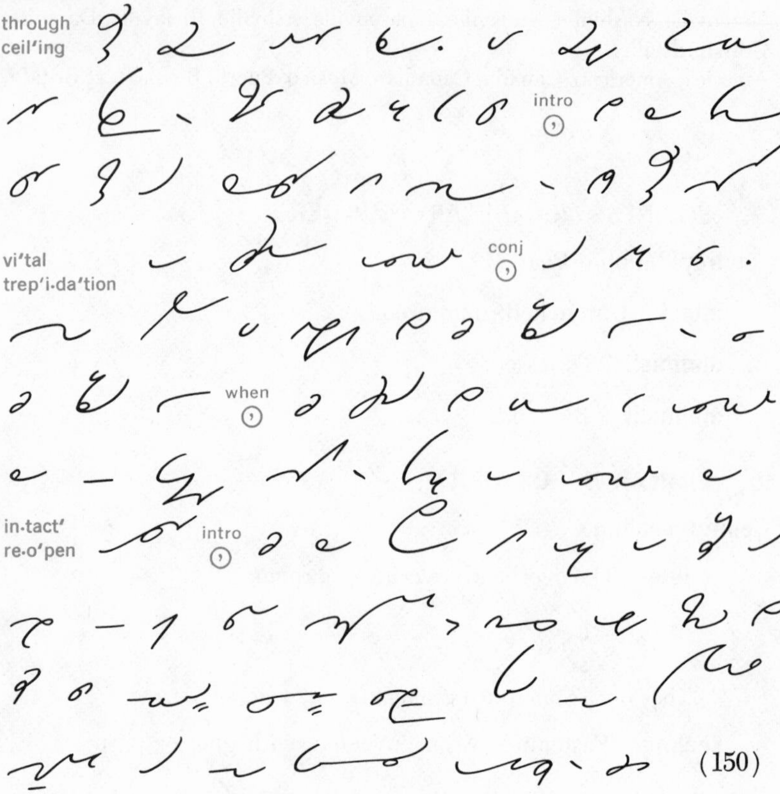

(150)

522.

sales
Mex'i·co

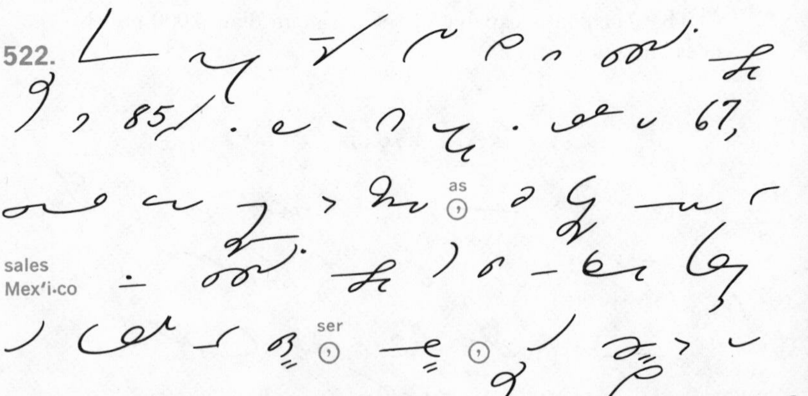

[Gregg shorthand outlines]

ease
op'er·a'tor

(135)

....

523.

spec'i·fi·ca'tions
sound'proof'

intro
①

es·tab'lished
sci'ence
re·sign'

di·min'ish
staff's

(103)

....

524.

suc·cess'ful
ex·ec'u·tives

[Gregg shorthand outlines]

par

intro

up'-to-date'
hyphenated
before noun

intro

intro

nc

(141)

. . . .

525.

intro

firm's
re·ceiv'a·ble
loss

conj

de·stroys'
en·trust'ing

in·cin'er·a'tor

(94)

526. **Transcription Quiz.** Supply the necessary punctuation and the missing words.

(121)

LESSON 68

● **Warmup.** Your warmup letter is on page 409. Copy the second paragraph of this letter as rapidly as you can and as often as you can.

Developing Word-Building Power

527. WORD FAMILIES

Rec-

1 *[shorthand outlines]*

-pend

2 *[shorthand outlines]*

-ser, -cer

3 *[shorthand outlines]*

-ish

4 *[shorthand outlines]*

-fer

5 *[shorthand outlines]*

---

1. Recall, recover, recovery, reconsider, require, recommendation.
2. Pending, depend, spend, happened, expend, suspend, expenditure, impending.
3. Answer, closer, nicer, dancer, racer, tracer, eraser.
4. Finish, furnish, astonish, abolish, accomplish, nourish, polish.
5. Suffer, offer, stuffer, rougher, safer, briefer, tougher.

Building Transcription Skills

528. BUSINESS VOCABULARY BUILDER

inferior Of poorer quality.

parcel Package.

grime Dirt or soot that has been rubbed in.

529. COMMON WORD ROOTS

Post-: *1. Having to do with the mails*

postage The charge for mailing a letter or other material.

post office The governmental department that handles the mails.

postmark The cancellation mark of the post office.

Post-: *2. Later; after*

postpone To put off till later.

postscript Something added later, after a letter has been completed. (In letters it is indicated *P. S.*)

postwar After the war.

Reading and Writing Practice

530.

Transcribe:
  $32,000
year's

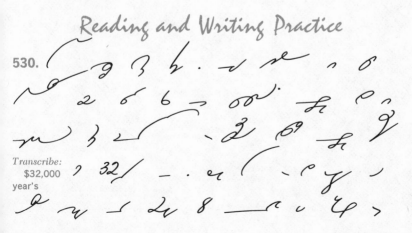

ex·pens′es
ef·fi′cient·ly

[Gregg shorthand outlines]

intro ⊙

a·chieve′
splen′did

(130)

• •

531.

[Gregg shorthand outlines]

when ⊙

guess
weight

when ⊙   bc ⊙

if ⊙

e·nough′
due

if ⊙

and o ⊙

eas′y·to·op′er·ate
hyphenated
before noun

[Gregg shorthand outlines] (141)

....

532. *[Gregg shorthand outlines]*

traf'fic
worn
ap·pear'ance

conj

par

grease
grime

proud
fa·mil'iar

if

(114)

533.

intro
skim'ming
eye
intro
u·nique'
stor'age
par
if
intro
intro
nc

(173)

534.

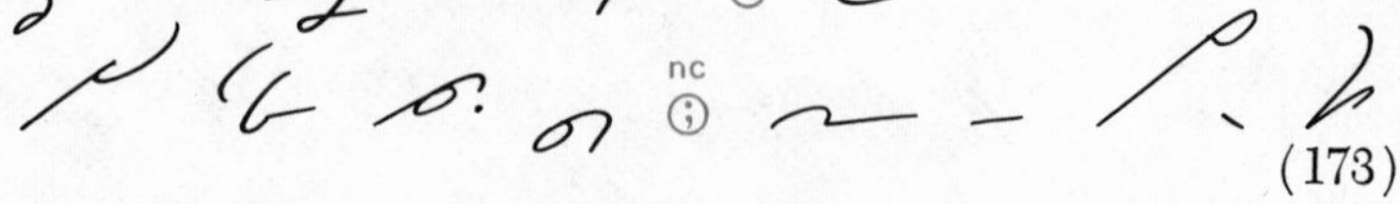
nc

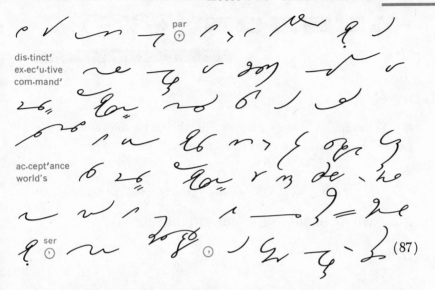

dis·tinct'
ex·ec'u·tive
com·mand'

ac·cept'ance
world's

ser

(87)

535. Transcription Quiz. Supply the necessary punctuation and the missing words.

(122)

LESSON 69

● **Warmup.** Write the third paragraph of the phrase letter on page 409 as rapidly and as often as time permits.

Developing Word-Building Power

536. WORD BEGINNINGS AND ENDINGS

Trans-

1 [shorthand outlines]

Electric-

2 [shorthand outlines]

Con-

3 [shorthand outlines]

For-

4 [shorthand outlines]

1. Transacted, transfer, transport, transmit, translate, transpire, transform.
2. Electric, electric typewriter, electric light, electric fan, electric machine, electric motor.
3. Constant, contribute, convenience, continue, contemplate, condition, contest.
4. Perform, performance, forward, information, enforce, effort, forget, force.

426

Building Transcription Skills

537. BUSINESS VOCABULARY BUILDER

desperately   Urgently; very badly.

peak loads   Times of greatest activity or use.

remodeling   Making over.

538. GRAMMAR CHECKUP

Learn, teach

learn   To acquire knowledge; to gain information.

You can learn to operate the machine in a matter of hours.

teach   To give or impart knowledge; to instruct.

I can teach (not *learn*) you how to operate the machine in a matter of hours.
I will teach (not *learn*) him a lesson!

Reading and Writing Practice

539.

ev'i·dent·ly
er'ror
fill'ing

[Gregg shorthand outlines]

des'per·ate·ly *[shorthand outlines]* nc · intro

[shorthand outlines] (100)

··

540. *[shorthand outlines]* as ·

[shorthand outlines]

[shorthand outlines]

[shorthand outlines]

[shorthand outlines] 68 /

[shorthand outlines] par ·

fig'ures
al·read'y *[shorthand outlines]* 74 /

[shorthand outlines] conj ·

[shorthand outlines]

an'nu·al
fur'ther·more'
em·ploy'ee *[shorthand outlines]* intro ·

[shorthand outlines] nc ·

[shorthand outlines]

[shorthand outlines]

[shorthand outlines] (173)

541.

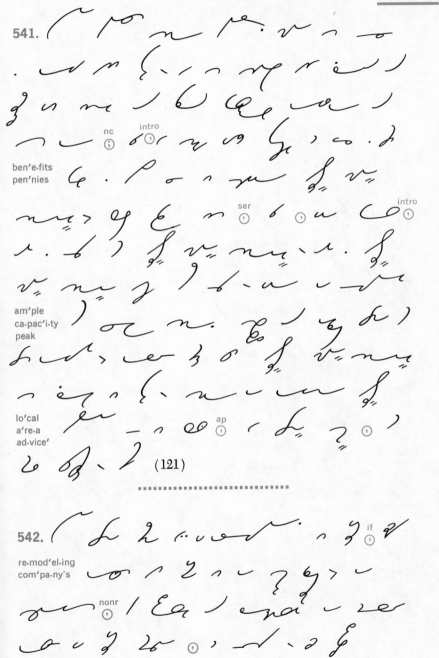

ben'e·fits
pen'nies

am'ple
ca·pac'i·ty
peak

lo'cal
a're·a
ad·vice'

(121)

542.

re·mod'el·ing
com'pa·ny's

[Gregg shorthand outlines]

ex·ec'u·tive
de·ci'sion

intro
⊙

(121)

....

543. *[shorthand outlines]*

re·ferred'
sta'plers
ter'ri·to'ry

intro
⊙

par
⊙

slight
in'con·ven'ience

ap
⊙

[shorthand outlines]

sta'tion·er'y
be·gin'ning
mu'tu·al·ly

(167)

544. Transcription Quiz.   Supply the necessary punctuation and missing words.

[shorthand outlines]

(144)

LESSON 70

● **Warmup.** For the final time, the phrase letter on page 409 is your warmup. In your best shorthand, write as much of the letter as time permits.

Developing Word-Building Power

545. SHORTHAND VOCABULARY BUILDER

Rd

1

-tation, Etc.

2

Tem, Dem, Etc.

3

Nt, Nd

4

---

1. Occurred, safeguard, desired, records, stored, card, neared.
2. Repetition, recommendation, additional, commission, determination, hesitation.
3. System, automatically, temperature, temporary, demand, damage.
4. Guarantee, plant, want, account, signed, designed, trend.

Building Transcription Skills

546. BUSINESS VOCABULARY BUILDER

basically   Essentially; fundamentally.

sturdy   Strong.

microfilm   A film of small size used for keeping a photo-graphic record of printed matter.

Reading and Writing Practice

547.

an'a·lyzed
con·nec'tion

conj

op'er·a'tor
bas'i·cal·ly
rough

oc·curred'
guar'an·tee'

(130)

548.

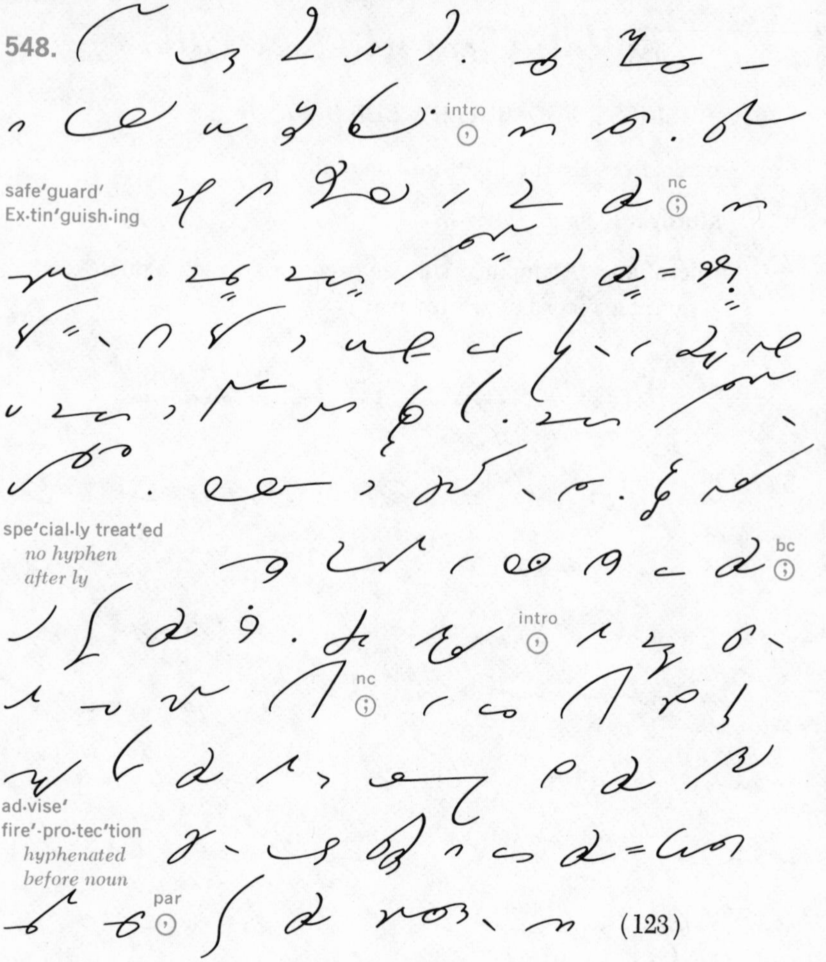

safe'guard'
Ex·tin'guish·ing

spe'cial·ly treat'ed
no hyphen after ly

ad·vise'
fire'-pro·tec'tion
hyphenated before noun

(123)

549.

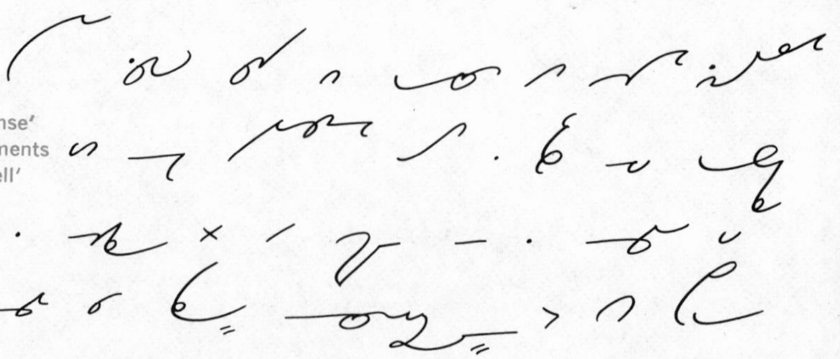

con·dense'
doc'u·ments
nut'shell'

[Gregg shorthand outlines]

(100)

---

550. *[Gregg shorthand outlines]*

ser ①

② *[Gregg shorthand outlines]*

up'-to-the-min'ute
hyphenated
before noun

e·quip'ment
de·struc'tion

③ *[Gregg shorthand outlines]*

④ *[Gregg shorthand outlines]*

20

30

if ①

neg'a·tive
rec'om·men·da'tions

(117)

551. Don't Waste the Pauses

[shorthand notation]

Mr. Davis

[Gregg shorthand outlines]

As a result *[Gregg shorthand outlines]* (257)

··

It goes without saying that a secretary must be able to type well and take dictation rapidly and accurately. These skills are basic and absolutely essential for her success in the modern business world. — Philip S. Pepe, Director of Business Education, Remington Rand Division of Sperry Rand

15

Aviation

On December 17, 1903, the good citizens of Kitty Hawk, North Carolina, rubbed their eyes in disbelief. They were sure they saw, off in the distance, something that looked like a big flying box. What they were witnessing, of course, was the birth of a great industry — aviation. That "flying box" was the Wright brothers' plane, which on that day

438

made four successful flights, one for a duration of 59 seconds at a speed of 30 miles an hour.

That flying box was the great-granddaddy of today's majestic jet airliner, which carries a hundred or more passengers from coast to coast nonstop at a speed of more than 500 miles an hour — with all the comforts of a fine hotel.

In those early days only the bold and adventurous had the courage to fly in the flying boxes; today millions of people — even some of the most timid — fly every year, for air travel is safer than riding in an automobile.

Even though the aviation industry has made almost unbelievable progress since the Wrights built their plane, it is still in its infancy; and we can expect to see some wonderful advances in aviation in the days ahead.

In the not-too-distant future no one will be surprised when it is possible to take a jet plane in New York at noon to keep an appointment in Paris an hour or two later. The traveler won't make an impression on anybody when he says that he was in Bombay in the morning, in Tokyo for lunch, in London for afternoon tea, and home in Kansas City for dinner! Nor will they look at him as though he had lost his sanity when he casually asks the airlines reservations clerk what time the next spaceship leaves for the moon!

The greater the aviation industry becomes, the greater will be its need for office help, of which the secretarial worker is an indispensable part. The letters in this chapter deal with various phases of the aviation industry. They are typical of the letters you would take from dictation if you obtained a stenographic position in some branch of that industry.

LESSON 71

Building Phrasing Skill

552. PHRASE BUILDER

Reading goal: 40 seconds.

After

1 [shorthand outlines]

Let us

2 [shorthand outlines]

Omission of A

3 [shorthand outlines]

Yet

4 [shorthand outlines]

1. After the, after that, after that time, after them, after which, after this, after those.
2. Let us, let us make, let us know, let us have, let us see, let us say.
3. As a result, at a loss, at a time, for a moment, for a few days, for a few minutes.
4. As yet, has not yet, has not yet been, have not yet, I have not yet, I have not yet been, I have not yet been able, we have not yet.

553. WARMUP PHRASE LETTER

This is your warmup phrase letter for Chapter 15. How fast can you read it? How fast can you copy it?

440

[Gregg shorthand outlines]

59571

27

27, 9

(131)

Building Transcription Skills

554. BUSINESS VOCABULARY BUILDER

low ceiling Dense clouds, fog, or smog close to the ground. The lower the ceiling, the more difficult it is for planes to take off.

take-off The rising of a plane from the ground.

accommodations Available space in a plane, train, hotel, etc.

Reading and Writing Practice

555.

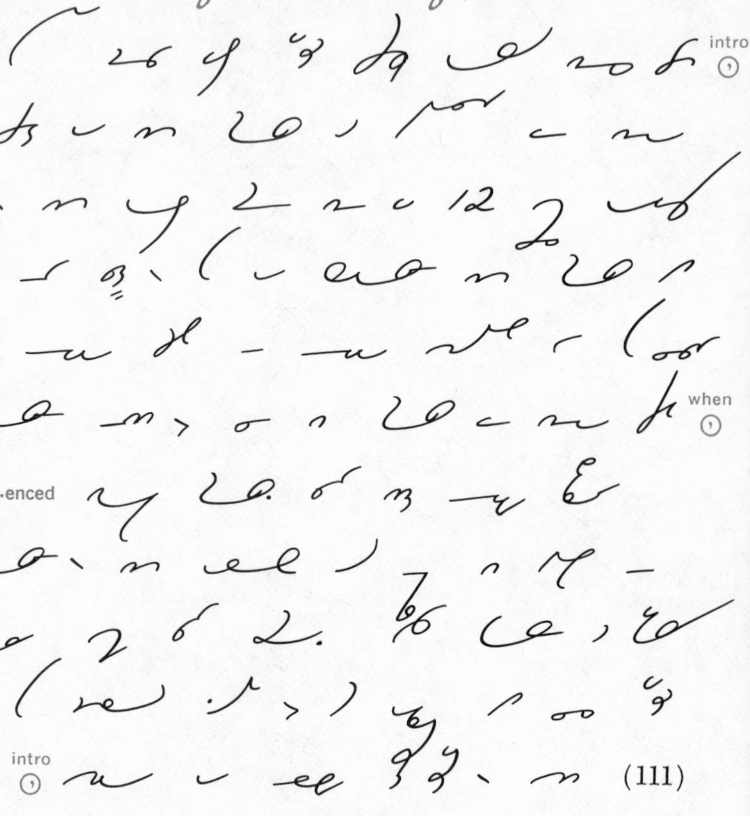

cit'ies
air'line'
world's
ex·pe'ri·enced
plane
skilled

556.

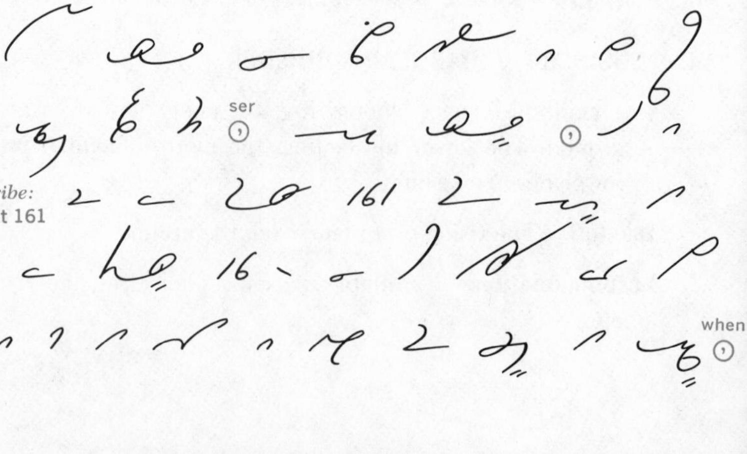

Transcribe:
Flight 161

touch
nec'es·sar'y

nc

if

(110)

557.

ceil'ing
ac·com'pa·nied
sleet

bc

par

safe'ty
proud

conj

sev'en-hour'
hyphenated
before noun

conj

(113)

558.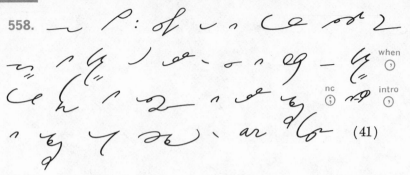

(41)

559. Transcription Quiz. Supply the necessary punctuation and missing words.

(140)

Office-Style Dictation, 3

Occasionally a dictator will say a word or a phrase and then change it. Upon reflection, however, he decides that the original word or phrase is better. The dictator might say:

> The accommodations are excellent—no, *good;* oh, leave it *excellent.*

The best way to handle this situation is to rewrite the restored word or phrase as though it were a completely new form. You write the word *excellent.* You then strike it out and substitute *good.* Finally, you strike out *good* and rewrite *excellent.*

Do not try to indicate that the original outline for *excellent* is to be restored; this effort may make your notes difficult to read, with the result that you might not be able to transcribe them correctly.

560.   ILLUSTRATION OF OFFICE-STYLE DICTATION

LESSON 72

● **Warmup.** Your warmup letter is on page 441. Practice the first paragraph, writing it as rapidly as you can and as many times as you can in the time available.

Developing Word-Building Power

561. BRIEF-FORM CHART

Your reading goal: 20 seconds.

1. Idea, ideas, subject, subjects, circular, circulars.
2. Put, puts, one, once, good, goods.
3. Regular, regularly, present, presently, order, orderly.
4. Enclose, enclosed, use, used, work, worked.
5. Big, bigger, great, greater, time, timer.

562. GEOGRAPHICAL EXPRESSIONS

446

1. Paris, Rome, Tokyo, London, Berlin, Vienna, Moscow.
2. France, Italy, Japan, England, Germany, Austria, Europe.

Building Transcription Skills

563. BUSINESS VOCABULARY BUILDER

concept   Idea of what a thing in general should be.

transatlantic   Crossing the Atlantic Ocean.

seasonal   Affected by the season or seasons.

564. SIMILAR-WORDS DRILL

Fair, fare

fair   Honest; just; also, not stormy.

[shorthand outlines]

You will be able to stay in good hotels at fair prices.
The weather in England is generally fair at this time of the year.

fare   The price of transportation or passage.

[shorthand outlines]

The fare is only $40.

Reading and Writing Practice

565. *[shorthand outlines]*

fas'ci·nat'ing
con'cepts

[Gregg shorthand outlines]

mir'a·cle
break'fast
climb

[Gregg shorthand outlines]

(120)

....

566.

ad·ven'ture
life'time'
To'ky·o

[Gregg shorthand outlines]

fare
Transcribe:
   $1,300

[Gregg shorthand outlines]

(Gregg shorthand outlines) (97)

567.

weath'er
fair

(shorthand) ① ①

nc

(shorthand)

② ①

ac·com'mo·da'tions
fair

(shorthand)

③ ①

fare
ef·fect'

conj
①

(shorthand)

if
①

(shorthand) 330 *(shorthand)*

12 *(shorthand)* (116)

568.

ap
①

(shorthand) ①

(shorthand)

[Gregg shorthand outlines]

ma′jor
first′-class′
hyphenated
before noun

bc

intro

[Gregg shorthand outlines]

sin′gle
car′ried

[Gregg shorthand outlines]

1940

par

cir′cu·lars
pre·par′ing

nc

[Gregg shorthand outlines] (144)

· ·

569. *[Gregg shorthand outlines]*

nc

[Gregg shorthand outlines]

par

[Gregg shorthand outlines]

thought′ful
hus′band's

[Gregg shorthand outlines]

nc

oc·ca′sion
a·ris′es

[Gregg shorthand outlines]

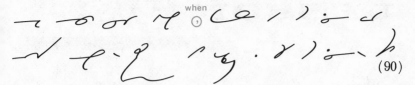

(90)

570. Transcription Quiz.   Supply the necessary punctuation and missing words.

(143)

LESSON 73

● **Warmup.** Your warmup letter is on page 441. Copy the second paragraph as rapidly as you can and as often as you can in the time available.

Developing Word-Building Power

571. WORD FAMILIES

-work

1

-man

2

-gent

3

-sure

4

Comm-

5

---

1. Work, network, framework, overwork, teamwork, guesswork.
2. Businessman, workman, newspaperman, foreman, postman, freshman.
3. Agent, negligent, intelligent, diligent, urgent, stringent.
4. Sure, assure, measure, insure, pressure, pleasure, treasure.
5. Commit, common, commercial, committee, committed.

452

Building Transcription Skills

572. BUSINESS VOCABULARY BUILDER

intermediate   In between.

formality   Compliance with formal rules.

coach   A plane for which fares are lower than for first-class flights because fewer conveniences are provided.

573. SPELLING FAMILIES

In some languages, a vowel sound is always spelled the same way. In English, however, we are not so fortunate; a vowel sound may be spelled a number of different ways. In this spelling family, you will study the useful words in which *i* is spelled *igh*.

Words Ending in -ight

height	flight	fright
sight	twi'light'	up'right'
light	might	cop'y·right'
slight	night	tight
de·light'	right	bright

Reading and Writing Practice

574.

wal'let-sized'
hyphenated
before noun

[Gregg shorthand outlines]

ac·cept'
per'son·al

par

wear
la·pel'

ser

par

(160)

....

575.

and o

jet'lin'er
com·mer'cial
busi'ness·man's

ap

880

flights
in'ter·me'di·ate

par

880

ser

[Gregg shorthand outlines] intro ⊙

[Gregg shorthand outlines] 27

[Gregg shorthand outlines]

[Gregg shorthand outlines] 880 **(139)**

. . . .

576. *[Gregg shorthand outlines]*

[Gregg shorthand outlines]

[Gregg shorthand outlines] 41 60

[Gregg shorthand outlines] intro ⊙

fare
budg'et *[Gregg shorthand outlines]* 10,
suit

[Gregg shorthand outlines] 24

[Gregg shorthand outlines] when ⊙

min'i·mum
for·mal'i·ty *[Gregg shorthand outlines]*

[Gregg shorthand outlines] conj ⊙

[Gregg shorthand outlines] if ⊙

[Gregg shorthand outlines] ser ⊙

[Gregg shorthand outlines] if ⊙

[Gregg shorthand outlines] **(129)**

577.

[Gregg shorthand outlines]

sched'ules
a're·a

intro
①

post'age-paid'
hyphenated
before noun

intro
①

(106)

▪▪▪▪▪▪▪▪▪▪▪▪▪▪▪▪▪▪▪▪▪▪▪▪▪▪▪▪▪▪

578.

[Gregg shorthand outlines]

be·gin'ning
ap·pre'ci·a'tion

intro
①

intro
①

ser
①

cour'te·sy
gen'u·ine

(85)

579.   Transcription Quiz.   Supply the necessary punctuation and
the missing words.

[Gregg shorthand outlines]

(177)

LESSON 74

● **Warmup.**   Your warmup letter is on page 441. Copy the third paragraph of this letter as rapidly as you can and as many times as you can in the time available.

Developing Word-Building Power

580. WORD BEGINNINGS AND ENDINGS

-cial

1 [shorthand outlines]

-ification

2 [shorthand outlines]

-ily

3 [shorthand outlines]

Ex-

4 [shorthand outlines]

---

1. Partial, initial, special, credentials, substantial, crucial, social, official, financial.
2. Notification, modification, ratification, specifications, simplification, gratification.
3. Family, easily, readily, steadily, momentarily, temporarily.
4. Excursion, extra, extreme, extent, extend, examination, excess.

Building Transcription Skills

581. BUSINESS VOCABULARY BUILDER

ascends   Goes up.

descends   Comes down.

partial   Inclined to favor one thing more than another.

582. GRAMMAR CHECKUP

Possessive with Verbal Noun

Always be careful when you find a gerund (the *ing* form of a verb used as a noun) that is preceded by a noun or pronoun; the noun or pronoun takes the possessive case.

> *John's* leaving caused me much unhappiness.
> I admire *his* taking the time to coach the team.
> I should appreciate *your* letting me know when you will leave.

Note: Be especially careful when the pronoun that precedes the gerund is *your.* It is so easy to transcribe the *you-your* brief form as *you* in this situation if you are not attentive.

Reading and Writing Practice

583.

Transcribe:
five o'clock

[Gregg shorthand outlines] (64)

· ·

584. *[Gregg shorthand outlines]*

first'-class'
hyphenated
before noun

[Gregg shorthand outlines] 12 21

[Gregg shorthand outlines] ②

[Gregg shorthand outlines]

conj ①

ac·com'pa·ny
ex·cur'sion

[Gregg shorthand outlines] ③

[Gregg shorthand outlines] 198/

[Gregg shorthand outlines]

intro ①

[Gregg shorthand outlines] (144)

585.

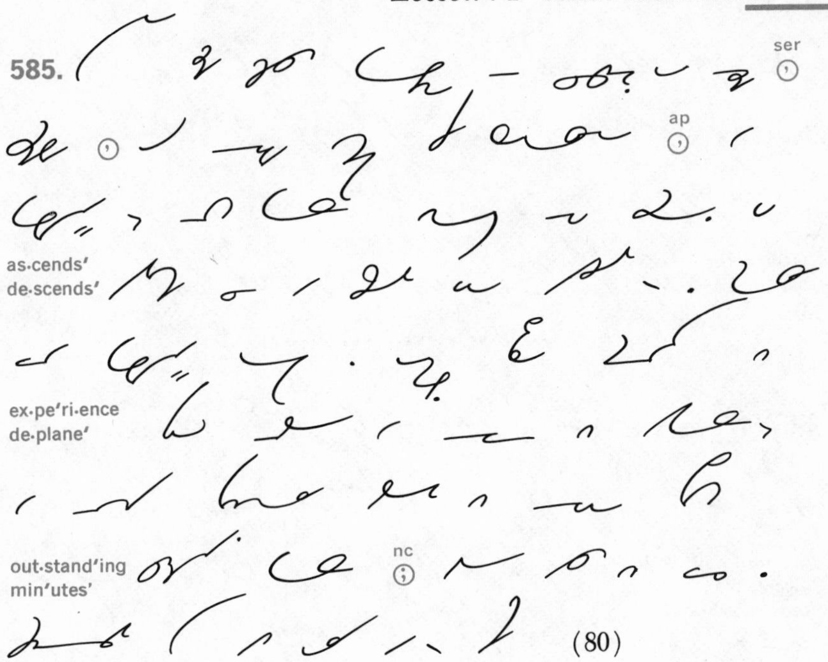

ser ap

as·cends′ de·scends′

ex·pe′ri·ence de·plane′

nc

out·stand′ing min′utes′

(80)

586.

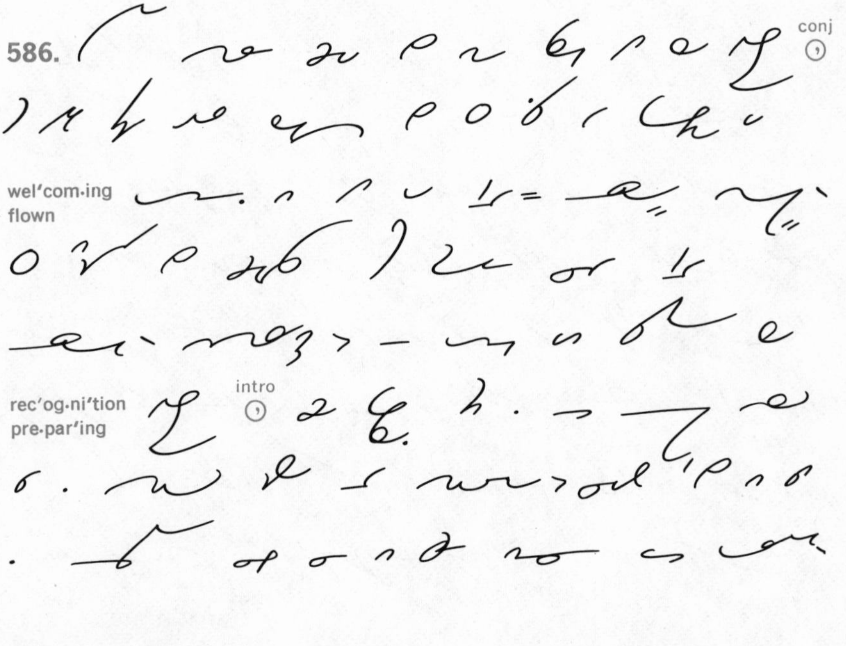

conj

wel′com·ing flown

intro

rec′og·ni′tion pre·par′ing

as

when

pleas'ure
per·son·al·ly

(134)

587.

his'to·ry
a·vail'a·ble
re·spon'si·ble

intro

nc

①

②

ap

③

when

[Gregg shorthand outlines] (145)

588. Transcription Quiz.   Supply the necessary punctuation and the missing words.

[Gregg shorthand outlines] (141)

LESSON 75

● **Warmup.** Your warmup letter is on page 441. Copy the entire letter as rapidly as you can. If time permits, write it a second time in your best shorthand.

Developing Word-Building Power

589. SHORTHAND VOCABULARY BUILDER

Ng

1 *[shorthand outlines]*

Ngk

2 *[shorthand outlines]*

Tern, Term, Dern

3 *[shorthand outlines]*

Ĭa, Ēa

4 *[shorthand outlines]*

Ol, Or

5 *[shorthand outlines]*

---

1. Long, longhand, bring, young, string, single.
2. Bank, blank, frank, drink, ink, trunk.
3. Turn, term, determine, return, returned, modern.
4. Area, associate, aviation, create, creation, brilliant, appreciate.
5. All, old, tolerate, or, more, store.

Building Transcription Skills

590. BUSINESS VOCABULARY BUILDER

spacious   Roomy.

tolerate   To endure, to put up with.

Reading and Writing Practice

591.

semi′pri′vate
as·so′ci·ates

[Gregg shorthand outlines]

and o

ser

San′ Fran·cis′co
for′ward

(101)

592.

bus′y
tol′er·ate

[Gregg shorthand outlines]

par

long'hand' lose

intro

and o

when

(124)

593.

re·duc'es dam'age

intro

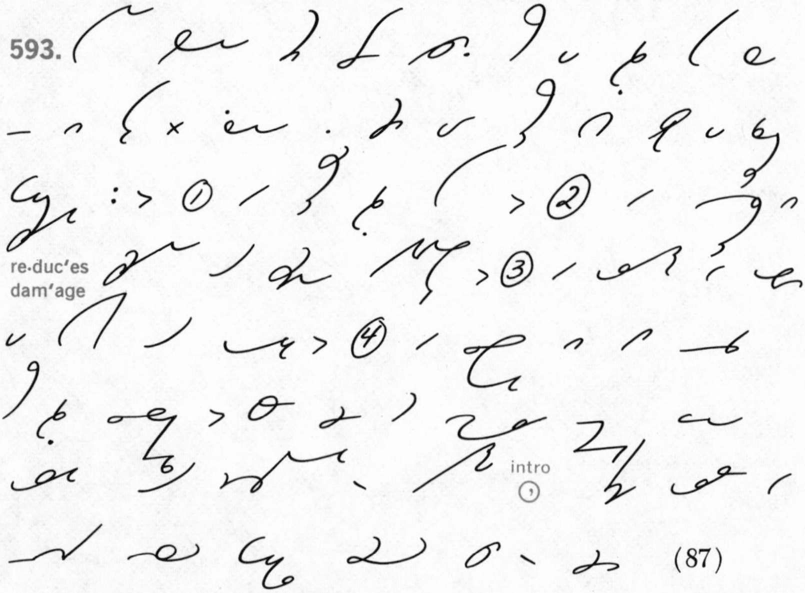

(87)

594.

re'al·iz'es
flew
past

a'vi·a'tion
na'tion's

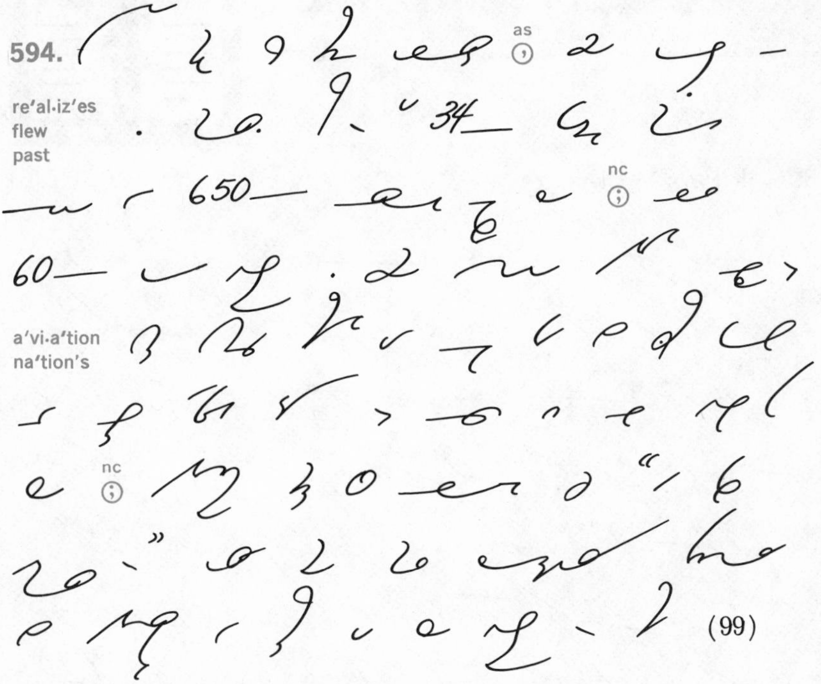

595.

ca·reer'
wheth'er

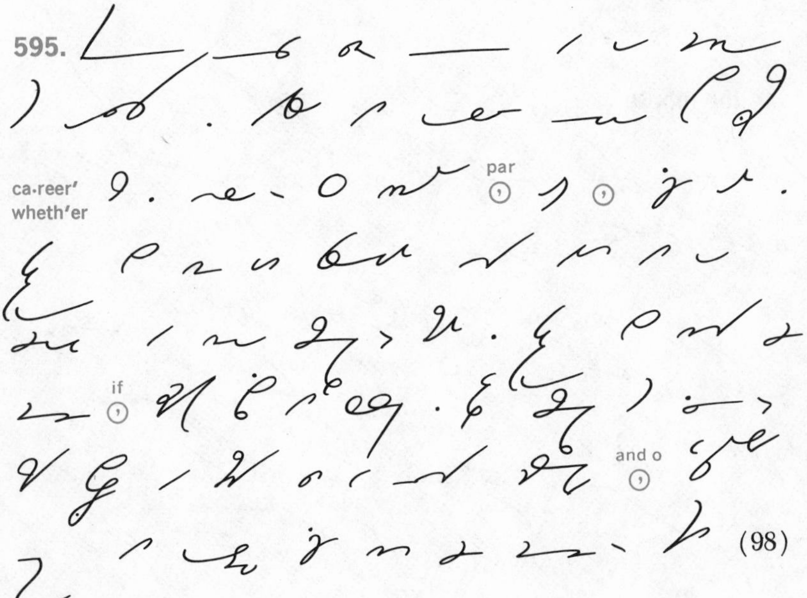

596. It Pays to Organize

[shorthand outlines]

In the month *[shorthand outlines]*

[Gregg shorthand outlines]

Betty proofread

(344)

16

Education

One "business" that never lacks for customers is education; at one time or another *everyone* is its customer — willingly or unwillingly! What is more, its customers are constantly increasing — increasing so fast, in fact, that new schools cannot be built and new teachers trained rapidly enough to take care of them.

Schools and colleges in the United States employ thousands upon thousands of teachers and administrators. And these institutions have need for vast numbers of office workers, too — bookkeepers, typists, filing clerks, telephone operators, and stenographers and secretaries. Educational secretaries as they call themselves find their work interesting and exciting.

A stenographer in a high school principal's office put it this way: "My work never gets dull — every day is different — and there are so many young people to work with that I keep young, too!"

A stenographer-receptionist in a private business school said she likes her job because "I greet all callers — businessmen, prospective students, and parents. I think the biggest thrill of my job is to see the change that takes place in a student — from the time he comes in to enroll until he graduates and takes an office position. He seems to 'grow' before my very eyes!"

The secretary to a physics professor, who is also a prominent author in his field, says that in typing her employer's manuscripts she has obtained the equivalent of a college education — and received a salary for it!

Yes, the rewards of working in education are many. Perhaps you will have an opportunity to learn more about the advantages of this field by working during your free hours or after school in one of the school offices, or, perhaps, as "secretary" to a faculty member.

The letters in this chapter will give you some idea of the type of material that a stenographer in a school system takes from dictation.

LESSON 76

Building Phrasing Skill

597. PHRASE BUILDER

Your reading goal: 25 seconds.

Glad

Much

Many

Miscellaneous

1. Glad to see, glad to say, glad to hear, glad to know, I shall be glad.
2. Very much, how much, so much, as much, much more, too much.
3. Many days, many times, many of them, many of these, many of those.
4. As soon as, as soon as possible, to me, to make, to know, let us, to us, to do, to do the.

598. WARMUP PHRASE LETTER

Your warmup phrase letter contains 130 words. How fast can you read it? How fast can you copy it?

[Gregg shorthand outlines]

(130)

Building Transcription Skills

599. **BUSINESS VOCABULARY BUILDER**

> **scope**   Extent; range.
>
> **hearty**   Warm; cordial.
>
> **remedial**   Designed to correct.

Reading and Writing Practice

600.

in·quir'y
re·ferred'

[Gregg shorthand outlines]

nonr

if

if

part′-time′
hyphenated before noun

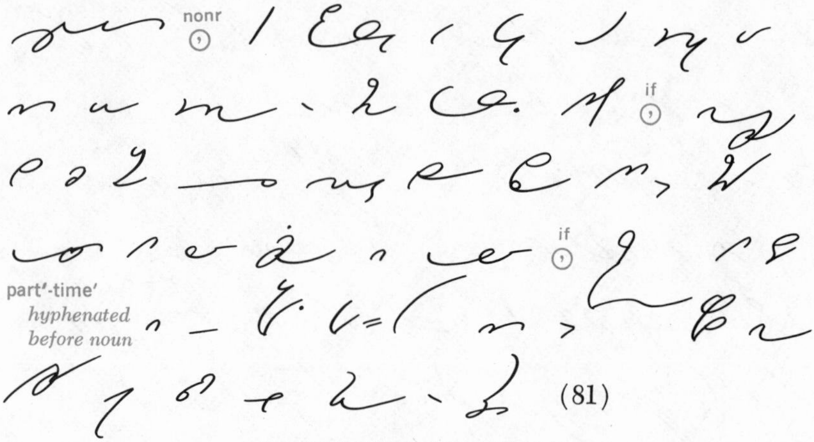

(81)

601.

heart′y
for′ward

nc

ap

nc

passed
ca′pa·ble

bc

when

and o

(88)

602.

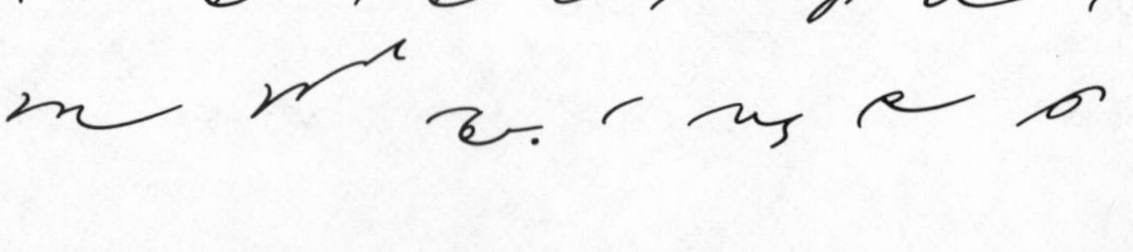

stu'dent's
par'ents'

(Gregg shorthand outlines)

as

if

de·ci'sions
ac'tu·al·ly
judg'ment

ap

Transcribe:
a.m.   10:30   bc

if

(124)

∙∙∙∙∙∙∙∙∙∙∙∙∙∙∙∙∙∙∙∙∙∙∙∙∙∙∙∙∙∙∙∙∙∙∙∙∙

603.

son's
urge   nc

par

bc

[Gregg shorthand outlines]

conj ⊙

re·me'di·al

ser ⊙

if ⊙

(133)

604. Transcription Quiz.   Supply the necessary punctuation and the missing words.

[Gregg shorthand outlines]

(118)

Office-Style Dictation, 4

A businessman may occasionally decide to transpose words or phrases for emphasis or some other reason. The simplest way to indicate the transposition of a word or phrase is to use the regular printer's sign for transposition.

The dictator might say:

> The radio is the least expensive and most effective advertising medium for our products — make that *most effective and least expensive.*

In your shorthand, you would make the change in this way:

You would then be careful, when you transcribe, to type the word *and* after the word *effective.*

605. ILLUSTRATION OF OFFICE-STYLE DICTATION

LESSON 77

● **Warmup.** Your warmup letter is on page 473. Write the first paragraph as rapidly and as often as you can in the time you have available.

Developing Word-Building Power

606. BRIEF-FORM CHART

Reading Goal: 25 seconds.

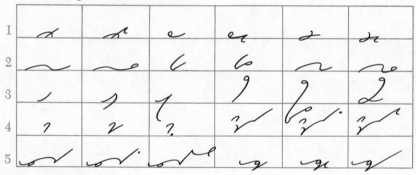

1. Quantity, quantities, year, years, send, sends.
2. Glad, gladly, part, partly, great, greatly.
3. There, therefore, thereby, every, everybody, everywhere.
4. Wish, wished, wishing, understand, understanding, understands.
5. Regard, regarding, regardless, request, requests, requested.

607. GEOGRAPHICAL EXPRESSIONS

478

1. Pittsburgh, Harrisburg, Greenburg, Parkersburg, Hattiesburg, Blooms-
burg, Newburgh.
2. Pennsylvania, Ohio, Indiana, Illinois, Missouri, Kansas, Mississippi, Iowa.

Building Transcription Skills

608.   BUSINESS VOCABULARY BUILDER

brochure   A pamphlet.

revealing *(adjective)*   Opening up to view, especially
something that was hidden or unknown.

incurred   Brought down on oneself.

609.   SIMILAR-WORDS DRILL

Accede, exceed

accede   To agree to; to grant.

We are happy to accede to your request for an extension of
time.

exceed   To go beyond; to be more than.

Some of the classes in this school exceed 40 students.

Reading and Writing Practice

610.

bro·chure′
ac·cede′

conj
⊙

[Gregg shorthand outlines]

(104)

611. *[Gregg shorthand outlines]*

tal'ent
ca·reer'

mon'ey-mak'ing
eight'-page'
*hyphenated
before noun*

and o

for'mer·ly
Transcribe:
$1

if

conj

ex·ceeds' [shorthand outline]

(121)

································

612. [shorthand outline] ap · [shorthand] 2 ·

Transcribe:
September 2
per·mis'sion [shorthand outline]

[shorthand outlines]

as ·

[shorthand outlines]

nc ·   intro ·   40

[shorthand outlines] nonr ·

[shorthand outlines] nc ·

[shorthand outlines] 20 [shorthand] intro ·

[shorthand outlines] ser · [shorthand] ·

com·mu'ni·ty [shorthand outlines]

[shorthand] par · [shorthand] nc ·

ac·ced'ing [shorthand outlines] ·

[shorthand outlines] (114)

································

613. [shorthand outlines]

rec'om·mend'
of'fered [shorthand outlines]

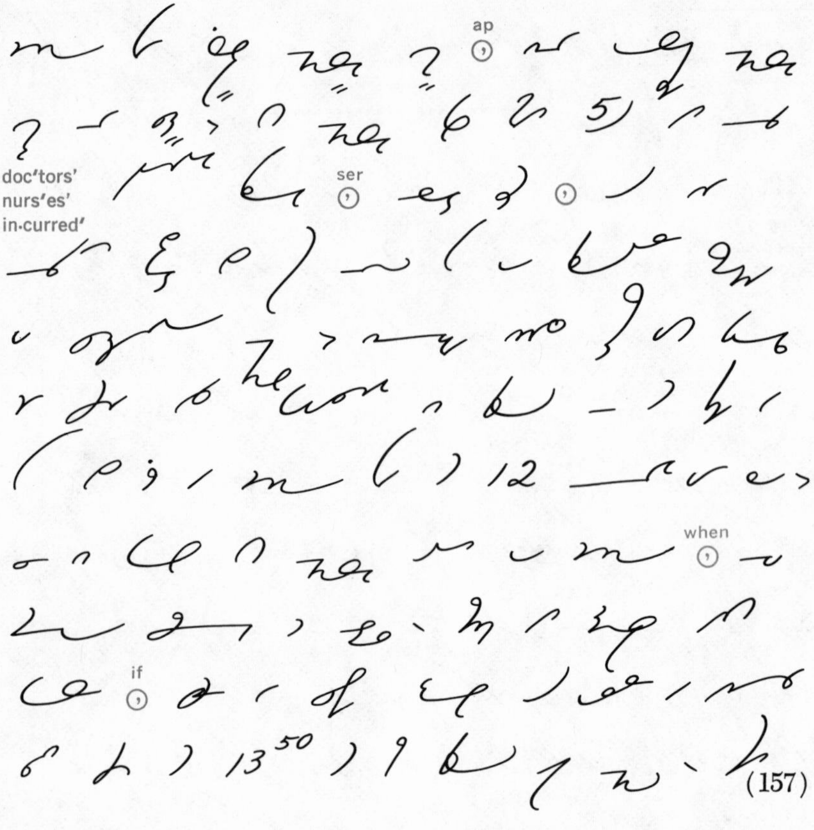
ap
doc'tors'
nurs'es'
in·curred'
ser
when
if

(157)

614.

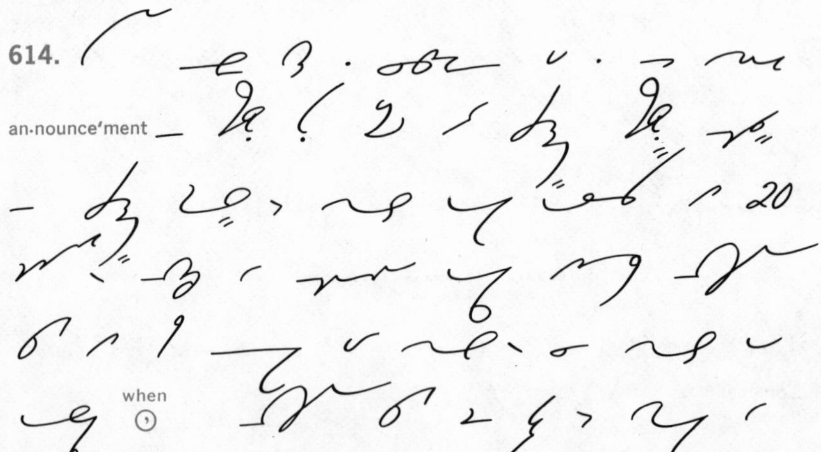
an·nounce'ment
when

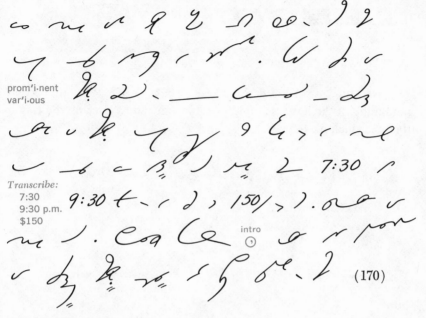

prom′i·nent
var′i·ous

Transcribe:
7:30
9:30 p.m.
$150

intro

(170)

615.   Transcription Quiz.   Supply the necessary punctuation and
the missing words.

(85)

LESSON 78

● **Warmup.** Your warmup letter is on page 473. Write the second paragraph of the letter as rapidly as you can and as often as you can in the time available to you.

Developing Word-Building Power

616. WORD FAMILIES

-ial

1 *[shorthand outlines]*

Sup-

2 *[shorthand outlines]*

-vity

3 *[shorthand outlines]*

-bility

4 *[shorthand outlines]*

-ple

5 *[shorthand outlines]*

---

1. Material, editorial, pictorial, secretarial, serial.
2. Supply, support, supplement, supplementary, supreme, supremely.
3. Activity, inactivity, brevity, gravity, productivity, captivity.
4. Ability, possibility, probability, inability, legibility, disability.
5. Example, people, triple, principle, ample, sample.

484

Building Transcription Skills

617. BUSINESS VOCABULARY BUILDER

comprehension Understanding.
council A governing body.
pictorial In the form of pictures.

618. SPELLING FAMILIES

Think twice before you transcribe a word ending with the sound of *ent* or *ant*. Most people pronounce both endings alike; consequently, pronunciation is of little help when you must decide to spell a word with *ent* or *ant*.

Words Ending in -ent

stu'dent	su'per·in·ten'dent	res'i·dent
pres'i·dent	ev'i·dent	ac'ci·dent
vice'-pres'i·dent	de·pen'dent	in'ci·dent

Words Ending in -ant

ig'no·rant	ac·count'ant	ap'pli·cant
war'rant	mer'chant	pleas'ant
re·luc'tant	serv'ant	sig·nif'i·cant

Reading and Writing Practice

619. *[shorthand outlines]*

if
⊙

be·lieve'
Karl's

[Gregg shorthand outlines] (81)

· ·

620. *[Gregg shorthand outlines]*

in'di·cate
sup'ple·men'ta·ry

[Gregg shorthand outlines] (97)

· ·

621. *[Gregg shorthand outlines]*

Coun'cil
fac'ul·ty

one'-hour'
  hyphenated
  before noun
as·sem'bly

[Gregg shorthand outlines]

choos'es
its

conj ①

ser ①

nc ⊙

intro ①

(135)

622.

As·so'ci·a'tion
va'can·cy

when ①

ser ①

ex·pe'ri·ence
pro·spec'tive

con·ven′ient
ap·pre′ci·ate

if
①

nonr
①

and o
①

(168)

623.

re·o′pen
nec′es·sar′i·ly

ap
①

ap
①

ser
①

①

intro
①

cr
⊙

(112)

624.

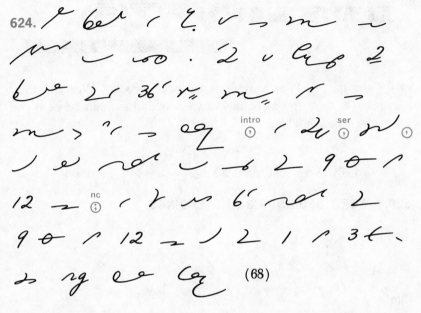

(68)

625.   Transcription Quiz.   Supply the necessary punctuation and the missing words.

(87)

LESSON 79

● **Warmup.**   Your warmup letter is on page 473. Write the third
paragraph of the letter as rapidly as you can and as many times as you
can in the time available.

Developing Word-Building Power

626. WORD BEGINNINGS AND ENDINGS

-hood

1 *[shorthand outlines]*

-ble

2 *[shorthand outlines]*

Al-

3 *[shorthand outlines]*

-ther

4 *[shorthand outlines]*

In-

5 *[shorthand outlines]*

---

1. Neighborhood, childhood, boyhood, parenthood, motherhood, likelihood.
2. Suitable, possible, notable, creditable, reasonable, reliable, eligible.
3. Almost, also, although, already, alternative, alternate, Albany.
4. Gather, other, whether, together, altogether, further, farther.
5. Increase, invest, inform, incomplete, intend, insure, income.

Building Transcription Skills

627. BUSINESS VOCABULARY BUILDER

    eligible   Fitted or qualified to be chosen.

    proof   A test print made from a negative.

    blemishes   Flaws; defects.

628. COMMON WORD ROOTS

  En-: *in, into*

    enclose   To put or shut in.

    enroll   To register in.

    enter   To go in.

    entrance   A way in.

    enact   To make into law.

Reading and Writing Practice

629.

phone
ad·mis′sion

for′ward·ing
du′pli·cate

nc

intro

wheth′er
el′i·gi·ble

[Gregg shorthand outlines]

out'-of-state'
hyphenated
before noun

conj

par

(127)

630.

ap

when

sur'gi·cal
Transcribe:
$500

ser

if

(107)

631.

(Gregg shorthand outlines)

par **intro**

eyes
blem'ish·es
por'trait

(shorthand outlines)

(110)

∙∙∙∙∙∙∙∙∙∙∙∙∙∙∙∙∙∙∙∙∙∙∙∙∙∙∙∙∙

632. *(shorthand outlines)*

Transcribe:
October 25
7:45

ap 25 ⊙ / 7:45

nc

" ' " —

conj

[Gregg shorthand outlines]

if
⟨,⟩

8-6161 (153)

as
⟨,⟩

cr
⟨·⟩

if
⟨,⟩

·····································

633.

ap
⟨,⟩

pleas'ant
di·rec'tor

par
⟨,⟩

intro
⟨,⟩

pro·ce'dures
i·de'as

intro
⟨,⟩

sched'ules
in·struc'tors

intro
⟨,⟩

[Gregg shorthand outline] (161)

634. Transcription Quiz. Supply the necessary punctuation and missing words.

[Gregg shorthand outline] (134)

LESSON 80

● **Warmup.** This will be your final warmup on the phrase letter on page 473. Make one copy of the letter in your best shorthand.

Developing Word-Building Power

635. SHORTHAND VOCABULARY BUILDER

Oi

1 [shorthand outlines]

Ū

2 [shorthand outlines]

Ow

3 [shorthand outlines]

Ī

4 [shorthand outlines]

1. Point, disappoint, poise, toil, annoy, annoyance, soil, boiler.
2. Interview, future, unit, unite, united, few, futile, fuse.
3. Brown, without, announcement, sound, found, pound, ground.
4. Apply, child, type, style, file, smile, grind.

Building Transcription Skills

636. BUSINESS VOCABULARY BUILDER

assurance Pledge; guarantee.

stock exchange A place where stocks and bonds are traded.

intriguing Engaging the interest to a marked degree.

intermission A pause or recess; rest period.

Reading and Writing Practice

637.

(Gregg shorthand outlines)

as·sur'ance
ad·mit'ted

Transcribe:
May 16

daugh'ter's
choice
ac·cept'ed

won't
e·nough'

(132)

638.

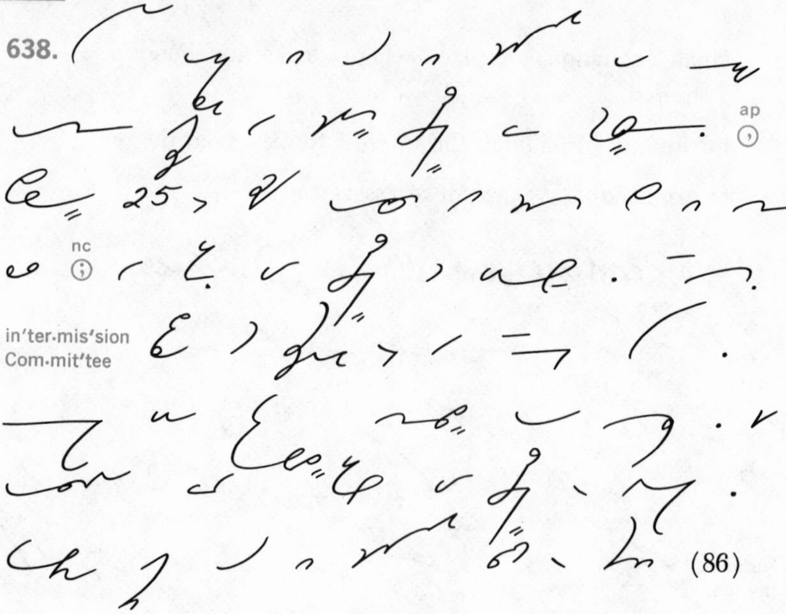

ap ;
nc ;
in'ter·mis'sion
Com·mit'tee

(86)

639.

es·tab'lish
vi'tal
young'ster
ser ;
;

(94)

640.

up'-to-the-min'ute
hyphenated
before noun

when

ref'er·enc·es
stu'dent's
lie

intro

(123)

641.

nc

(58)

The Secretary on the Job

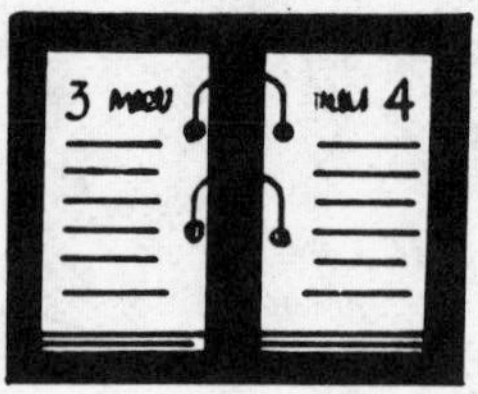

642. "But That's What You Said"

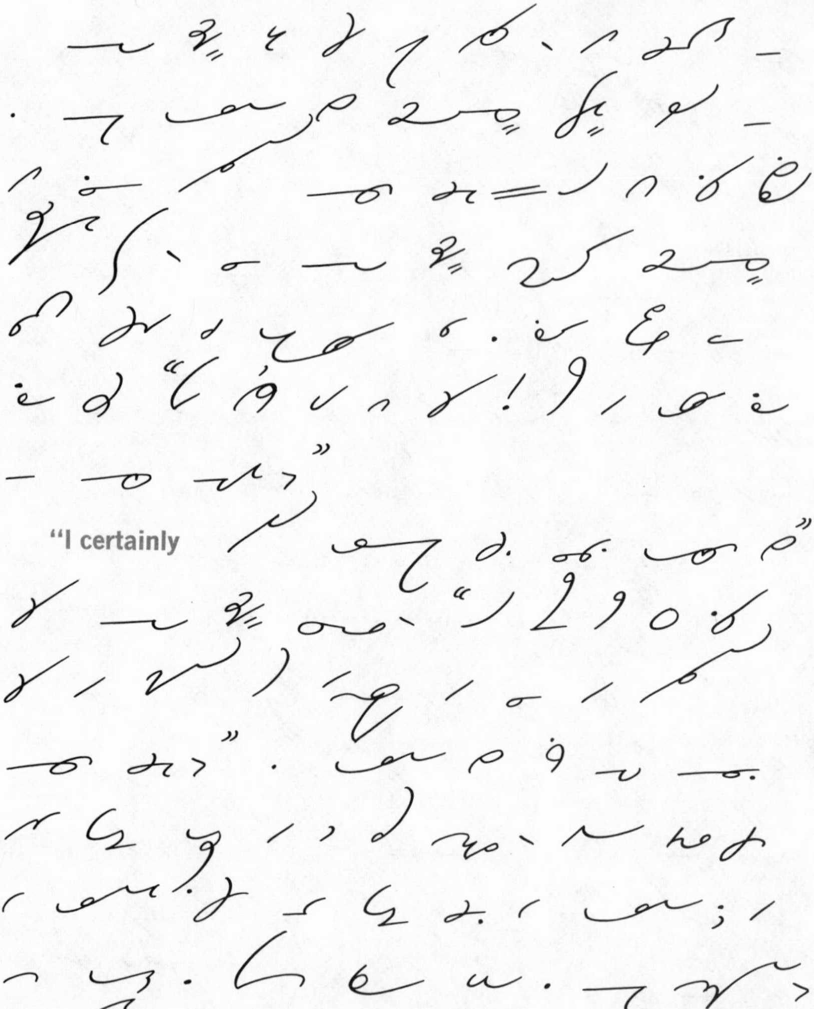

"I certainly

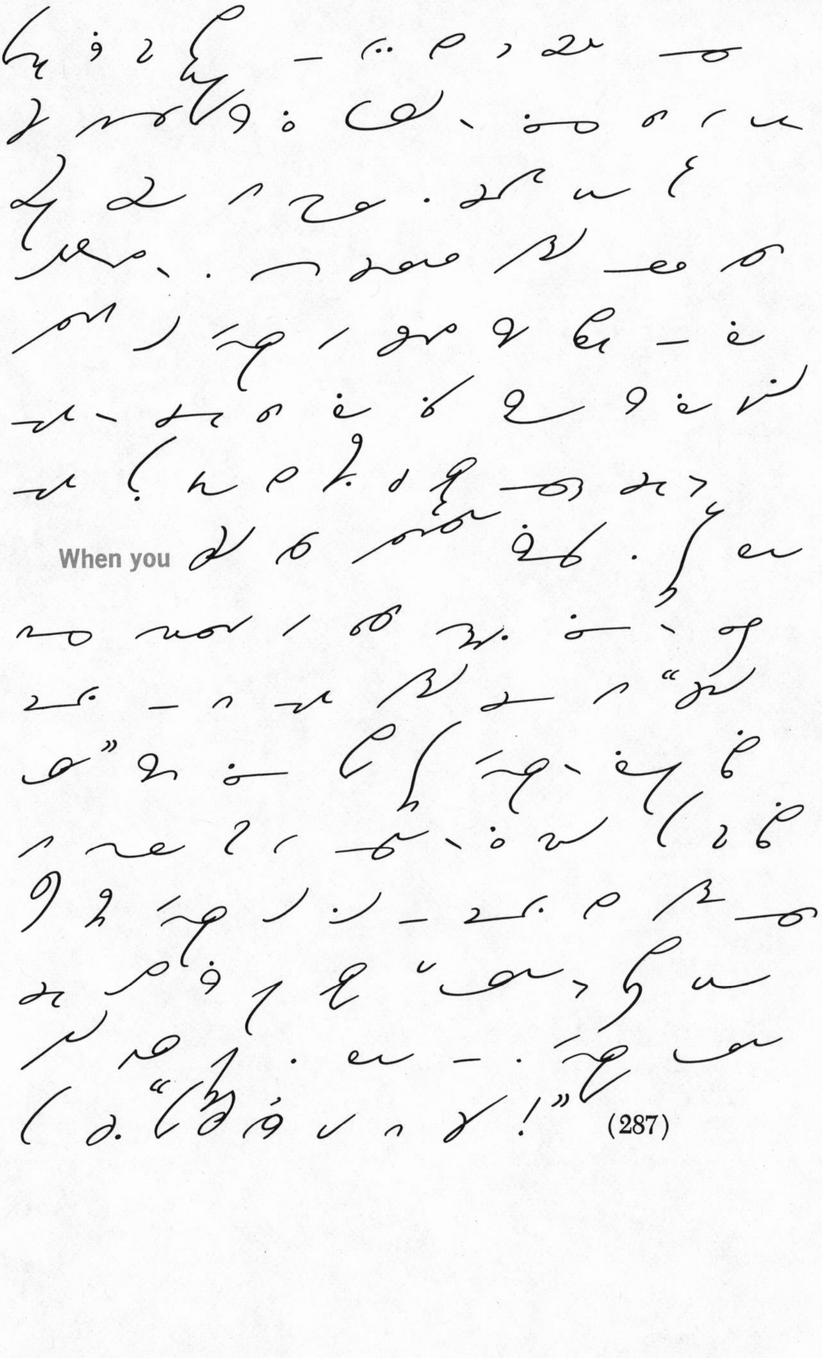

When you

(287)